OF INDIAN ORIGIN

Writings from Australia

OF INDIAN ORIGIN

Writings from Australia

Edited by

Paul Sharrad
Meeta Chatterjee Padmanabhan

Orient BlackSwan

OF INDIAN ORIGIN: WRITINGS FROM AUSTRALIA

ORIENT BLACKSWAN PRIVATE LIMITED

Registered Office
3-6-752 Himayatnagar, Hyderabad 500 029, Telangana, India
e-mail: centraloffice@orientblackswan.com

Other Offices
Bengaluru, Bhopal, Chennai, Guwahati, Hyderabad, Jaipur, Kolkata, Lucknow, Mumbai, New Delhi, Noida, Patna, Vijayawada

First published 2018

ISBN 978-93-5287-295-4

Typeset in Crimson 11/13
by Shine Graphics, Delhi 110094

Printed at
Yash Printographics, Noida

Published by
Orient Blackswan Private Limited
3-6-752, Himayatnagar,
Hyderabad 500 029, Telangana, India
Email: info@orientblackswan.com

CONTENTS

ACKNOWLEDGEMENTS

The editors would like to thank the writers, their families and publishers for permission to reproduce our selected materials. Every effort has been made to trace copyright holders and to obtain their permission for the use of copyright material. The publisher and editors apologise for any errors or omissions made, and would be grateful if notified of any corrections that should be incorporated in future reprints or editions of this book. The editors may be reached at: psharrad@uow.edu.au.

Grateful acknowledgment is made to Shayne Kearney for her research assistance.

INTRODUCTION

This anthology is a celebration of short fiction and poems by writers of Indian origin either living in or sojourning through Australia. A small but increasingly growing number of writers of Indian heritage are contributing to the larger Australian literary landscape—a scene that has dramatically changed from the early twentieth century, with more ethnic voices becoming part of the mainstream, and literary discussions turning from national to diasporic to transnational frameworks. Many who come from Culturally and Linguistically Diverse (CALD) backgrounds choose to shape their writing on the basis of their hyphenated identities, thereby contributing to the model of a multicultural Australia (even if they also question the reality behind the ideal of equally accepting all cultures as part of the national fabric). Others prefer not to be confined by labels and see themselves as projecting sensibilities that are inherently borderless, and their work as exploring the human condition from no specific geographical region. To take but one instance, Michelle Cahill was received into the general Australian literary scene with a book of poetry that did not push her ethnic identity; she went on to edit an online magazine specifically designed to promote multicultural writing in an effort to counter the ongoing concentration of attention on mainstream (Anglo-Celtic-European) Australian writing. Despite the complications of and resistances to simplistic labels, literary work from minority groups in Australia has attained recognition by means of, as well as in opposition to, categories such as 'migrant' and 'multicultural', and in recent decades has used and challenged the catch-all banner of 'Asian-Australian' (which to some extent has been inherited from North American literary movements). Writings by Australians of Indian heritage assert specific differences from Chinese and Southeast Asian ethnicities. (For example, no writer of Indian heritage tells of reaching Australia by fishing boat as a refugee, and unlike other 'Asian-Australians', most can invoke some connection to an Australian readership through shared legacies of British colonialism.) Asserting a specific regional identity (Goan, Bengali, Fiji-Indian) further problematises the categories of both 'Asian' and 'Indian'. *Of Indian Origin* offers an introductory overview of a newly visible literary presence, both within Australia and within the global space of diasporic Indian writing. It reveals both commonalities across 'migrant writing' in general and the increasing variety of experiences that make up contemporary Australian literature.

In 2003, the Indian poet and critic Makarand Paranjape could name only eight Australians of South Asian origin who were publishing literary work, and he reflected the general opinion about Asian-Australian writing. This collection shows that much more has been going on, especially in recent times. In 2016, for example, Witchcraft Press published Manisha Anjali's *Sugar Kane Woman,* a poetry collection about Indian women living in exile in Fiji, and Giramondo Publishing launched *Letter to Pessoa,* a book of short stories by Indian-Australian Michelle Cahill. 2016 also saw Roanna Gonsalves enter the literary scene with her debut collection of short stories, *The Permanent Resident,* published by University of Western Australia (UWA) Press. And Suneeta Peres da Costa's novella *Saudade* will be published in 2018 by Giramondo. Indian- and Asian-Australian poets are also being published in literary magazines such as *Mascara Literary Review,* which is interested in the work of contemporary migrant Asian-Australian and Indigenous writers. *Peril Magazine* is another forum for Asian-Australian arts and culture. In 2017, Melbourne celebrated the Jaipur Literature Festival by inviting a number of Indian writers to present their work and write about Melbourne. With increasing Indian migration to Australia, there is greater awareness of Indian culture (attested to by 'Parramasala', the annual Indian community festival held in Parramatta outside of Sydney, and by regular participation of Australian writers in events such as the Jaipur Literature Festival and the Kolkata Book Fair). It is now possible to find spaces in 'mainstream' Australian literary culture for Indian voices and to break open the 'South Asia' box which previously packed together writings from India, Sri Lanka, Pakistan and Bangladesh and represented them as an undifferentiated collection of minority writing. 'India' itself is problematised as an identifying category when we consider the voices of Indo-Fijian writers in Australia (several included here) who, despite their double separation from a cultural 'homeland', still remember with nostalgia old Hindi film songs or capture a scent or sight from visits to the land of their forebears. This anthology shows that even the still small field of 'Indian-Australian' writing is by no means a homogeneous entity. Nonetheless, discussion of this new field is framed by the history of relations between the two former colonies and now nations, Australia and India. We briefly sketch the main elements and discuss the texts that are included so readers have some basis for appreciating their content and their creative strategies to both represent diasporic and transnational experiences and to be heard in the wider Australian context.

Australia as a nation has had a long history of interaction with India, right from the arrival of the first shipload of settlers in 1788. For a number of reasons, this history has been largely manifest in the nation's literature through the eyes of its white, mostly Anglo-Celtic settler population which moved from colony to colony in earlier times and which has travelled overseas in more recent years. Some of the results of this history of material and cultural exchange have been collected in works such as *Of Sadhus and Spinners: Australian Encounters with India* (2009), edited by Bruce Bennett, Santosh Sareen and Susan Cowan and published by HarperCollins. As yet, however, there has been no concerted attempt to show the other side of the story—the literature of Australia by writers of Indian origin or ancestry. This is mainly because until the last decade there have been too few published voices to constitute a significant Indian-Australian literary community.

Indians have been in Australia since before the 1840s. British families given land grants in the colonies, after service in India, brought with them their Indian servants. Later, Indians went as contracted labour on sugar plantations and vegetable farms. People from the Punjab in particular managed to settle down and some entered popular memory as 'hawkers'—small traders travelling through country towns to supply outback sheep and cattle stations. From the 1860s, camel handlers from the North and West of greater India were engaged to carry supplies through Australia's central deserts. They were given the generic label of 'Afghans'. One of the first recorded pieces of writing by an Australian resident of Indian origin is from Khwaja Mohamed Bux, a Perth merchant who sold silks and textiles from his native land of Kashmir. Apparently the only Indian in Perth in the 1880s, he wrote letters to the colonial government requesting permission to bring his family members to Australia to help run his business.

Early immigrants were few in number and not necessarily literate (or literate in English) and, as historian Margaret Allen has discovered, the few texts archived are mainly complaints to the government that fellow British citizens were being discriminated against in some way. There are also some accounts by Indian travellers to Australia: Fazulbhoy Vikram kept a journal of his travels in the 1880s, Christian convert N. L. Doss toured churches to lecture on mission work and published his impressions of the major cities back in India in 1888, and T. N. Mukharji recorded his involvement with organising displays of Indian material culture in Calcutta and Melbourne in the 1880s. The first literary book published in Australia by a citizen of Indian background which was accorded national recognition was a 1965 collection of stories titled *Time of the Peacock* by Mena Abdullah. Of Kashmiri origin, her family took up a sheep farm and thus inserted themselves into the 'bush' culture that was central to the national ethos. This recognisably mainstream cultural space and an overall vision of happy coexistence of Irish, English and Indians allowed the assertion of cultural difference to be tolerated by the majority. Her book also gained acceptance in part because of the editorial collaboration with and 'sponsorship' of an Anglo-Australian writer, Ray Mathew. Mathew moved to the US in 1961, so *Time of the Peacock* had the distinction of being published simultaneously in Sydney and New York. We have chosen two examples of Abdullah's lesser-known work as a poet that are characteristic of her ability to tell an evocative story with economy and humour, clearly placing Indian characters in Australian society and culture.

Until the 1970s, relations between Australia and India were framed by policies and attitudes derived from the British Empire. As a 'white settler' colony anxious to protect its relatively high standard of living, Australia at the Federation of its various colonial states in 1901 instituted protectionist labour and immigration laws that borrowed from Durban's legislation to control the influx of cheap 'coolie' workers. This set of laws became known as 'The White Australia Policy' because it prevented the entry of people of colour (indeed, of people of *any* colour, 'white' included, who were deemed inconvenient by the predominantly Anglo-Celtic Christian society). The Restriction Act was repealed in 1947, at a time when Australia needed an influx of labour. The number of Anglo-Indian writers represented in this collection shows the effects of the 'White Australia Policy'. Anglo-Indians (the term including both people of British background raised in India and children of British-Indian intermarriage) were granted privileged entry because of shared colonial culture and some quantum of European ancestry, but they were also made to feel anxious and resentful because of 'colour' discrimination. Prevention of immigration by 'undesirables' (people of political beliefs or cultural backgrounds seen as a threat to Australian Anglophile conservatism) was maintained by the imposition of a test in a language deliberately selected to exclude the applicant. Such practices were finally revoked in the 1970s, with a points system for entry based on the kinds of workers the nation required.

It has to be remembered that the mainstream 'white' Australian literature was for a long time dominated by British culture and looked down upon as 'colonial'. It took some time to establish itself as a local product distinct from British publishing and Eurocentric critical disdain. The study of Australian literature at the university level was not firmly in place until the 1970s, and the various national literary projects grouped under 'Commonwealth Literature' produced comparative work such as C. D. Narasimhaiah and S. Nagarajan's pioneering collection, *Studies in Australian and Indian Literature: Proceedings of a Seminar* (1971).

When a new Australian national canon was sufficiently evident (and evidently focused on 'dead white males'), minority groups began to protest against its exclusions. It was the post-war European immigrant groups whose voices dominated—Italians, Greeks, Poles and so on (examples include Peter Skrzynecki's 1985 anthology, *Joseph's Coat: An Anthology of Multicultural Writing* and the 1988 collection *Beyond the Echo: Multicultural Women's Writing*, edited by Sneja Gunew and Jan Mahyuddin). It was as part of 'migrant writing' anthologies that some Indian-origin voices were able to appear in print, but even when 'Asian-Australian' writing became a subject of discussion as part of a wider shift to policies recognising multicultural variety, the demographic favoured writers from Southeast Asia and China. Writers like Ee Tiang Hong, Simone Lazaroo, Beth Yahp, and later Brian Castro and Alice Pung belong to this group. It is to be noted that it is minority group cultural activists who push new writing into public visibility. In 2008, Alice Pung, for example, compiled *Growing up Asian in Australia*, an anthology that included Indian voices. It became an important resource book for high school students in Australia. Sunil Badami, Shalini Akhil and Aditi Gouvernel were featured in that book and have continued to write and perform. In this collection, Akhil and Gouvernel again depict experiences of 'growing up Asian', but Badami's story is selected to show how not all work is confined to expressing the 'migrant experience'.

Arguably, Indians should have established a literary presence decades ago given that most immigrants after 1950 were professionals with a good command of English. However, the engineers and doctors who arrived in Australia during the outflow of skilled labour (partly inspired by a widespread demand for scientists during the 'space race' era) were not necessarily of a literary bent and had to concentrate more on establishing their social and economic position, perhaps penning the occasional memoir of being 'diasporic' and sometimes publishing their work back 'home' in India. Many memoirs, short or long, exist as anthologised fragments or self-published documents. Like some of the pieces in this collection, they record life before migration and the difficulties of settling into a new country, but most have the quality of 'in-house' family or spontaneously personal accounts—short documentary sketches that have sociological significance but lack the sense of expressive craft that might carry them beyond their immediate purpose. Moreover, publication of such pieces has usually been through community or private publishing with small print runs, making locating copies today a difficult task. Exceptions are professionals with some literary background who record first-person accounts of arrival (Vinay K. Verma's poem 'New migrant', included in this anthology, is one example) and sometimes record subsequent distress and disillusionment (Manik Datar's 'Point of No Return', also included in this anthology). A national taste for biography and tracing family origins has permitted some 'ethnic' voices to gain mainstream attention in Australia. The standout instance in recent times has been Saroo Brierley's story of tracking down his Indian birth mother, published by Penguin in 2013 as *A Long Way Home* and released in 2016 as the film *Lion*. Latika Bourke was also adopted as a baby. In 2015 she published *From India with Love: Growing Up Australian and the Journey of Self-Discovery that Led Me Back to My Indian Roots*, published by Allen & Unwin. A year earlier, Robynne Nelson published *Dharmalan Dana: An Australian Aboriginal Man's Search for His Aboriginal and Indian Ancestors*, in which she records her father tracking down the story of his grandfather, an Indian who migrated from Mauritius. Other examples of 'life writing' can be found, but this collection has focused more on fiction, poetry and modified versions of non-fiction.

It has been the 'second-generation' offspring of migrants who have felt more involved in the cultural life of Australia. Greater ease with the English language in all its nuances has made it possible to engage more fully in the social, cultural and intellectual life of Australia. The children born or raised in Australia often feel less pressure to establish themselves economically (which was the task the first generation had taken upon themselves), and have hence benefitted from a greater freedom to pursue their own creative endeavours, including writing. Australia too has experienced a shift in how it views and thinks about migrants, multiculturalism and ethnic identities, and this has enabled different experiences to be aired in literary circles. The possibilities of choosing professions other than medicine, law and accounting, and the availability of creative writing courses at universities and as a career option are some of the other major changes that have potentially enabled a larger assortment of younger writers to become part of the Australian literary scene. For some, arriving as children of migrants, the enforced encounter with Australian society created upset and questioning that prompted literary expression. This tension is apparent in Glenn D'Cruz's 'Where are you coming from, Sir?' and Aditi Gouvernel's depiction of schoolyard racism in 'Wei-Li and Me'. Writers born in Australia with a parent originally from India do not draw on the 'culture shock' experience or that of being migrants or children of migrants, but traces of Indianness are evident in their work, as in the case of Robert Wood and Anupama Pilbrow.

Both first- and second-generation writers work with the double vision of the physical present home and the mental or cultural past home, but those closer to the migration experience often reveal a more agonistic attitude. Theorists of diaspora speak of melancholia as a characteristic psychological condition and literary mood, with its difficulty of bringing into expression inexpressible, sometimes actively repressed, emotions. Writing by those long settled or by second-generation writers frequently takes on a more ironic or even playful tone. The distinction is not a clear or fixed one, though. Melancholy is evident in Christopher Cyrill's 'What Withers and What Remains', where a young man discovers the loss felt not by his father, who migrated to Canada, but by his uncle back in Lucknow. In other work, melancholy appears in tales of young Indian-Australians finding themselves overseas in New York (Suneeta Peres da Costa) and Nepal (Michelle Cahill) or New Delhi (Aashish Kaul) and is not consistently tied to nostalgia for the home (Australia or India). The character in Brij Lal's 'Kismet' is also melancholic, but that is the result of his failed love affair rather than his change of country. This does not mean that living in a society where the dominant ethnicity and culture are different from your own is free from emotional strain—we can see even in her relatively brief sojourn abroad the tension building quietly inside the poet Maria Preethi Srinivasan. Her inner explosion is dramatically externalised at the end of Manik Datar's story, when the despairing protagonist, here only recently migrated, is driven to throw a brick at one of the government buildings in the national capital.

For the children of migrants, the focus becomes more localised, as the parent rather than India itself becomes the repository of Indianness. Rihana Sultan's comic use of the generation gap in 'Not a House But a Home' is a good example. The challenge for second- and third-generation Indian-Australians—if they do not simply ignore their grand/parents' heritage—is to incorporate into their own selves an India remembered from visits 'back home', as can be seen in Sumedha Iyer's 'Over the Rainbow', or one constructed from 'second-hand' experiences in their diasporic homes. Then the task for the writer is to express this in ways that go beyond the kind of touristic representations other Australians might produce. Younger writers may choose to produce a 'global' writing that readily fits within mainstream literary publishing, keeping their identity to one side. They may write from a position of in-betweenness that either cheerfully reconciles differences (see Shalini Akhil's 'Destiny') or manifests itself in restlessness (as in Michelle Cahill's 'Sadhu'). All of the above is as true of Indian heritage writing in Britain or North America as it is for Australia. It is hard to generalise about regional differences with any great degree of validity, but if we think of the work of Bharati Mukherjee or Jhumpa Lahiri, we might hypothesise that Indian-Australian writing tends to be less solemn or tendentious. Perhaps the Australian stereotype of 'no worries' egalitarianism smooths some of the sharp edges of identity politics in other countries, but that can only be a vague speculation.

Not all writing—not even that dealing with moving from one country to another—reflects relations at the scale of the national. Texts can function in and across spaces such as the body, home, suburb or region, and our responses may also depend on the spaces—physical, social or cultural—that we read from. If we look at the material in this collection, we can see a number of sites commonly selected: often a space of transition, from India or Fiji to Australia (the airport is a primary space of transition in Bernadette Inez Earle's 'Leaving: 1969'). There are other spaces of transition from being foreign within Australia to becoming part of the society (with the barriers inherent in this process). The schoolyard is one such space in a couple of works. Such a process is scaled down at times to the domestic and familial, and at that level the common trope of food and cooking appears as a means of negotiating identity. Mena Abdullah's 'Hadji-Jack' shows gifts of food as both signs of hospitality and tactics of distancing the outsider; a girl learns to accept her Indian identity by cooking with her grandmother. A few pieces included in this collection engage with spaces on the subcontinent, sometimes as sites of departure and sometimes as spaces of sojourn, of possible self-discovery, but they are also scaled right down to the figure of the isolated subject. It is perhaps significant that language and cultural practices rather than skin colour or public politics are more commonly the points around which conflict occurs, though this is not to say that race and politics are not sites of contest in the national drama—as Roanna Gonsalves's 'Curry Muncher 3.0' makes clear. Several pieces interestingly sidestep such matters by investing in literary reference and reworking of legends as an intertextual space in which transformations can be effected.

The angst and protest possible in any writing by racially marked minority groups living in white majority societies is frequently controlled or deflected in this collection through narrative strategies. Child narrators are common and they keep darker adult experience at bay or allow it to be implied under a surface of innocence. Humour or fable are also deployed to assuage extreme reactions to the stresses of the everyday. Moses Aaron's stories, Shalini Akhil's would-be Wonder Woman, Manisha Anjali's fever-stricken child, Aditi Gouvernel's feisty schoolgirl and Rihana Sultan's comic description of a father's hoarding are all examples of these devices. If irony, rather than anger, seems to be a common expressive mode, it may be explained by themes of conflict and discrimination having already been worked over by earlier generations of multicultural writing from other ethnicities. It may also have something to do with the more comfortable social position of this group of writers. Indians have generally been regarded as 'good migrants' who are more readily integrated through their having professional qualifications, sharing some colonial heritage (cricket!) and possessing a mastery of English. Professor Iyengar's verse 'postcards' resulting from his trip to Australia to visit his university-lecturer son is a case in point.) This is by no means the experience of all Indians coming to Australia. But, as with all immigrant groups, those being exploited behind the counters of petrol stations or fast food shops generally do not have the time to write stories and poems. Perhaps they will in the future.

Professor Iyengar's visit as an academic studying Commonwealth Literature and Maria Preethi Srinivasan's doctoral study in Australia carry echoes of Australian-Indian contacts via the 1950s Colombo Plan. This produced a major influx of people to Australia from the subcontinent for periods of higher education followed by a return home or movement to other countries. Tertiary education remains a major reason for immigration, though increasing numbers of family visits to settled professionals signal the likelihood of an increasing tourist trade, which may generate literary versions of the exotica already found in Bollywood treatments of Australia (beginning with *Salaam Namaste* in 2005 and followed by many films such as *Love Story 2050, Bachna*

Ae Haseeno, Shaadi Ke Baad and *Chak de! India*). In amongst that, there is the increasing global movement of people, so that many settling in Australia for several years or more not only revisit India at regular intervals but also move on to other jobs overseas. Perhaps the most famous Indian sojourner in Australia is Man Booker Prize-winning Aravind Adiga, who completed his high-school studies in Sydney before heading to America, Britain and eventually to Mumbai.

Another factor mitigating a literature of migrant outrage or diasporic nostalgia is the origin of the writer. Anglo-Indians tended to come to Australia early and assimilate more readily, and many saw Australia as a haven from the uncertainty of newly independent India. Patricia Pengilley's protagonist who wants to escape her 'Chee Chee' identity in 'The Case of the Vanishing Princess: Sally's Tale' is a case in point. Goans also had a marginal position until their Portuguese colony was incorporated into India and so were less likely to romanticise their origins. Some, like Michelle Cahill, went to Australia as twice removed from India, having been raised in both Kenya and England. Fiji-Indian Australians also remember Fiji rather than India (a Fiji that has been for them a site of economic and political struggle, even if some writers do reveal a nostalgia for the simple rural life of their childhood). The multiple distancing of such writers induces a sense of ambivalence and wry satire, as can be seen in some of Sudesh Mishra's poems.

The age of the writer is another determinant of content and style. Younger people, and those born in Australia, in particular, are more likely to have absorbed local cultures and studied Anglophone literary works. Sunil Badami's story, for example, is completely absorbed in an Australian Christian setting. Literary education also overrides personal attachments—Subhash Jaireth, a relatively early migrant, but a university-educated one, writes a subtle tale about textuality which mocks *Midnight's Children,* and the younger Suneeta Peres da Costa manages her expatriate experience by assembling a picture of her reading.

Selection for this anthology has been made only from works in English. This is partly owing to limitations on the language skills of the editors, and partly because it is only work in English that circulates visibly in Australian publishing. There are some Hindi, Punjabi and Tamil (to mention only the three main language groups) poems and stories published in Australian community newspapers and in India. Malaya Gangopadhyay is but one example of someone in Australian academia who has published stories and essays in Bengali in Kolkata. One day, these works will also be collected and recorded as part of Australia's transnational literary networks. This collection is also framed by our focus on work with some claim on literary intent and style. There are blog-style pieces of 'hippie' travel writing or personal memoir—Darren Assey's *Between Borders and Buses*, published by Beyond Yonder in 2008, being one example, or Singapore-born Komi Sellathurai's blogs. This kind of writing will no doubt proliferate and blur textual boundaries, but at this point it sits outside of our limits. One shift in our focus falls also on creative rather than academic writing. Australia has had many distinguished scholars of Indian heritage (Purushottama Bilimoria, Vijay Mishra, Debjani Ganguly, and Partha Chatterjee, to choose only from the Humanities). As most readers will know, there are also well-known Australian writers of Pakistani, Sri Lankan or Bangladeshi heritage (Yasmine Gooneratne, Chandani Lokugé and Adib Khan to name a few), but we have confined ourselves to an Indian context if only because its writers are generally less familiar to readers both inside and outside of Australia.

We have also mostly avoided using 'stand-alone' published novels and autobiographies on the principle that these are likely to be available, perhaps familiar even, to readers, and because excerpts rarely do justice to the originals. Consequently, many early works by writers now known for more recent books are included, partly with the intent of providing a panorama of the development of the field. Following his early stories, Christopher Cyrill published two novels: *The Ganges and its Tributaries* (McPhee Gribble 1993) and *Hymns for the Drowning* (Allen & Unwin 1999). Shalini Akhil published a comedic novel, *The Bollywood Beauty* (Penguin 2004) and Suneeta Peres da Costa is best known for her novel *Homework* (Bloomsbury 1999). Rashida Murphy had her first novel, *The Historian's Daughter*, published in 2015 by UWA Press. Some other published works that have attracted interest over time have been David McMahon's *Vegemite Vindaloo* (Penguin 2006), Bem Le Hunte's *The Seduction of Silence* (Flamingo 2000) and *There Where the Pepper Grows* (2005) and Christine Mangala's *The Firewalkers* (Aquila Books 1991). Kavita Nandan published *Home After Dark*, a novel set in Fiji,

Australia and India through the University of the South Pacific in 2015. While, too, there is work being done in Australian theatre and film by people with Indian antecedents, this material tends to be either fleeting in duration or hard to reproduce reliably and economically, so we have concentrated on print-published material that has had some impact on the national arts community. The one exception is an example of the increasingly popular genre of performance poetry, a mode that has made room for many minorities and involves actual voices, rhythms, movement, sometimes percussive or musical accompaniment. This is the favoured medium for Anupama Pilbrow.

Material could be organised in a number of ways. Since most of the writing selected circulates in Australia under a broad 'multicultural' or 'South Asian' rubric, we have not 'ghettoised' writers into smaller ethnic or language groups. Perhaps the main determinants of style and content are the distance between the writer and the migration experience, and the years in which material appears. We have steered a middle path by arranging selections according to the dates of each author's earliest selected publication. Additionally, the poems in this collection have been formatted to match the style and layout when first published.

All anthologies are provisional, this one especially so. We think that our selection makes for both enjoyable and instructive reading on its own terms. We hope that it will further the existing if still small interest amongst Indian readers in the literature of Australia and that it will in turn increase Australia's awareness of the wealth of talent amongst its growing Indian-origin population. This collection also provides a unique overview of how Indian-Australian literary writing has developed over half a century.

MENA KASHMIRI ABDULLAH

Born in 1930 to immigrant parents of Muslim and Hindu backgrounds, Abdullah was raised on a sheep farm in northern New South Wales. She is best known for her collection of short stories, *Time of the Peacock*, published by Angus & Robertson in 1965, which was prepared in collaboration with the Australian author Ray Mathew. The book provides a mostly idyllic picture of a rural childhood that encompasses various ethnicities and religions, not least being her mother's Hindu faith and her father's roots in Islam. Abdullah also wrote many poems during the 1950s for the well-known national magazine *The Bulletin*, which promoted a popular literary expression of Australia as a nation of knockabout rural workers.

'Hadji-Jack' first appeared in issue 18 of *The Bulletin*, published on 3 April 1957, and 'Chupatty Chant' first appeared in issue 12 of *The Bulletin*, published on 20 July 1955.

Hadji-Jack

Hadji-Jack the hawker man, set out for
    Inverell
With praying mat and Koran to convert
    the infidel.

When he reached that busy township, he
    wandered up and down
And preached and read the Koran to the
    people of the town.

But, alas for his intentions, it was plain
    to man and beast
The reaction of the townsfolk was strange,
    to say the least.

He preached to Ben the barman. Ben
    said, 'Good on you, Jack!'

Gave him some pipe-tobacco and slapped
    him on the back.

He lectured Widow Watson on the loath-
    someness of ham.
The widow smiled and gave him two jars
    of home-made jam.

He won six eggs from Mrs. Brown, some
    rice from Mr. Chan,
A dozen navel-oranges from Father
    Harrigan.

At last, footsore and convertless, he
    sought the homeward track
With the gifts of the good townsfolk in
    a bag upon his back.

He shook his head, a puzzled man, and
    sighed and murmured, 'Well,
Perhaps I come here next month and
    convert the infidel.'

Chupatty Chant

For as long as I can remember, twenty years
    or more,
My mother made chupatties sitting cross-
    legged on the floor.
With her sari falling round her in gleaming
    folds of white,
She would mix the dough and knead it, her
    fingers quick and light,
And the bangles danced and jingled like bells
    upon her arms
As she shaped the flat chupatties between her
    clapping palms.

She was there throughout our schooldays
when, holding back our tears
Like hunted forest children we fled the white
child's jeers.
We'd creep in and sit beside her, in silence, for
we found
There was comfort in her nearness and that
homely clapping sound.
For though the heat was wearisome and though
the day wore long,
My mother made chupatties and sang a Hindi
song.

I well recall the morning that the shed went up
in flame.
My father ran down shouting and calling
Allah's name.
Rashida grabbed a sugarbag and Mena took
the pail,
And little Lal-Muhammad came following on
our trail.
The baby, big-eyed Jamila, crawled crowing
to the door—
And Ama made chupatties sitting calmly on
the floor.

There came a time when rabbits tunnelled
through our land's good heart,
So round the boundary-fences we took the
Poison-cart.
My father puffed and sweated beneath his
broad hat's shade
While we tagged along beside him, more a
hindrance than an aid,
All through that steaming summer and when
winter cold winds fanned—
And Ama made chupatties to warm the heart
and hand.

Now living in the city, we may sit and take
our ease;
There are no droughts to worry us, no dust and
flies to tease.
For those nagging inland problems we do not
give a rap,
There's water for the asking had by turning on
a tap;
And we have a modern kitchen with gadgets
by the score—
But Ama makes chupatties sitting cross-legged
on the floor.

MARY HOLLIDAY

There is little information available about the author Mary Holliday. She was born in Calcutta, and after completing her education and teacher training in Darjeeling she married an Australian and moved to Sydney. In addition to writing short stories she had a novel, *Open Season for Fury,* which was published in 1991 by Indus.

'Phoenix Unbidden' first appeared in the collection *The Tracks We Travel,* which was edited by Jack Beasley and published by the Australasian Book Society in 1961. It also appeared in a popular series of annual story anthologies, *Coast to Coast.* The publisher was attached to the left-wing Realist Writers Group. The story is of interest because it shows a total assimilation into the national Anglo-mainstream with its adherence to rural domestic drama and demotic idiom, even if it implies a critique of the infuriatingly self-centred stereotypical Aussie bloke.

Phoenix Unbidden

'Where's the spray outfit, Lil? There's a fire over at Dobson's.'

His boots shattered the music and he strode into the kitchen letting the wire-door[1] bang behind him.

'What did you say?' She looked around, dragging her attention from the radio.

'If you'd only turn that cacklephone off, you might hear me speak once in a while.'

'Well, I'm lonely, stuck in this gloomy old house—'

'Yes, yes. Never mind all that now. Where's me knapsack spray?'[2]

1 Australian houses (pre-electricity or pre-air-conditioning) had a solid door and a door of fine wire mesh, or 'fly wire', to keep insects out and the house well ventilated.

2 Most farms had 'knapsack sprays'—metal canisters strapped to one's back. The canisters had a hose and a pump handle and held water for putting out fires or controlling weeds.

'I wish you'd take your boots off,' she began, 'stamping all that chook-dirt[3]onto my kitchen floor—'

'Will you listen a minute! There's a fire at Dobson's. And I got to go. Now where is my spray kit?' He bent down to fling open the cupboards, pushing the neat contents to one side. 'Nothing's safe in this place. A bloke can never find a thing. When I lived here with Gran, I knew if I put a thing down there, there it would be when I wanted it.'

'Yes, and from all I've heard about your Gran—'

'Cripes, what the hell have you done with it?'

'Your knapsack spray is in the truck where it ought to be,' she replied heatedly, glaring across at him. 'What would it be doing in my kitchen anyway?'

He thumped out of the kitchen, leaving the cupboards open, and she followed, catching the wire-door before it swung shut.

'Is it full of water?' he asked over his shoulder.

'Of course it's full of water. What good is an empty tin at a fire?'

'Little marvel, ain't yer?' Suddenly he grinned at her and clambered into the truck.

'And if you don't want your back burnt,' she said, ignoring his peace-offering smile, 'you'd better wear that old army shirt on the rack behind you. I put it there in case.'

'You think of everything.' He reached for the shirt and began to put it on. 'Aw, you mean kindly I suppose. And I guess I'll get used to it in time, if it don't kill me first. But honestly, Lil, can you be a little less like a schoolma'am, do you think? You fuss, fuss, fuss from morning to night. Gee you're hard to get on with at times.'

She said nothing but watched him button the sleeves. Then she looked across at their neighbour's land, which lay separated from their own by a ravine filled with boulders and ancient grey gums. Now a smudge of smoke arose from it into the dazzling sunlight. It wavered for a moment towards her, then shakily straightened and faded into the noon-day sky.

'Is it dangerous, do you think?'

3 A 'chook' is a hen or rooster.

'Not if it stays where it is.' He pointed with his hand. 'It's the State Forest over on that side of Dobson's we've got to watch. If a wind should fan the fire out of the gully, it could get the long stuff edging it on Dobson's place and so work back to his chooks, his orchard and house to say nothing of the forest. And then it would be a fair cow of a thing[4] to control in all this heat.'

'Looks like he's cutting a break[5] now.'

'That'd be him all right. Waits till it's too late and the horse has gone. Aw, he makes me sick. When I had the bulldozer out to cut me own breaks, he said he could have his done too. But not him. He's too lousy to pay Will Wilcocks the three quid to do the job. I'll do it myself with me rotary hoe, when I'm good and ready, he says. Cripes that bloke's mean.'

'The wind is blowing our way, Fred. And you can smell the smoke too.'

'You don't call this a wind, do you? Anyway, you have nothing to worry about here. The gully always has a blaze every so often. Can't remember how many times I've seen it burning.'

'When will you be back?'

'When you see me,' he said. 'And don't wait tea. Better see if the chooks have enough feed. They should be right tonight. Blast Dobson. I meant to top off the bins this afternoon.' He started the engine. 'Well, can't be helped. Give us a kiss, love. And take care of yourself.'

'But will you be all right?'

'Can a duck swim? Aw, stop fussing, will you? Why shouldn't I be all right? You silly old chook.'

He accelerated and the truck shot forward, roaring out of the shed. He drove at his usual break-neck speed as if all roads were his property and every other car on them trespassing on private ground.

Lil watched the brown dust settle lazily, thinking of her husband with a feeling of amused exasperation mingled with affection. Their life together was as uncertain as a switchback at Luna Park,[6] one moment

4 An expression used to imply something will be stubborn or difficult.

5 'Cutting a break' means to plough up land so there is no vegetation to burn, thereby halting the spread of a grass fire.

6 Luna Park is a well-known funfair in Sydney featuring a roller coaster.

up and the next moment down. She knew she would never have peace with him for longer than ten minutes at a time, but life without him would be infinitely flat and insipid, like eating an egg without salt.

She noticed now that the acrid air was sprinkling her with frail black confetti and falling about her clean line of washing. So Lil decided to take it in before it smelt of smoke and would have to be re-boiled. It was a good thing Fred was not here to see her, she thought, because he loved to pick on her over the daily wash. No part of her routine annoyed him more and she would be glad when the baby came and she could wash with impunity. Perhaps he would leave off bawling out, 'Gawd, woman, you only washed yesterday. It's not necessary to do it every day. I'll put a board on top of the tubs, then you can sleep down there. Good grief, we won't get any wear out of the clothes at this rate. My shorts are going at the seams as it is. If Gran were here now, she'd say you had a bad conscience.'

Lil gave up replying to him. They had wasted the first months of their marriage haggling over Gran's ideas. She would gain nothing by saying that times had changed, that some said Gran never troubled herself with water, and that most of the old woman's suntan would disappear with a little soap. To Fred, Gran was an angel, albeit with a fiery sword, which from all accounts, she never hesitated to use. She had reared her orphan grandson the hard way, moulding him in her own strong image, breathing into him her own impatient fire, and when she had died, she had died happy in the knowledge that even if her body lay rotting in Nabinga cemetery, her battle-axe spirit marched on in Fred.

Lil carried the basket of clothes into the house. She could never call the place her home, although she had been living there almost ten months. Everyone referred to it as 'Gran's place', as they had done for years past. Everything, she thought, had belonged to Gran first, and the dead woman would yield over nothing to the young girl who had taken her place. Least of all Fred. He was so ingrained in Gran's ways that nothing must be changed. Even the battered furniture she had used for half a century, and which filled Lil with despair, must not be rearranged, let alone sold.

But when the baby came, Lil thought, things would be different. Gran would have no part there. With a son in the house, Fred could forget the past, and enjoy the untouched future ahead. And Lil would be part of that.

She smelt the smoke in the kitchen as she entered, and placing the basket on the table, she decided to shut all the windows in the house. But her eyes fell on the dirt Fred had brought in, and habit drove her to clean the floor first. Then she rearranged the cupboards, replacing neatly everything Fred had pushed to one side, and when she had finished, she looked with satisfaction at the orderliness of the room.

But the smoke was more pronounced now. A stiff breeze beat the curtain up, parallel to the floor as it blew in through the open window. She struggled to her feet as quickly as her heavy body would let her and went over to shut it. The strong current of wind hit her, catching her breath and choking her with its foul air.

Then she gasped in horror at what she saw.

The whole gully was enveloped in flames. From end to end, stretched as far as the eye could see, and spreading as she watched it, the fire twisted and crackled, attacking branches and surrounding and destroying every living thing it touched. Like some nightmare monster, it roared in elation, gobbling with insatiable greed and growing huge and bloated, but still moving with incredible speed. The ruthless wind stoked its insane frenzy, thrusting the struggling timber into its burning embrace, then lifting the flames, the wind caressed them briefly, leaving them to beget a dozen new fires in as many dry places.

The sky was hidden by the smoke, but now and then the sun was seen dimly, like a large circle of blood. The jagged, leaping wall of scarlet hid Dobson's farm and the opposite hill. She was alone, facing its fury, isolated in her terror.

She began to shiver, her hands turning to ice in the heat. Swaying and moaning gently, her body dissolved to nothing and her mind became a void. She was incapable of movement, incapable of thought. She watched the holocaust approach her and made no effort to move from its path.

Then she saw the fire jump the firebreak, and the fowl houses began to smoke. The sight jolted her into action. She would have to release the birds. For a fraction of a moment she hesitated, fearful to go out, then she seemed to hear Fred's voice shouting that 'Gran never was scared'. They would roast alive if she did not open the pens and if the fowls were lost through her negligence, she knew her husband would never let her forget it. Trembling violently, she opened the back door and staggered down the steps.

At once the heat hit her, scorching her body, draining every drop of moisture out of her and filling her with an unquenchable thirst. But she struggled down the path, surrounded by noise and confusion, pushing through the shimmering heat, which danced out to meet her in rose-coloured, glowing waves. The earth was steaming. The shadows had turned red. Hazily, Lil realised that the neat plump fruit trees were brittle and brown, and their smooth green leaves shrivelled and yellow. Her swollen body seemed to have increased threefold, and she forgot her terror in her anxiety not to trip and fall on the many branches, which had been ripped off and were being carried past her on the fierce wind. But she dragged her leaden legs onwards towards the billowing smoke. Her eyes burned, smarting so much that she could hardly bear to keep them open, as the tears streamed down her cheeks. Once she stopped to tear off her apron and held it around her nose, in an effort to keep out the ash.

An age later she reached the fowl runs but the fire had spread to all but the ones nearest her. Lil ran into the first one, but the birds, nesting on their perches, seemed asleep until she saw in horror that they were quietly allowing themselves to be roasted alive. Stupefied by the heat, they were as incapable of action as she had been.

Grabbing a grit-bin, she rushed among the hens, beating it in an attempt to stir them. One or two fluttered down but made no effort to leave the smoking pen or escape through the open door. The ground beneath her feet was smouldering and one of the supports was now alight, so Lil, pressing the apron closer to her face, fled up the path she had come. Fred could not now reproach her; she had done her best.

She groped her way back to the house, forcing her aching eyes open, her legs shaking with weariness and her whole being longing for sleep. Once she stumbled and might have fallen to her knees, allowing herself to succumb to the insidious heat, had not a knife-sharp pain pierced her into wakefulness and sent her struggling mechanically on up the eternal path. She became aware of two solemn orange eyes, unblinking in the gloom and watching her as she approached. She was almost on top of them before she realised they were the headlights of the truck and that Fred was back.

Pulling her apron from her face, she began to call his name, her voice croaking and unreal, until his dirty figure emerged and two rough hands pulled her to him.

'My God, Lil, where were you?' he shouted through his soiled handkerchief, which hid his face like a mask. 'Why weren't you in the house? Struth,[7] what a fright you gave me.'

'The chooks,' she gasped. 'I tried to save them.'

'Good grief! In this blaze? Are you mad? You should not have moved till I came. But are you all right?'

'Yes, I think—'

'Good. Here then. Take this spray. Keep the jet on the wall. When you weren't here, some burning timber was blown onto the verandah. Keep the timber damp. Don't stop till I tell you.'

He slipped the can off his shoulders and put it on a chair, which stood with some other pieces of furniture on the gravel path. Placing the spray in her hands, he moved it up and down, directing the strong jet of water onto the old wooden wall.

Then leaving her, he wrenched off a long branch and bound away, beating about him, trying to drive out the flames, which were rapidly eating his home.

She watched him disappear and reappear in the smoke, too weary to even hold the spray. So she presently put it down and quietly sat on a kitchen chair.

What did it matter, she thought, if the old house was burnt. No amount of paint or glass louvres could hide the fact that it had served its time. Disappearing in a gigantic bonfire, it was a fitting pyre for the cantankerous spirit who had built it sixty years ago, and besides, it saved a lot of argument with Fred about pulling it down.

'I'm sorry, Lil,' broke in the voice of Ron Marsh. 'Too bad we couldn't save Gran's house. But with only me and Fred, see, there was nothing much we could do. It already had a hold on when we come, and the boys were all over at Nabinga Forest—'

7 'Struth' is short for 'God's truth' and is used as a mild oath.

'Give us a hand with this furniture, mate,' cut in Fred, rushing up and throwing a stool onto the truck. This blaze is coming in all directions and we'd better get down to the highway.'

They bumped down to the main road, where Fred came to a halt, and the three of them silently looked back. Even one of the hedges bordering the drive was ablaze.

'All gone, Fred. Fowls, trees and Gran's place. Cripes, it's tough.' Ron spoke solemnly, sympathetically. 'You understand, mate, about the boys. The blokes had to stop the forest going, or the town would not have been worth a bumper.'

'Of course,' replied Fred. 'Well, what the hell. It's all insured. That's one thing. Now let them pay, I think I'll put in for three thousand chooks; the place can carry that number easy. And those trees were so old. They had to go sooner or later, I suppose. It was only Gran's house.'

'Yes,' said Ron turning to Lil, 'I am sorry you had to lose your home.'

'My home?' Her voice sounded flat. 'That wasn't my home. It was Gran's. I was minding the place that's all: minding it for a ghost. I was the glorified housekeeper, kept everything just as the mistress left it. Only thing was I couldn't give notice and leave.'

'Lil, what's got into you?'

'Fred, let her alone. She had a bad time.' Ron interposed quickly, with a bachelor's fear of family discord coupled with an acute embarrassment at the sight of a pregnant woman weeping.

'You never loved me, Fred,' continued Lil, ignoring Ron. 'You never cared that I tried to save your silly chooks, and that I might have been killed. All you were worried about was the precious house of Gran's.'

'The woman's mad,' retorted Fred, 'Of all the bloody nonsense—'

'It is not nonsense, it's the truth. And what's more, I'm leaving you and I'm going right now.' Wildly she threw open the door and pulled herself out. But once on her feet, all her energy left her, and she leant weakly against the cabin, tears streaming down her smudged face, loud sobs shaking her tired body.

'Listen, mate,' whispered Ron, 'we'd better get her to the hospital.'

'Good idea,' said Fred. 'Come on, love,' he continued to his wife, speaking in his gentlest manner and holding the door open for her, 'hop in and we'll see what the quack says.'

'Leave me alone, will you.' She slammed the door shut.

'Do you feel OK, Lil?'

'No I don't. I feel awful. I think I'm going to die.'

'Lil, are you in pain?'

'What do you think?'

'Cripes, I am not a thought reader, am I? Well, answer me. Are you in pain?'

'Of course I am in pain, you idiot.' And then suddenly, in spite of her misery, she found her good humour returning.

'I'll get the doctor, mate. You stay here,' cried Ron.

'Hand me the tarp;[8] it's underneath all the furniture at the back. And throw me the penknife in the glovebox. One thing I don't have to do is build a fire. Just put me spray tin on the stump to boil.'

Then Ron called, 'I'll be quick and lively' and sped away down the road.

'Good on yer,' called Fred, grinning. Then he turned to his wife. 'Whatever did you frighten the life out of Ron for? He'll be grey before he gets to town. Besides, I could have got you in under ten minutes meself, if you got in the truck.'

'Do you know what to do, Fred?'

'Too right I do. Who do you think used to help Gran, when I was a little bloke, and she had to sit up with the cows? Grandad's heart used to play up on him, so I used to have to pull me weight. I wanted to be a quack meself, one time. Only thing was I didn't like school. Now you lie there, and give me your hand, love, and don't worry. Gran taught me all I should do.'

Presently she said, 'Fred, I think I meant it just now when I said that I was going to leave you. It's just that I can't stand any more Gran. You've fed me on her for months, from morning to night, until I am no longer trying to please you but some dead old woman I never even met.'

8 Short for tarpaulin; the cover for a truck's load.

'But what've you got against Gran? Why be so jealous? And anyway, she was a second mother to me.'

'But don't you see, we must live our own lives? At any rate, I must. If you can't break away, Fred, then I will. And I will wash the clothes when I like, and eat what I like, when I like. I got to hate her so, I felt she was coming between us.'

'Lil, love, you weren't well. But if it pleases you, I swear I won't mention Gran again, or tell you a thing about her. Now how's that? Make you happy? And when we get the insurance money, I'll build you one of those ready-cut homes you're always talking about, and a washing machine, so you can play with water all day long. And I'll even wipe me boots before I come in.'

When the truck returned, Fred called gaily, 'Say, doc, I'm not paying your fee. Did the job meself. And Lil behaved better than the cows.'

He held up triumphantly a noisy bundle wrapped up in his soiled khaki shirt.

'Get an earful of this kid, will you. Arrived in a hurry because she heard we had roast chook for tea. Cripes,[9] did you ever see such a temper? All right lady, I'm sorry we didn't have the red carpet down, but you picked a bad day. Will you see the way she's laying into me?'

'And your wife?' asked the doctor, 'How is she?'

'Good-oh. Nothing to it. Just a case of blistered feet.'

Then he lowered the screaming baby into his wife's arms and the four of them gazed intently on the baby.

'And who do you reckon she's like, doc? Her mum or her dad?'

The old man pushed his hat back and slowly smiled.

'I don't think she is like either of you. I'd say she was the living image of your Gran. Even her rages are like Gran's, on the loud scale. And Gran would have chosen such a day as this to be born.'

'Do you hear that, Lil?' shouted Fred in excitement. 'By crikey, doc, you're right. It's a wonder I didn't see it before. Of course, she is like Gran. So we'll call her Kate, after the old girl. And if she turns out like the old lady, cripes, what a time we are going to have!'

[9] A mild swear word or exclamation of surprise which may be used as a substitute for 'Christ!' or 'Jesus!'

VINAY K. VERMA

Born in 1949, Verma moved from Calcutta to Australia in 1970 to pursue a career in journalism, notably as a cricket writer. He was the first to publish a biography on Kapil Dev, titled *By God's Decree,* and his chronicles are held at the Melbourne Cricket Ground. Verma began writing poetry in the late 1960s and was part of the younger generation of writers who wrote in English in Calcutta. He published several books of verse there, his last being *God Owes Me Royalties,* which was published by Writers Workshop in 2011. His work was also published in Australian literary magazines. He passed away in 2011.

'whales for breakfast and dolphins for tea' is from *apple jack blue bean and river mountain,* published by Poetry Guild, Calcutta, in 1973, and 'negative personality' appeared in *poppies and ashes,* which was also published by Poetry Guild, Calcutta, in 1968. His poem 'New migrant' appeared in volume 20, issue 5, of the magazine *Eureka Street* in 2010.

whales for breakfast
and
dolphins for tea

whales gurgling their throats
early morning
throwing the sea at the sky
making espresso with the backlash
of their tails
it's breakfast time

dolphins slicing the waves
toasting and buttering the sea
with froth for evening tea

as I trace patterns
on the beach of your thighs
the sun glinting on little hairs
like the underside of mushrooms

it's so peaceful
I hear the starfish crooning
I hear the winds on the sleeping ocean floor
the sun catches little bits of glass like tinsel
setting the sands on fire
as I stretch and doze in the blaze of your passion

I wake with the sands sober now
and the sea blushing at us in the distance
where the sun straddles the horizon
as we walk towards the night
my shoes unlaced
and shirt buttons open

negative personality

living in " " & question marks
bracketing ourselves
into so many adjectives
everyone and everything is a pronoun
hes shes theys and thems
I tells you (love)
wes becoming one of those thems
(my she) wes fullstopped at the ends
of theyses and themses paragraphs
the only nouns in
this flood of pronouns
are you (my she) and
me (your he)
these theys clutch at commas
and call each other adverbs

lets forget this wintry land
of punctuation and pronouns
and walk hand in hand
thru the twilight of nouns

New migrant

It was not escape and it was not freedom
the pouch of stemcells unnoticed at customs
my currency and negotiation
I was oppressed and an oppressor
tetrapak[1] crumpled emotions
dustbinned and years later
recycled I no longer bartered
my expertise for reward
my morality was not tax deductible and
my love had no caveats
undirected and scattered on soil that was not mapped
unexpecting and receiving
more than I deserved I finally
learnt to measure in sensations.

1 A plasticised cardboard tetrahedron packet designed to hold milk and fruit juice which can be efficiently stacked.

AMITAVA RAY

The poet and novelist Amitava Ray (1952–2011) was born in Calcutta. His first work, titled *Apocalypso,* was a book of fiction published by Writer's Workshop in 1975. By then he had been living in Australia for just over a decade. In 1980, after completing his Masters in Philosophy, he released his novel *Baby Tiger* with the 'new wave' publisher Wild & Woolley. He returned to India in 1982. His prose pieces contain surreal elements that create a bizarre and disruptive reading experience aimed at deliberately pushing readers out of their comfort zones. This style of absurdist excess was typical of a period of radical experimentation in Australian writing when sex, drugs, etc., were part of the country's social upheaval. It is interesting that Ray's so-called 'migrant' voice was involved in this cosmopolitan revolt long before migrant writing was viewed as anything other than autobiographical.

'Journey' is taken from his poetry collection *Cactus and Rain,* published by Mita Ray in 1984. The prose pieces 'Naked Ladies' and 'Mona Lizard' are excerpts from *Baby Tiger*. Ray invokes Baudelaire and Shakespeare's Iago to raise an implicit critique of reading simple realism (a long-standing tradition in Australian writing).

Journey

(for Boolan, friend of many journeys when there was nothing else to do)

The light was drawn
across the closed railway line.
Stranded on the platform, no particular place to go.
We took two tokes each
and as if by magic
the train came   it rode
a hard-working child
growing pregnant swelling from station to station.
We needed the money but the coins rolled

end to end of the cabin.
We could not chase them.

The mediterranean faces
watched.
The blue eyed ones watched us looking at the coins hungrily.

As if by sorcery, your sorcery,
a warm blanket awaited us at the end of the line.

The abandoned child bride train
whiplashed into the mythology of stoicism
has given us birth.

Naked Ladies (excerpt from *Baby Tiger*)

To begin at the beginning …
The clown went mad, went into the lion's cage where he slew the lion with a knife, then went crazy and started feasting on the lion's entrails. A little while later in the afternoon, the ballerina came into the cage. At first she was repulsed by the clown's blood-covered body, but then she found her hands moving all over his body till her right hand stopped on his genitals. His cock went hard, she drew him closer to her and they made love passionately. Later they slept like two children, using the lion's liver as a cushion. Yet later in the afternoon, the ring-master came into the cage, kicked the two lovers awake and asked them to report to his office after they had cleaned themselves up.

'What the devil are you trying to pull?' the ring-master was furious. 'I know all that stuff about "le Coeur a des raisons que la raison ne connait pas"[1] but Giacomette, do you know how much a lion costs? Next it will be elephants.'

1 'The heart has reasons that reason does not know.' A phrase originally coined by the Enlightenment philosopher Blaise Pascal.

'I'm sorry but I was hungry and Rosemary Durer is very attractive.'

'Look, you're too avant-garde for us. We're an extremely traditional establishment here.'

❖

'The Moor is of a free and open nature, that thinks men honest that but seem to be so.' Call me Giacomette. Clowns are often called that. I'm an absolute amateur at everything and you'd be doing me the biggest favour in my life by killing me. I love negresses and fucking in pools of blood. My heart is gorged with blood like that of a drowned man. Rosemary Durer took it out of the rib cage and put flowers in it.

Saracen bells and savage cymbals—that's Rosemary Durer for me.

'You have no idea how lucky you are,' said the ring-master. 'This is an extraordinarily coveted position.'

'The trouble is though,' I said, 'that the number of tricks I can pull is extremely limited.'

'Well you'll just have to invent a few new ones or else you'll get fired soon I guess. The best thing that you can probably do would be to cut off your prick, thereby creating a falsetto voice. Falsetto voices are extremely valued amongst clowns. Cut off your prick and I'll raise your pay.'

That's the sort of humour the ring-master has!

Mona Lizard (excerpt from *Baby Tiger*)

Look I'm not a genius or anything. I'm just the man on the street who doesn't like being on the street. I'm only writing this to stay off the streets. Somebody's going to lock me up one of these days for wilful damage to awful poetry but before they do I just want to state the situation.

Everybody always treats you like a leper if you want to be a writer; they treat you like a cockroach if you say you want to be a poet. I never tell anybody that I want to be a pornographic poet, that I want to fuck their brains, that I want to blow up their heads with dynamite. I'm not that eager to be exterminated.

My situation is paradoxical. You see, I'm blind but I still see. I see the stage, I even paint and set it up. Why, yes I can even give directions to the actors who appear on the stage from time to time, but I don't know what they say about me in the green-room.

Oh well, fuck them!

Now for a little more spleen. Do you know why I hate you, dear reader? It's because you want the truth. You are like a starving peasant who just wants a bowl of spaghetti or rice with perhaps just a little bit of salt. I want to give you delicacies. I am involved in a strange process. Like a gorgon I turn to stone when I see my own reflection and then I thaw and turn to flesh only to turn to stone again and again and again …

K. R. SRINIVASA IYENGAR

Professor Iyengar (1908–1999) was an Indian who pioneered teaching Commonwealth and Indian English Literatures at the university level. In addition to publishing critical studies on William Shakespeare, Gerard Manley Hopkins and Rabindranath Tagore—and penning the biographies of Sri Aurobindo and Swami Vivekananda—he also wrote poetry and published a verse account of his three-month trip to Australia. The trip took place in 1979, when he visited his son who taught at universities in both Queensland and New South Wales.

The three selected poems are from *Australia Helix: A Spiral of Verse Sequences*,[1] published by Affiliated East-West Press in 1983. The writer was in his seventies when he recorded his impressions of Australia, and interestingly projects his own culture onto the sights he encounters, fusing surfers with Coromandel fishermen and looking for spiritual ideals to redeem what he sees as a materialist 'Culture of the Average' (to cite the title of one of his verse essays). As a literature professor, Iyengar also filtered his views through standard Australian works on university syllabuses at the time—A. D. Hope's poetry (especially his 'Australia') and the fiction of Patrick White.

Unfinished Continent

Do I dare fling my gaze on this vastness
    and contain it for a while?

Like a mighty mastodon long asleep
    resisting the stir of day,

1 'Australia Helix' is both the title of Iyengar's collection and his own metaphor for a complex and evolving new society. It plays on the idea of 'Australia Felix', an expression coined by Major Thomas Mitchell during his 1836 explorations of western Victoria. Major Mitchell used the term, which is Latin for 'fortunate' or 'happy', to describe lush pasture. 'Australia Helix' also echoes the idea of Australia as the lucky country, as enshrined in Henry Handel Richardson's trilogy *The Fortunes of Richard Mahony*.

With the head bent, eyes closed, body inert,
    and some heaving in the air:

This sheer enormity of coastline, bush,
    waterways, hills and deserts,

This museum of forgotten life-forms
    fascinating to muse on:

How can I foist a trite formulation
    on this baffled adventure?

An odd grain of sand or tremulous leaf,
    a flashing crystalline pearl,

A single gaze, leap whelp, whine or whimper,
    a warble, warning or a screech,

Every fling or flick by reptile, spider,
    fly, lizard or soldier-ant,

Every atom of action, thought, life-force—
    somehow comprehends all, all.

If the seed is the preordained harvest
    and the spasm the finished man,

How shall we hold the North against the South,
    the hollow against the rind?

Here as I watch the puzzled Kangaroos
    or the wistful Koala bear,

Here as I resist the mosquito swarm,
    or the pressures of the past;

Amidst these storied concrete accretions
    as I feel o'erawed and trapped,

An instant's violent tearing of forms
    obliterates indifference

And there are no borders or barriers,
    only Australia Helix.

Opera House Visited

I decided I would make the effort
    and see the Thing for myself.

You might say it's an emerald of a site,
    almost three-dimensional:

Bennelong Point and skyscraper banners,
    and framed by the arching Bridge.

As you get close, go up the flight of steps,
    the cloak of strangeness slips by,

And what had seemed a mighty nautilus
    yawns a leisurely welcome.

The crawling cranky creature—no ugly
    duckling but a stately swan!

This was a multimix Home of the Arts,
    And no mere Opera House

The Rocks and the Shells,[2] the land and the sea,
    a muddle or mosaic?

Closer and closer, ascent and descent,
    a labyrinthine linkage:

Halls, stairs, theatres, studios, foyers,
    library, restaurants, bars—

A teasing commingling of varieties—
    ballet, choir, drama, pop, jazz!

Pause for a while to relish nostalgia
    or sniff futurology.

2 The 'Rocks' is the district across the harbour from the Opera House. The 'Shells' refers to the 'sails' of the building's roof.

A hundred attitudes had coalesced here,
  and all the technologies.

As you take your fill of the Nolan[3] fish,
  all evolution unrolls—

Whale, tortoise, boar, lion, dwarf, and all the men:
  hero, flute-player, Buddha!

What a Herculean push of labours
  and mating of superskills!

Praise the architect and master-builders
  of this Temple of the Arts.[4]

A Camp of God

How did the choice fall on the greenland site
  in Helensburgh, Wollongong?

What clicked—was it anxious search, or the play
  of chance, or the wind of Grace?

A stretch of slow rise and garden wildness
  commanding the countryside,

It awaited this transfiguring hour
  through all the drift of past time.

Has the Lord of the Seven Hills decreed
  his own global dispersal?

Wholeness remains Whole whether multiplied,
  diminished or divided.

3 Sidney Nolan, a painter most famous for his series on Australian outlaw Ned Kelly and for his huge canvases of the rough country in northern Australia.

4 For the Australian reader, the Opera House poem curiously slips past conventional views of a grand icon (hinted at in the concluding stanza) to convey a feeling of multifarious disorder.

What's a consecrated temple image
but the realisation

Of the Divine's mystical tremendum
as a radiant Presence?

The eyes of faith and the heart of ardour
recognise the Living God.

And the elected Realm is here, a Camp
of God[5] in human space-time.

Still a long long way to go, and battles
to fight, and marshlands to cross;

And the human instruments—albeit flawed,
weak or at cross-purposes—

Receiving the immaculate charges
of high aim and engagement,

Half-perceiving, driven more than driving,
must achieve consummation.

With the great Remover of Obstacles
first sanctifying this spot,

The pathway will be cleared for the descent
of the three-splendoured Divine:

The ineffable harmony of Light,
Largesse and sovereign Grace.

5 A Hindu temple complex, constructed in bushland to the south of Sydney. It has a large building dedicated to the deity Venkateshwara and a smaller complex devoted to Lord Ganesh Chandramouliswarar, Tripura Sundari, Subramanian and the Goddess Durga.

PATRICIA PENGILLEY

Born in 1926 in India, Patricia Pengilley moved to Australia as a young adult and spent many years teaching deaf children in Victoria. She often travelled back to India and her reworking of a storytelling tradition reflects her Anglo-Indian background.

The selected tale first appeared in the anthology *Beyond the Echo: Multicultural Women's Writing,* edited by Sneja Gunew and Jan Mahyuddin and published by University of Queensland Press in 1988. The decade leading up to the Australian Bicentenary (1988) of colonial settlement saw a radical revision of the national self-image under the impact of feminism and agitation for recognition and equality for indigenous and ethnic minorities. *Beyond the Echo* was a pioneering marker of this change in the literary sphere. Pengilley's story was reissued in her own collection of linked tales, *Midnight Voices,* which was also published by University of Queensland Press in 1992.

In 1996, Pengilley self-published *Kite with Severed Strings,* a childhood tale set in the Nilgiris district. In 1999, PenFolk published her autobiography *The Tiger and the Kangaroo Went to Sea: On Becoming Australian,* and Action Press published a poetry collection she and Janet Paisley wrote titled *Landscapes.*

The Case of the Vanishing Princess: Sally's Tale

This event took place in 1947.

Dad says that ever since my Aunt Kitty started stirring the family for stories of the British Raj, everyone has been bitten by a bug—to search for old paraphernalia and become maudlin with worn-out tales and family memorabilia.

To anyone who says to me, 'Have you started … ?', I laugh and say, 'Me? Hell … don't ask me to write … never could … can't spell … can't compose … can't formulate … literary moron!'

'Dictaphone it,' said Aunt Kitty.

Damn! That old bird never lets up. Damn! For an attack of archaeological-family-blues was coming on. To be honest, Dad's tale of the family rubies really got to me. Why has he been so secretive about it all these years?

So here goes—dictaphone. Well, this is typical . . . typical . . . I always do things differently . . . never could be the same as everyone else in our family. I mean . . . to begin with . . . I look different. 'They' were all fair . . . brown-haired . . . blue-eyed . . . English-bound. Me? I'm dark. And never hankered for the White Cliffs of Dover. If Chinese women had their feet bound up,[1] our Indian-born English families had their minds bound up . . . trussed up like mummies with bandages stamped 'Rule Britannia'. All born bleating 'Home Sweet Home'. Home bleeding England.

Well, about 1947 the family was planning to migrate; planning 'TO BE OR NOT TO BE . . . THAT IS THE QUESTION'. Of course, the real question was: TO BE WHOM BLOODY WHO?

I had just sat my Cambridge School Certificate. I told you, we were English-bound. Dad was some big nob in the Telegraph Service in Bombay at the time. Well, most kids were pondering what they were going to do next, school, thankfully, being over. Hell, I hadn't got there—yet. I wasn't even sure how someone as dark as me was going to get into bloody white Australia.

This realisation had hit me hard that December. These days, this sort of experience is poetically described as a moment of truth; I would say my moments of truth have been ghastly dilemmas.

And this is how it all started. One night, I had planned to meet Wendy, my friend, in a Cinema Ice-cream Parlour. A new kind of peach melba was the 'in thing'. Later we were going on to a cocktail party at Lulu's home to celebrate the end of school and exams. And, well . . . her parents were out.

I can remember I had borrowed Mum's black dress and her high-heeled shoes. By hitching this dress up with a silver belt, pulling the bodice out over my boobs, making sure my shoulders were showing, I felt cute, grown up. I was sure the dangling silver earrings from the

1 Traditionally, for Chinese women, small feet were regarded as beautiful and aristocratic. Many girls had their feet tightly bound for life to prevent growth.

bazaar gave me a touch of class. Every time I think of those earrings I can feel the damn things pinching. I was sick-to-death-of-being-going-on seventeen, the youngest in the class.

I was eating a peach melba, hopefully in a seductive fashion, when an ape of an English sailor came barging in, breath stale, bulging with alcohol, and made some suggestive propositions. Coolly, I swirled the high stool around and turned my back on him. Actually I was feeling pretty scared and wondering if I had overdone the growing-up bit. And I began to regret borrowing Mum's things without asking her, especially when a group of watching soldiers sniggered.

'Tart,' the sailor snarled behind me. 'Tart ... dirty *Chee Chee*. Go back to the gutter!'

Suddenly I was mad ... mad with rage. Didn't know I had it in me to be so angry. I was sick of these morons in the forces pretending the war gave them the right to everything, so I just turned around, faced him, toppled the remaining ice-cream down his tropical uniform and jumped on his toes. That tactic had been tried out on me in my last netball match, and I had been longing to do it to someone else ever since. To my surprise, he squealed like a village pig, his eyes popping out like press studs coming apart ... snap! I hadn't meant to hurt him so much. Oh God, of course, I'd forgotten about Mum's high heels. He had begun to look as if he would punch my nose and some of the fellows started to hold him down and shout: 'Get! *Chee Chee*.'

I didn't wait. I meant to walk out slowly, swinging and twirling my bag. I would have liked to have been able to drawl something like: 'Come up and see me sometime. Cry baby!' like a Mae West film, but I tripped on the broken heel and hobbled out. Curses! When I got out in the street I ran, just in case they were all after me. You never know with these things. Fortunately, I bumped into Wendy. She was just getting out of a tonga. So I pushed her back into the seat and yelled, '*Juldi juldi* tonga-wallah ... drunken sailors in bar!' Well, that was a mild exaggeration, but I thought that would satisfy Wendy and get the tonga moving. 'We'd better go straight to Lulu's,' I told Wendy.

'What's the matter, Sally?' Wendy was peering at me through her thick glasses. 'You look strange ... awfully ... cheap. Your make-up is streaming everywhere. Wouldn't your mother mind you wearing so much?'

I mumbled something about Mum and Aunt Betty being away for a few days, and only Dad and I were at home for the time being. I mopped my face, let the belt out a little, covered my shoulders and decided Wendy was a prude about some things.

'Wendy,' I said eventually, 'why the hell is *Chee Chee* such a dirty word?'

Wendy looked solemn, owl-like, as if she was answering a question in the Cambridge School Certificate. 'Sally, why do you always use such bad language? I suppose the British would rather half-and-half babies never happened. And if "it" happened, why throw it into the gutter? And Indians, high-class, self-respecting Brahmins, would say: "Leave it in the gutter." I guess we have to decide now to be either English or Indian, Sally. Well, that is what Dad says. And I agree with him. This is not the time for in-betweens. Mum says there ought to be a separate state for the Anglo-Indians.' And so she went on and on.

So I was an in-between, gutter scum. I had become miserable; it was worse, I told myself, than the fate of a Jew. I mean, a Jew even in a concentration camp was a JEW. This is ... nothing ... Even Wendy called it ... IT.

When we arrived at Lulu's, we had to settle the tonga fare. Wendy was very meticulous about such matters, and never let anyone get away with a thing, which was a pity for this left me short of money. I had to keep enough for a tonga home and I was supposed to supply the cigarettes for the party. Lulu's cousin, Phil, was teaching us how to smoke properly. I mean, we were accustomed to puffing away like blasted steam trains behind the lavatories. So telling Wendy not to wait for me, I sneaked around the corner, still hopping from time to time, and tried to negotiate the sale of a few cigarettes out of a packet. The old man in the wayside shop was not having any and offered me beadies instead. Beadies are smokes for coolies, made, I swear, from tobacco scraps and bits and pieces scooped off the floor of a tobacco factory and rolled into leaves. I took them for a joke. Decided Lulu would look a treat, smoking a beadie in her mother's elegant sitting room.

When I eventually got to the place, there were about seven girls sitting around brandishing ghoulish-looking cocktails. There was Lulu, her cousin Phil, Shanti (my best friend), Wendy and a couple of ring-ins. Shanti was looking unhappy. She was an Indian Christian and very upright. Lulu meanwhile had started to mix a cocktail for me in a very sophisticated way. Her sister had an American boyfriend and she kept on and on, quoting his recipes. I knew Shanti's parents wouldn't approve and Shanti cared; I knew mine wouldn't approve and I didn't care a ... a dime ... or so I told myself.

'Let's make whoopee,' gurgled Lulu, sounding like the cinema. She had been unable to find the tomato juice for the Bloody Marys, so she was toppling raspberry fizz into glasses. I guessed Lulu's mother had left out the fizz as a suitable drink for her daughter's party.

'While parents away, children will play!' cooed Phil. She had brought out a gigantic cigarette holder and wanted to know who had the fags.

I felt damn foolish but admitted I had brought beadies. There was a strangled silence. Shanti glanced at me, horrified.

'Beadies!' Lulu sounded shrill.

'What a joke,' said Wendy, trying to help. She didn't look as if she thought it was funny. The cocktails were doing something to her weak eyes. They were flying in all directions, out of control.

'Sally's always up to something, just for a lark.'

Everyone agreed it was a lark except Shanti. So Phil tried to pop a beadie in her holder. This brought on a kind of group hysteria, especially when Phil sprawled on a settee like the Empress Josephine. 'Someone told me that opium is injected into beadies,' she said mysteriously.

Lulu talked about the adventurous who were going places: England, Canada, USA. Her sister was going to be a GI bride.

I didn't want to admit we might be migrating to Australia. 'What will you do with your colour?' I could hear Phil say, looking all innocent and doe-eyed.

So I said, 'I think I'll stay ... why not? I have roots in India. Guess? One of my Indian ancestors was a princess!'

That stopped all the 'aside' conversations. No one, but no one, talks about their Indian ancestors. A princess! Everyone ogled a bit. Even Wendy's eyes momentarily stopped wandering. Shanti, sipping her lemonade, remarked: 'You're all crazy tonight. I think we should go home before Lulu's parents come back.'

Her common sense annoyed me. She was supposing the princess to be the offspring of a Bloody Mary and a smelly beadie.

'Let's go when I'm finished,' I said. Holding the glass in one hand and the beadie in the other, and forgetting about the terrible taste of the beadie, I felt … like … a … princess … It was not … bad … not bad … at all.

'Remember how my Aunty Kitty got to Australia? She sold a ruby necklace. I believe it belonged to the family. You see, Great Grandpappy married a young Coorg princess and a prince gave her the rubies, a dowry, naturally. Aunt Kitty always said the rubies were the gift of a prince.'

I was fibbing like mad, making up the story as I went along. At that time I wasn't sure about the rubies, everyone had been so damned secretive then. I didn't really know much about our families or anything, so I thought I was doing rather well until Phil burst out laughing. 'You're joking; you must be! We all know none of our parents can face up to an Indian in their midst so they invent a princess, like a fairy story. Like fairy stories, the princess vanishes away … phoo …' and she blew an imaginary candle out and upset her cigarette holder.

'What a scream,' said Lulu for the umpteenth time. She seemed to have gotten into a groove, except this time she made it sound really sad as if she didn't want Phil to elaborate too much in case she had to banish the beautiful princess.

'Sh! Sh! Sally, you're er-er … allowed a v … vanishing princess,' said Wendy, who really was sloshed. Her eyes were now glued into a cross-eyed position.

'Children … we better go home. Before Auntie comes home,' said one of the ring-ins.

I kept thinking of what Phil had said. She had hit the bloody nail on the head. No self-respecting parent would admit to anything … except a royal … Indian.

'Should we buzz off?' asked a voice somewhere in the midst of thick beadie smoke. I heard Shanti insisting she take Wendy home, so I slipped out, leaving them arguing about the method of transport: taxi, tonga, rickshaw, or a dad's pick-up service.

Considering all things, I didn't think calling in any of the fathers was quite the wisest move. Anyway, I suddenly wanted to get home very quickly. I had started feeling pretty lousy. Perhaps Bloody Marys charged with raspberry fizz and washed down with beadie fumes didn't quite agree with me.

Fortunately when I arrived home, Dad was, as always, changing for dinner, whether he played tennis after work or not. This gave me the chance to slide into my bedroom and take off Mum's clothes. I had hardly scrambled out of them when Dad was outside my door.

'Sally ... Sally ... are you in? Are you ready for dinner?'

Dinner! Christ, I was going to throw up.

'No,' I croaked, 'I'm going to bed ... I'm ill ... just leave me alone ... something I've eaten has upset me.'

'Some soup,' said Dad, sounding like Mum, 'some soup and toast.' Jesus, why can't parents leave you alone?

'Starvation fixes it,' I muttered and hoped it would. It felt so bloody permanent.

'Fill in the form for the Australian authorities when you're better,' he said kindly, moving away. 'I've left it on your desk and, oh, we'll need another photograph.'

I sat down on the chair and stared at the form. Not another ... and a photo to examine our colour. No one was allowed to have an Indian grandparent. Those were the regulations. I was OK, but how about Dad and Mum with their grandparents? God how I hated the whole mess. We had won the war, hadn't we? Then why were we running off like frightened deer to a country where colour was so important? I tore up the form and wrote my own.

TO WHOM IT MAY CONCERN

NAME : Chee Chee
AGE : Don't care
COMPLEXION : Take one European
Take an Indian
Cocktail them
Add an olive ...
Then lump it or like it.
EYES : Not blue
Not brown

NATIONALITY	: Mongrel
COUNTRY OF BIRTH	: No man's land
OCCUPATION	: Vanishing princess
AMBITION	: To be a human being

I pushed this under the door. I knew Dad would eventually return, pick it up and stand outside, silent, scanning it. This made me feel so sad I went off to the bathroom to throw up.

MEETA CHATTERJEE

Born in 1959 and raised in Mumbai, Meeta Chatterjee spent time in Dubai before migrating to Australia with her journalist husband. She has Masters degrees in English Literature and Education, and a Doctorate in Education. She is a lecturer in academic language and literacy. She co-convenes the blog 'Southern Crossings' and is working towards publishing a collection of her poetry.

'On Writing a Poem' appeared in *The Indian* in 1988. 'Erasure' and 'Landscape: Travelling through South Australia' were published in *The Journal of Literature and Aesthetics* in 2004 and re-published by *Mascara* in 2015. 'Bakhtin Said' has not previously been published.

Erasure

Those who saw her go, deny that she was naked.
She tugged the sky off the clothesline, wrapped it
round herself and walked into the river—they said.

Fourteen days later lamps and rumours
flared on the banks of the Ganges.
Fishermen say that she strode into the village
stark naked, on full moon nights.
She ignored offers of clothes,
tied her wet hair into a bun
and walked past the living.

Some say she visited the temple, clanged
the bells to crescendo and then
dissolved into the flame of an oil lamp.
Others had seen her behind the abandoned house
beckoning drunken gamblers.

'Very unbecoming of a Brahmin girl—even in death.'—
They shook their heads.
Others claim that they have seen her big with child
waving her voice at the wind—
her songs naked too.

In her own home, no one speaks of her.
They've blacked out her pictures from
family albums and
scrubbed her off collective memories.
But on some cold winter evenings
when the sound of the conch
scatters and scatters
through the incense-filled prayer room,
images of my dead eighteen-year-old aunt dance
on grandma's eye-lashes
asking to be grieved.

Landscape: Travelling through South Australia

The coastline disappears—
bewitching in its flouncy, racy skirts and the promise of bare skin.
The smell of seeds in the rainforest is memory.
The sky is a chalice, upturned on land—the last drop gone.
Occasionally the soil desperate for seed and water
parts its itchy legs stealthily
to irrigation and grows guiltily pubic.
But mainly, the land blisters and throws up dead animals on the
    veins of roads.
Bones jutting, skin broken and broken again, the land endures
    the sun roaring its orange pulp of heat.
At nightfall, the sky and land meet like wounded saints—too tired
    to sleep.

Bakhtin Said …

Bakhtin said that
words are nanopatches which sit in the brain and radiate contexts.
words are cartilages that interconnect dreams,
if you squeeze a word, it gives out little ampoules of lived-in
 experiences,
if you hang a word out to dry, it shrinks in the cold of scrutiny,
if you wear one, it becomes a badge of your colour, race and
 sexuality.
if you cut a word open like a fruit,
it oozes acid sweat beads like pomegranate seeds
lining the velvet of your mouth with tartness
or floods it with the honey crystals of mangoes
or settles your cavities like kiwi fruit seeds.[1]

If you let them, words will spin and pirouette,
showing muscle and grace in rhythm.
Though sometimes they flop onto the floor
like a clown in a deliberately large costume,
laughing and being laughed at.

On Writing a Poem

I have spent nights sitting on the edge of inspiration,
trying to bait the right reflections.
Taut in concentration, I have shaken word trees,
jabbed endlessly at images, rhymes, approximates,
pushed metaphors inside out,
just to draw meaning out of their little rivers—
only to find a lifeless pile of bubbles.
I have looked endlessly for velvet phrases to cover my ecstasies.

[1] 'Kiwi fruit' here refers to Chinese gooseberries, known by their other name for being grown in and exported from New Zealand.

Paining over dimensions and objective correlatives for my
    emotions,
I have recoiled from shining loads of blankness.

But sometimes the right words just flutter in
and sit on the page like uninvited birds.
Feeding on my mirths and hurts, they dance:
their footwork perfect, their mudras fitting.
And then suddenly cocking their heads to one side,
They beat their wings.
A poem takes shape and flies.

SUDESH MISHRA

Now Professor in English at the University of the South Pacific in his birthplace, Fiji, Mishra was born in 1962 and completed his Honours BA and then a doctorate in Australia. He has taught in both Scotland and, for many years, in Australia, and his poetry has been published internationally. His collections are *Rahu* (1987), *Tandava* (1992), *Memoirs of a Reluctant Traveller* (1994) and *Diaspora and the Difficult Art of Dying* (2002). Two of his plays were included in *Beyond Ceremony: An Anthology of Drama from Fiji* (1992).

Mishra's poems often carry echoes of Yeats and Eliot. 'Mt Abu: St Xavier's Church' is selected from *Memoirs of a Reluctant Traveller*, published by CRNLE/Wakefield Press. 'Feejee III', 'Dear Syd', 'Self-Reflection' and 'Indian-Australian Association: Annual General Meeting' appeared in *Tandava*, published by Meanjin Press. Note, in Fijian words, *d* is sounded as *nd* and *b* as *mb*.

Mt Abu: St Xavier's Church

There is an Anglican Church at Bazaar
With broken stained-glass windows and a belfry
That will crumble in less than two or three
Years, if the raja or the ruling sarkaar
Continues to tread the path of negligence.
Should I be indifferent after the fact,
Being one with many axes to grind? What
Perverted sense, what religious romance
Gave rise to this house—while in Calcutta
They sold you, Father, across the water?[1]

[1] This refers to the forceful indenture of poverty-stricken Indians to labour on Fijian sugar plantations.

Feejee III

To renew my own decay I return annually
From the exiled pages of Vidhya Naipaul,
Re-acquaint myself with residual friendships
And the debris of relations who gather my success
In the vacant shell of a tactless crustacean,
                and through me toast themselves.
After all, they say, you resemble mother's father's
Pedagogic brother. I empty a vitamin pill
And shut myself in the capsule, hoping desperately
To transmute into someone blissfully average,
Like that cousin who botched basic school,
But knew success with a much-neglected girlfriend.
Before envy's gelignite disrupts your shell
                (For she's with child by him in marriage,
So you heard from a casual friend, who made a point
                Of mentioning the fact casually),
You shed all pretensions and ride out the anger
At the local bordello. Only the post-coital cigarette
Tells just how fictional are the experiences
Of Stephen Daedalus. In six weeks your liver
Is as susceptible to flame as Badlu's gas station;
                And the surviving neurones confirm
The journey back to a land you'll never call home.
                And so the snake devours its tail
                And so the third-eye on itself prevails.

Dear Syd[2]

I live behind the chequered grilles in Nasese,
Where all the trash cans are pink and joggers
Pullulate like geckos on the kerb,
And the kerb becomes a luminous stage

2 After returning to teach in Suva, the capital of Fiji, Mishra wrote to the poet and his former PhD supervisor, Syd Harrex.

For the act of chasing papery moths
Till someone turns the lights off. For two weeks
I have dwelt in a subliminal dark,
Groping at the faucet, trying to turn on
A childhood in the phalanxed sugarfields
Of Nadi. After ten homecomings I find
I'm indigenous to the sky; while the sea,
That hirsute swashbuckler, breaks crockery
All over the reef. O to lunch alfresco
With naiads mad on strawberries as breakers
Strap the obstinate earth. O to be cast
Adrift on a barrel of the darkest Hermitage,[3]
A seraphic gull blithely oblivious
To destination and destiny. My wishes
Are romantic, to say the least, but what
Visions to prise, old friend, from an island
Where tyrants, like washerwomen, follow
The logic of the clothesline; where each new day
A moustachioed bandit[4] poses as sheriff?
Thus I give myself to the arched suavity
Of the conch, or, hermetically sealed
In my sweltering chalet, listen to Bach
And Pankaj Udhas.
                    The morning rain thins
To the beat of a typewriter; I dream
Of the hatchet-scene in Dostoyevsky
And am stricken with guilt. What to boast of
Having killed the dissident in my soul?
What to boast of after such confessions?
The resident poet's a castaway, they'll say;
And I will be silent, having grown wise
In my ostrich view of things. But the rage
(That gets others lancing at the abscess
In their mongrel's foot) is inside me too;

3 A costly red wine from South Australia.

4 The 'bandit' refers to Sitiveni Rabuka, a military officer who led the first coup in Fiji in 1987. He was later elected the Prime Minister of Fiji.

And in nightmares the cries from the broken Syria[5]
Break me like no book—the splintering hull,
The seething ocean, the human struggle;
Afterwards the wash of the sea and a silence.
These images won't let me be, macheteing
Through my equanimity, sinking the coracle
Bobbing inside the archipelagic heart.
So, a hoon[6] in a black Holden,[7] I fly west
Over humps and potholes, through villages
And resorts where veritable Fridays
Hobnob with veritable Crusoes. The smell
Of burning cane obsesses me to the point
Of distraction; twenty miles from Nadi
I stop to watch sooty flakes of cane fall
Upon the dome of a sky gored by bulls.
Twenty miles from home I break with grief,
And all the rhymes go sour like toads
Bespattered on the road.
                    Only a grandfather,
Leaning on his malacca cane, could explain
Why such sights move the bourgeois soul; only
A grandmother cracking clothes over river-stones
Could say why I stopped along a dark highway
To watch the communion of ash and sky
In a silence that was as consummate
As the sound of crying in an empty church.

5 The Syria was a ship which carried indentured labourers to Fiji. In 1884, it was shipwrecked off the coast of Viti Levu and 59 people lost their lives.

6 An unruly young man, generally linked with reckless diving.

7 The Holden is Australia's national car.

Self-Reflection

A stiff wind fills up the neighbour's laundry.
What philosophy to wring from this, or
From a scalloped ocean that will forever cry
And tumble question marks along the shore?
Poets always fuss about something: a bride's
Haughty upper lip or unclean slogans
On toilet seats. If anything survives,
After the holocaust dirties our linen,
Poets will, and cockroaches, and the Reagans.
We bards live in a rarefied heaven
Where verse grows in drawers with rats' droppings,
And nothing disrupts the beady-eyed facts
Of our nocturnal comings and goings;
Nothing that touches you touches our little truths.

Indian-Australian Association: Annual General Meeting

Minutes

South says North's smeared with turd;
North says South *is* turd;
West, lachrymose with fervour,
Will brook no schism on the grounds
Of regionalism. East asks
Whether he'd brook schism on the turf
Of turdism. The Sikhs,
Through sheer force of habit, opt out—
Improvise a room, a gathering
In ethereal Khalistan. Meanwhile
The Fijians sit tight and contemplate
The wine, the women, the guffawing clock.

MANIK DATAR

Manik Datar was born in 1953 in a Marathi-speaking family in Calcutta. She moved to London and then Australia, where she lived in Darwin and Alice Springs before settling in Canberra. She has written in Marathi and English and published stories and autobiographical sketches, the best known of which is 'My Sister's Mother', anthologised in *Of Sadhus and Spinners*. Her work often explores themes related to home and resettlement.

'Point of No Return' was originally published in *Voices* volume 5, issue 4, in 1995.

Point of No Return

The tailor designer from Fine Man Suitings, emporium for foreign-returned gentlemen's sartorial needs, beckoned me to a bar stool of ancient walnut, well-worn with the contours of many hapless ones. The tailor himself settled down with the air of one who enjoys storytelling and stitches clothes in order to have listeners.

'You are already knowing this Sir, an educated man like you, fashion is coming six months later to Australia.'

He rotated an imaginary earth in his hands.

'Fashion is starting in America and when it is hot season in America it is cold season in Australia.'

Incredibly, I was mesmerised by the sheer nerve of this exposition with which the man explained away the ridiculous flares he had produced. I informed him that my friend in America did not wear anything like these. The tailor raised his palm like Ganesha, in a classical gesture of reassurance.

'Perhaps your friend is not being fashion-conscious person,' and lolling his head from side to side he added, 'but this I am knowing, bell-bottoms is coming again, only now it is bell from bottom to top.'

It was like this ever since Bodomama's, that is, Uncle's, papers arrived, sponsoring me to Australia. Suddenly I am as popular as

Tendulkar. Everyone I know claims a relation, a neighbour or a colleague who has been abroad, be it to Britain in the forties, Germany in the sixties, USA in the seventies or Dubai and Sharjah in the nineties. They all offer advice. I am to learn, to earn. I am to save and return. Yet no one warns how I am to spend Sunday when time itself splits open like a chasm beneath my feet.

❖

I notice how the boat hire man offers life-jackets only to children on his paddleboats. He must assume I can swim. Where, might he have imagined, could I have learned to swim in Calcutta? In the Hooghly amongst the shifting sandbanks and jute barges? At the exclusive Officers' Enclave swimming pool? Not that it matters. For I realise that at this moment, in Australia, there is not one individual amongst all the 18 million people who would care if I capsize. Except, perhaps, the boat hire man. Bobbing around in his paddleboat, as if in Brownian motion, I feel as significant as a microbe.

Breaking away from the flotilla of adolescents laughing and shouting like a Coca-Cola commercial, I steer towards the arch of Commonwealth Bridge.[1] All around, Canberrans toil at Sunday leisure. Chubby fathers pedal their children in cycle-rickshaws. Young men pull at oars as seriously as any fisherman at Mazerhat, the fisherman's mart. Women, young and old, tramp for hours in the sun whilst fuel and water is already reticulated to their homes.

I feel a spasm of envy when I see a couple paddling together holding hands, sharing a joke. Rita and I would have been married by now. If she were here—her beautiful black hair centre-parted, filled with red *shindur* of a bride—she would have let me kiss her now, here in the middle of the lake, away from public gaze.

A moorhen skids beside me and swims along some way. For a moment I am bewitched by the present. Then as easily as breathing

1 One of the two main bridges across Lake Burley Griffin, it leads up to the new Parliament House. The name is derived from the fact that Australia was a set of individual colonies until Federation in 1901, when they came together as the Commonwealth of Australia.

in and breathing out I wish Rita was here to share the moment. I am overawed by the black swan that glides by, complete with its red beak as described in my geography text.

'*Hansa,* Goddess Saraswati's emblem,' I say aloud.

Like a baby grappling with its world I have an urge to name all things I see—birds, plants, places, whims of weather, foodstuffs, objects of everyday use—for in the naming of them in Bangla I can testify to their reality.

My childhood friend Ranjan had said, '*Besh korechheesh, jahchhiz je. Ja. Tui aar aashbi na.*' Very good. Go. But you will not come back. His words emblazon my life-path like a curse from an ancient rishi.

To Ranjan I had said, 'Can't you see, I'll finally be able to do something for our country. I can specialise in architectural conservation. I'll make contacts within UN, get heritage funding, enlist the support of our expatriate community. You'll see, our *karya,* our project will continue.'

Catching myself as if in sympathy with Ranjan's anger, I think, 'Hah! After all, these cameos of poignant beauty are the same everywhere. Is there not poetry in the vignette of a sparrow fluttering its feathers in the puddle under the tube-well, where a little boy with nothing but a tombac amulet has taken his bath? Is there not magnificence in the flame of the forest flowers on the gul-mohur tree?'

The last three weeks I have wowed and gee-whizzed and goshed like a tourist. Now, fatigued, I crave the familiar. I'm reminded of Dutta at the office, asking of Australia, 'Are there people there?' I understood he meant to say, 'Are there our people, Bengali people, there?' Nevertheless, I was taken aback. Today I comprehend his question. For my gaze wanders, then fixes on dark faces. Stupidly I wait for those faces to break into Ranjan's grin or Rita's smile. Later I shall go to the Indian cultural program. People there will most likely ask me about India. My knowledge will have currency once again, my tongue a listener.

❖

Since Bodomama sailed for Australia in 1969, family lore portrayed him as unpatriotic for leaving our country, dishonourable for not returning, and irreligious for not attending his father's death anniversary ceremony.

I would lie under the mosquito net on winter nights, or on grass mats in the breezeway in summer, listening to the hum of adult conversation. Half asleep I would conjure pictures of an uncle described as a brain drain. Twenty-five years later when this uncle offered to sponsor me to Australia the same family said: 'Chittababu's son is in Chicago, even Lalji's nephew has gone to Leeds. Of course you must go.'

There is irony, too. Rita told me she adored my optimism for Calcutta. The way Ranjan and I cycled through every laneway as though searching for that special Durga-puja festival spirit in everyday life.

'Rita's horoscope,' her mother used to declare whenever she saw me, 'states categorically that she will marry well, but she will live across the black waters, the ocean.'

Now, said her parents, they could see their way open to approaching my parents with a proposal for a formal engagement.

Immediately, Rita's relations and neighbours and acquaintances of relations and neighbours began supplying her family with tales of life abroad. Evidently there were no stories on Australia. From this it was construed that Australia did not rate highly as a foreign destination. Yet the story of the man in America who never returned to marry the girl he was engaged to prompted Rita's parents to insist on a wedding before I departed. An astrologer who could locate a suitably auspicious date in his almanac was found, and Rita and I were happy.

❖

Paddling till I perspire, I find it is not difficult to get under the bridge. Grey waves chop at my boat. I remember Sarkarbabu's comment when I showed him the tourist brochure on Canberra.

'A bush capital, eh? An oxymoron, my dear fellow,' he drawled. Indeed, I marvel at how Canberra contrives to hold back the bush.

The thrill of lifting my gaze to the untainted grandeur of the National Library and the High Court is spiked with a shot of pain as I see in my mind's eye the contrast with both such buildings in Calcutta, places I knew so well. The National Library in Belvedere was the Viceregal Palace; Lord Curzon's ballroom is now the Public Reading Room.

Monsoonal gardens advance like jungle, choking boating lakes with lantana. With what bittersweet mixture of anguish and pride I used to watch this helix, an equal triumph of nature and human spirit, as the thinnest of tendrils gained roothold and twined around in the bricks and mortar of the Raj.

Purple-brown juvenile leaves of the tropical trees unfurled slyly out of the cracks as workmen balanced on bamboo scaffolding, daubing the edifice with plaster and paint. The earth rejuvenated, imposing decay upon civilisation; yet, through this reclaiming shone the grandeur of human endeavour.

Out of this present of shuttered crumbling Victorian villas and the metre squares of domestic real estate staked out with canvas awnings across her footbridges, Ranjan and I visualised a restored future for our city.

❖

I paddle on in Canberra, a city gloating with glory. My paddles churn the lake like the great mythological churning of the oceans which brought forth the celestial ambrosia. Only, I bring up resentment. It irks that I should be sent off with a few pickles and a hand-knitted jumper on a move that destroys the stuff of which dreams are made.

My fingers trail in Lake Burley Griffin.[2] Idly I wonder if I will see fish. What sort of fish? Not fish like those that swim in a salty estuary so far away? Always questions, dancing in my skull like street urchins teasing a madman. Are Australian youth told by their families to forsake their land for another? I know so little of my peers here. What tales of Yesu Christo did they listen to on their grandparents' knees? What had they carried for lunch in their tiffin-boxes? And girls and women behave so oddly, with such little decorum, how do men know what to say?

2 Walter Burley Griffin was the architect who designed the artificially created national 'bush capital', which was founded in 1913.

I glance at my watch and squinting at the sun calculate as I do so many times a day—it's eleven here, they would just be rising for their Sunday. Perhaps Ma and Baba would be going to the village; they haven't visited Jadudada for a while. Has Mejda remembered to pick up Nanda's wristwatch I put in for repairs? And Rita? A bride. I turn the boat.

What of the little happenings in our *pada*, our street—its daily worries and their solutions, those events in metropolitan Calcutta that do not get into the *Telegraph* at the High Commission? Like a serial addict beached on the low tide of imagination I pine at what must now remain an episode unfinished.

Perhaps it might have been different if Bodomama and Aunt had remained in town, instead of jetting off four days after I arrived, he for a medical conference in Uppsala and she to help her sister with a new baby in Edmonton. So too, might my fate have been different if Rita's father had not been with us when we were faxing my papers to Bodomama in the Telephone Fax 'n Photocopier shop.

Or if we had not heard the woman in the shop shrieking with grief. We were the only other customers waiting on the cane chairs provided. Fan blades swiped the air. The woman's brother stood with her in the telephone booth, speaking the necessary English into the handset. Australia was mentioned a few times and arrested attention in the shop. Rita's father fell into conversation with the woman's sister-in-law, waiting beside us.

Over a year ago the woman's husband went to Australia, the sister-in-law explained. He was to have gone for a year, for study. Naturally her sister-in-law could not go. She was expecting their second child.

The receiver replaced, the brother swung out the door. I noticed the telephone meter read the sum of a week's salary for the shop assistant, a sobering thought as I imagined the sweet nothings Rita and I would say whilst she waited to join me in Canberra.

On hearing that I was heading for Australia, the brother took over the tale. 'How many times I am telling her, "Your place is with your man." After the baby there was the matter of money, of course there was. But I got together the fare from my contract in Bahrain, but that government said she has a shadow on her chest, she needs more tests. She had more tests. Then the *saala* swine of a brother-in-law said, "Why send her now; I'm returning soon only." Then he started telephoning my office saying, "Do like this—just send me her fare money. I need one more month and I will get this degree." That became two months, three, like this. We were of course fools for believing him in the first place.'

The woman herself huddled in a muffled silence as we grouped around in the laneway.

'Now she is receiving this document. In that country he is not divorcing by saying *Talaaq. Talaaq. Talaaq.* He is serving papers. Has she been a bad wife? Of course not. I, too, have our family honour to think about. She has been a good wife—earning and saving and bribing this one and that so her husband can get the extension he wants. For this he is divorcing her, for one year separation from husband. Court paper is saying my sister can dispute this. But the telephone officer is telling I need lawyer to dispute. Bhaisahab, where I am finding Australian advocate? Hun? Besides, if I had that kind of money do you think I'd waste it on a lawyer? Of course not.'

At this threat his sister started keening as one widowed.

After this event, I found to my total disbelief that Rita's family had called off our marriage—ostensibly until I returned on furlough. Ma's weeping was legendary. 'The shame. My son! Rejected by the girl's side,' she whimpered.

❖

The past reels on like a silent movie on the back of my eyelids. It screens on even as I serve customers in Bodomama's restaurant, polish my shoes or learn for the first time to navigate through a city with a map. In between, like providing subtitles for the audience, I try and caption the new plot for myself. My life as a palimpsest.

I worried lest someone at the cultural function knew of our families, had heard how Rita married Hari, that buffalo-like philistine, but nevertheless a banker in Oman.

John, Bodomama's restaurant partner and chef, did explain, 'Look mate, in Australia all jobs are honourable. What's more, how d'you reckon your uncle put himself through medical school? He waited on tables and drove taxis, that's how.'

Still, I worried that people would have seen me waiting on tables in Bodomama's restaurant and would be imagining that I was a career *chai-pani-wallah*, a tea boy.

I need not have worried. For I stand and wait by the back wall of the school hall hired for the function, and I sit in a chair in the middle of the room eating my snacks, but I rarely get past '*Namaskar*' and the odd handshake. Clusters of Punjabis, Hindi speakers, Maharashtrians and Tamilians reserve tables for their friends. I try and locate Bangla speakers. I recall Bodomama's advice: 'You really must stop thinking in terms of Bengali and non-Bengali. Many of our people don't mix in general functions, but I suggest you don't limit yourself to Bengalis alone.'

There is laughter and flying telegraphese like on Sundays at home. This is where I learn that brown faces, too, can lie. For there are many people my age milling about, but their faces express gargoyle-like animation I cannot read as yet. Their heads bob up and down as they speak and I have not the shorthand to follow them, these Indians brought up in Australia.

'You must be knowing …' I begin several times. Foolish I feel and clumsily I realise that belonging comes with incremental dues paid over years. My discerning gaze picks out new arrivals. Thin men. Guys with outfits similar to my Fine Man Suitings. A man and a woman standing conspicuously as a couple, she with no gaggle of women friends to swirl around her.

The show commences. A folk song. A skit, and a ten-year-old singing that jingoistic melody *Mera juta hai Japani*, 'my shoes are Japanese, my pantaloons are English, on my head I wear a red Russian cap'. His father accompanies him on the Yamaha. The audience taps to the beat. One two three four. The music saws at my nerves. The lyrics end in 'yet my heart remains Indian.'

Rapport between cast and audience emanates mellow indulgence. I sense not catharsis but feeble enactment of Sundays long past.

Distilled sophistication resumes. Small talk. I eavesdrop on people in designer jeans and in outfits of bead and mirror-work furbelows discussing my country as though it were a vacation spot, one amongst many.

❖

Sunday is extinguished. I slip off the bus shivering. With involuntary reflex I think Ma and Baba would be returning home—if they had gone to see Jadudada. Ranjan might at this moment be with Nishad and Kabi. Perhaps they would have adjourned to the cinema.

I stride on to Bodomama's restaurant, wondering why it never occurred to me before that I could indeed make friends with Australians, white Australians. I wait at the traffic lights in a friendly crowd. Electric lights festoon trees like some extraordinary night fruit. Pastel shades of pink and blue caress the city's dome. The crowd surges across the road. I gather strength from its momentum, a certain buoyancy from my anonymity.

Canberra seduces. I begin to forgive her vagaries, her tulip beds[3] that smell of manure and not flower petals, and her cold nights which sneak upon warm days. I appreciate her courteous bureaucracy and clean streets. Besides, I want to paddle a canoe and learn to swim and breathe fresh mountain air. I want to trace the Southern Cross and to …

Walking past lettering that marks the silhouette of the Family Court,[4] then skirting past a construction site, I idly notice half-a-dozen bricks lying about, and my mind swings to a boy, no more than twelve perhaps, rolling a hunk of loose cobbled road-metal along the pavement. I see him manoeuvring it to the family's kitchen, a windbreak for his mother's mud stove.

Suddenly, ambition-duty-pleasure-loneliness whirl in dissonance and grip my mind, tearing it apart like a tornado. Fear, like the lightning, bolts across my mind, and confusion thunders. At first I sob. Then, like

3 Canberra is known for its annual Spring festival, Floriade, which features extensive beds of tulips of all colours.

4 The Family Court is a special wing of the judiciary for settling divorces, adoptions, domestic violence, cases, etc.

the monsoon which rips open the Calcutta sky, my heart, too, cracks and a deluge gushes down my face.

I am in hiding.

I believe I ran to the bricks and picking up a few I lobbed them at the glass of the Family Court, whereupon an eerie siren splintered the night, joining the howling within me.

CHRISTOPHER CYRILL

Born in 1970 in Melbourne to Anglo-Indian parents from Calcutta, Christopher Cyrill fictionalised his upbringing and move to a new suburb of Melbourne in his first novel, *The Ganges and its Tributaries*, published by McPhee Gribble in 1993. He has taught creative writing at various universities in Australia and for many years was a fiction editor for HEAT magazine and Giramondo. A prolific writer, he has had a number of his works appear within Australia and internationally. His other novel is *Hymns for the Drowning*, which was published by Allen & Unwin in 1999. The novels capture an existential melancholy—part youthful ennui and part diasporic restlessness.

'What Withers and What Remains' is an early piece sampled from *Smashed: Australian Drinking Stories*, a collection edited by Matthew Condon and Richard Lawson and published by Random House in 1996.

What Withers and What Remains

My uncle had wanted to be a policeman. He is a tall man and when he was in his teens he made himself a set of weights by filling old ghee tins with concrete and setting iron poles between the tins. He trained day and night, drank buttermilk and ate at least two eggs with every meal, hoping to impress his examiners with his physique, preparing for the tests of strength the job would require of him. At dinner this evening, as his breath quickened and he reached for his pillbox, I could see along his arms, see where the muscle had withered and the flesh hung from the bone like wineskins and also the muscle that remained. He applied to the Lucknow Police Corps and sat and passed the exam but on the eve of his induction his mother had persuaded him to become a teacher.

My uncle lives on the grounds of the small Catholic school he founded and I have lived with him and his twin daughters for four months. We live near the Aminabad Markets, close enough to see the Lucknow Square clock tower, a brick spire with a broken face where hawkers sit in the surrounding weeds and roast corn. I sleep in a hammock in the room where my aunt's body was placed for the viewing. On each wall hangs a framed picture of her and in the corner of the room stands a statue of Mary garlanded with lotus flowers.

I rarely sleep more than five or six hours a night. I find it easy to fall asleep but often I'm woken by nightmares and when I wake I stay awake. I lie wide-eyed and afraid. I've had a recurring dream since I was a child of being pursued through a street of complete darkness. I never know what pursues me until the end of the dream when I realise that I am fleeing the dark, the dark which seems physical, as if it had hands and torso and feet, the dark that I am within until I wake.

One night last week my uncle and I hailed a rickshaw to Arjuna's restaurant near Lucknow station where my uncle pays half-price. My uncle was carrying a small hessian bag with him and he smelt of tiger balm and brylcream.

We rode through the narrow dirt streets between roped cows and thin brown dogs scavenging in rubbish heaps laced with dung. My uncle held a handkerchief scented with rose water over his mouth and nose. As the rickshaw driver passed through crossroads my uncle pointed out a grey building with smoke coming through a broken window, which he said was where my father had won his first boxing bout. I told my uncle that Lucknow looked like a city that had come through a civil war and he said that he would have left the city years ago if it wasn't for his school. Then he added that the previous autumn there had been a Holy War. Hindus and Moslems had rioted and fought with knives and sticks and stones over the desecration of a mosque and in the riots a friend of his had been trampled to death and my uncle talked of his friend's death in a way that made me regret having spoken at all.

We arrived at Arjuna's and my uncle paid the driver and told him to return in three hours. The driver looked away as he was paid. We walked into the restaurant, which was decorated with large fern trees and fraying tapestries, and the waiter called my uncle 'Mr. Tallow' and called me 'Sir' and offered us the middle table. We sat down and my uncle waved away the menus and ordered in Hindi. He tapped his watch and said something else in Hindi after he ordered. He then took a bottle in a brown paper bag out of the hessian bag. The waiter returned with two shot glasses and two long glasses and a jug of water. My uncle unwrapped the bottle.

'This bourbon I kept saying was for a special occasion, you know, but no special occasion has come. Well, they've come and gone for the last twelve years. More than twelve years old, this bottle.'

My uncle poured two shot glasses and I said thank you and we drank. The drink left a sandy taste in the back of my throat and made my eyes blur and it had neither the sweet aftertaste nor the dark mahogany colour of bourbon. I wondered if the liquor was safe but kept drinking, not wanting to offend my uncle and hoping at least the alcohol would help me sleep.

My uncle drank a few shots and sipped water. He said that he had taught the waiter when he taught at St. Francis' College.

'Very smart boy, except in Latin. We thought he'd be an engineer,' my uncle said, as the waiter laid plates of mutton curry and potato chips before us.

My uncle pointed to two other men, who were sitting in one corner of the restaurant, their faces partly hidden by the leaves of a fern tree, and he said that he had taught them and their children.

I looked around at the tapestries hanging from the walls, tapestries depicting scenes from the *Mahabharata*, the headgear of kings and the chariots of gods strung with gold beads, the red, white and black thread of Draupadi's gown unravelling, a wheel of fire laced with yellow ribbon.

My uncle drank and nibbled at his food and then he smiled and began speaking of my father. He told me about the time they had raced on second-hand bicycles up and down the Hazratganj, the main street of Lucknow, hoping to impress the woman who was to become my mother. My father had told me the story and in my mind I spoke the punch line along with my uncle, '... and she was walking down the street with someone else.' As he said this he raised his hand in the air and waved goodbye to an imaginary woman and I heard the pills in his top pocket rattle in their box. He told me then of his wish to be a policeman, and how my father's only ambition before he took his law degree was to play hockey for India.

My father died close to a year ago, never having seen the school his brother had founded. The school is built within the same rectangle of flats where the brothers were raised, my uncle acquiring the bottom floors in the years after my father's migration, breaking down walls, hiring a guard and dogs to protect the desks and the chalkboards and cement bags that he had trucked in from Delhi. In the years that I was attending primary school, my uncle was building his school, for Catholic girls between the ages of five and twelve, with the help of my father's cheques.

My father sent a cheque once a month along with short letters about our Vancouver winters, the starfish snow and the pink dawns above the Cascade ranges, the shop on Kramer Street that made the best halva, the photographs: *Michael the day of his birth, Michael and me at the Cape Chidley lighthouse, Michael at the National Hockey trials.* My father never once mentioned himself in his letters to my uncle. I wrote short notes to a man I was named after, retelling what my father had told him, and I paid for the stamps. My uncle had framed the photograph of my father and me embracing the night of my twenty-first birthday, the night my father recited Tennyson's 'Ulysses' from memory to a crowd of dinner guests either stunned or bored, and I wondered if people were preserved by the things that they preserved.

As I sat with my uncle that evening, as he drank more and talked less and the plates of food cooled before us and were taken and reheated and set before us again, I thought my uncle had missed his brother for all the years of my life in a way I could never imagine.

I was too drunk to eat by the time the bottle was empty. My uncle ate only a small bunch of grapes that came with dessert, leaving the tender green stalk in a bowl beside the bottle. The stalk looked like a bonsai tree. The waiter packed the food in plastic containers.

Outside the rickshaw driver was waiting. He said a storm was coming and helped my uncle into the rickshaw. He then put his hand on my shoulder and helped me in. The wind pushed the canvas top of the rickshaw up like a sail. My uncle leaned back and fell asleep. I asked the driver if he knew the way home and he smiled and nodded. He started pedalling as the rain began to fall. I sat back and watched him. He was pedalling fast and cars stopped for him as we passed the clocktower and turned left into the main thoroughfare of the markets, where the streetlights hung on loose wires and swung in slack arcs on the wind. It began to hail. The driver covered his head with his hands and the rickshaw rolled to a stop.

In the swinging light I saw pedestrians run under the awnings of stalls, tucking their groceries and packages under their arms. Rickshaw drivers leaned in under the canvas hoods with passengers. A woman tapped her children on their backs to hurry them up. A man tapped the hindlegs of his herd of cattle with a stick. Then the lights went out.

I sat in the dark and felt the movement of people around me, heard the grunts of a bull and the shouting of drivers. Water dripped into my hair. The hail glistened. The lights came back on. My uncle sat up, his eyes blinking, his arm reaching for mine.

When we arrived home my cousins looked as if they had been crying. They dried our heads with towels and scolded my uncle for being out so late. They did not talk to me. I offered my towel to the driver and thanked him and one of my cousins paid him. Again, he turned away as he was paid.

That night I lay in the hammock and tried to stay awake. I wondered how, after a lifetime of nights and mornings when I awoke trembling from darkness I could not outrun in my dreams, I had found myself drunk in a storm in the dark of a street I could not name and I had not been afraid. I felt as if I had been there too many times before to be afraid, as if my nightmares had prepared me for the moment.

The next morning my uncle could remember nothing. He sat and looked at the egg paratha on his plate and asked me if he had paid the bill and the driver. He then asked me what we had talked about and I said he told me that he had wanted to be a policeman. My twin cousins looked at him strangely, as if he had told a lie.

SUBHASH JAIRETH

Born in 1950 and originally from the Punjab, Jaireth trained in Moscow and taught in Roorkee before taking up a position at James Cook University, Townsville, in 1988. He has qualifications in translation, journalism and geology, and in 1996 he completed a doctorate on Russian drama. His Hindi poetry has appeared in *Before the Bullet Hit Me*, edited by Vani Prakashan in 1994. His English poetry has appeared in *Conversations of Love*, published by Penguin in 1996, and *Yashodhara: Six Seasons Without You*, published by Wild Peony in 2003. His verse narrative, *Unfinished Poems for Your Violin*, was published by Penguin in 1996. Two collections of stories—*To Silence: Three Autobiographies* (2011) and *Moments* (2015), were published by Puncher & Wattman. His novel *After Love* was published by Transit Lounge in 2012.

'Jack and Jill Went Up the Hill' first appeared in *Influence: Australian Voices*, edited by Peter Skrzynecki and published by Anchor in 1997.

Jack and Jill Went Up the Hill

Once upon a time there lived a writer. A conjurer, to be more precise. He was neither here nor there. He was a comma between two, a hinge, a pause, an existential hiatus. He told stories, and was very good at that, as good as the cunning Shahrazade who mesmerised death by telling a thousand and one stories. But he was not Shahrazade. He was a man, a silly but daring man. 'Don't worry,' he would like to say, 'I'll walk straight into her mouth and pull her fiery tongue out.'

Yes, he was crazy. 'Are you mad? Why rush-to-die?' his friends would ask. But he would merely smile and keep on writing. He wrote about girls who suddenly stopped growing, and men who turned into goats. He wrote about film stars who behaved like politicians and politicians who thought they were stars. He wrote about a poet who composed jingles and another poet who became a poet-in-residence[1] of a brothel. Yes, this brothel was the last straw. It brought his end. The writer died, but don't ask me how or why.

Let me instead tell you a story about Jill and Jack. They lived in a largish town of bureaucrats and politicians. The town had an artificial lake in the centre with a phallus-like fountain jet raining putrid water. The government wanted to call the town 'Shakespeare' but after deliberations settled on a more down-to-earth name.

Jill worked in a bookshop and Jack was a librarian. They both liked books. He liked to hold them, and place orders for them. She also liked to hold books, but just before selling them. Yes, you are right: they both wore glasses. She had brown hair, thin and straight, and he was bald. If you were able to look at him from the top, I mean, take a bird's eye view, you would see the contours of the driest continent,[2] surrounded by thin streams of red hair.

They also liked book readings and attended them regularly. One night after a reading during which they had plates of spicy garlic and a few glasses of red wine, they decided to walk home. The cold was refreshing. By the time they reached home, they were ready.

They made love in the drawing room in front of the telly, and then once again in the kitchen. The first session was on the chair. They were both dressed. He was watching the telly and she was watching him and the telly in the mirror. The second time they were naked and pretending to watch each other. They had not made love for a long time and they were surprised at the number of 'O!'s they were able to muster.

At night, he woke up and saw her looking at him. What happened next is quite interesting and because I want you to participate in it, I'll write it as a proper 'scene'.

Place: *Bedroom of her house. Near the northern wall, a futon double bed. Behind the head of the bed, a window through which the lower half of a full moon is visible. In the southern wall, a similar window and*

1 A slyly humorous comment on the fashion of 'community arts', whereby writers are awarded government grants to work for a period embedded in youth groups, prisons, etc.

2 Jack's head is compared to a map of Australia—a desert interior with a coastal fringe of trees.

a table. On the table a vase with dried native flowers. On the western wall, a poster of Matisse's 'Reclining Nude'. *The door is in the northern wall. Time: 3:22 a.m. Jill and Jack are in bed. Jack is stretched on his back and Jill is lying with her head on his hairless chest.*

Jack: Did you enjoy?
Jill: Did you?
Jack: No, I mean, did you enjoy the book?
Jill: The book?
Jack: Yes, the book.
Jill: Oh, the book.
Jack: Yes, the book I gave you last week.
Jill: Oh, that book!
Jack: Yes, that book!
Jill: The one about the 'longnose', 'the snotnose' and 'the piece of moon?'
Jack: (*satisfied*) Yes, that one. Did you read it?
Jill: Read it? (*grunting*) I devoured it.
Jack: Really?

Jill takes Jack's hand from underneath his head and drags it to where it matters. The foreplay for the third session begins, interrupted by comments about the book.

Now, this was a very famous book which had won the Booker Prize. Jack gave it to Jill because it was a paperback and because he loved her and knew that she liked books. It was Jill's birthday and he was able to secure the only copy in town. Jack wrote the following on the inside cover of the book:

Dear
To ^ Jill
Happy Birthday
Lots of love
Jack xO xO xO xO xO xO

It seems to me, and you'll surely agree, that Jack initially forgot to write the word 'Dear', because it was added later between 'To' and 'Jill' with the sign '^'. The 'x' of the sequence of six 'xo's after Jack is easy to decode, but what about the capital 'O'? A zero perhaps, or a black hole or …

In the morning when Jill was having a shower and Jack was reading the local newspaper, he saw the book on the floor. He took the book and read the note again. He was not pleased. The note oozed blandness. It irritated him, and the noise from the bathroom did not help. He closed the book, thought for a while, and opened it again. This time it opened at page twelve. This page was on the left-hand side and its lower corner was folded in. Twelve. The number stuck on his tongue like a thick garlic paste. He tried to press the corner straight. He couldn't do it. He smoothed out the corner, closed the book and stood on it, with his two feet and full weight, but the corner resisted. The page retained the imprint—a warp in the narrative on the page and outside the page. By now, he was standing naked with the book in his hand. He took a bookmark from the bag. It was one of the recent ones, which a friendly bookseller had sent him. It had the *Mona Lisa* printed on both sides. He put the bookmark beside the warp on the page and left the book on the bed.

'That's a lovely bookmark,' said Jill. She was making the bed. He was in the shower.

They had breakfast together and talked about this and that and then she drove him to work.

They did not talk to each other for several weeks after that night. They did meet at book readings and launches but parted after a formal peck on the check. Once or twice they rang each other but were welcomed by the answering machine and did not bother to leave a message. No, I'm sorry, he did leave a message twice. During the same period, he was invited by an Asian country to talk about his library's policy on acquiring old manuscripts. It was a pleasant trip, more so because he bumped into one of his Asian students. She was polite, gentle and entertaining.

Jack and Jill made love again, after exactly one hundred and forty-four days. But they did not talk about the book. They either did not want to or had forgotten about it. Books are books, and life must go on. That's right. Life went on.

You see, it was a love—not a marriage—of convenience. They both needed it. It was like interjections by the chorus in a Greek tragedy or a song in a Bombay film or a clown show in the circus. They lived amongst books, surrounded by them and the smell of freshly printed paper. I always found them smelling like books. Jill laughed when I told her that Jack smelt of stale books.

I know you'll agree if I tell you that we all tell small lies, and that, if this natural gift was taken away from us, life would become a nightmare. Jill and Jack knew the value of small lies and did not mind using them. Their lovemaking was also a colourful pattern in an elaborate tapestry of lies. They would fake bursts of passion, sensuous foreplay, and cataclysmic orgasms. They would invent new positions, and talk about them, improvise them to suit their own bodies, size and smell. You should know that they both were past forty and needed this uninvolved lovemaking.

One afternoon when they were making love standing in front of the bookshelf in her study, a book fell from one of the shelves. Yes, it was the famous Booker Prize-winning paperback. They both looked at it. He smiled, she wanted to laugh but was overcome by a big sneeze. The sneeze released them from their entangled position and the session ended abruptly.

She picked up the book and it opened at page one-hundred-and-forty-four with the *Mona Lisa* bookmark looking at them. They turned to page twelve and saw the fold on the lower corner.

In the evening they went for a walk up the small mountain near her house. They carried a toy-size bucket and a small spade. At the top they found a spot under a blue gum, dug a hole and buried the book there.

That night they did not sleep but made love, interrupted only by pots of herbal tea. We are unwarping the warps, they whispered to each other.

So, the famous book died, read first till page twelve, and then till the one-hundred-and-forty-fourth, and was buried on the top of a hill under a blue gum. The author, however, did not die. He just disappeared. There were rumours about occasional sightings but they were hard to confirm. He became a human UFO appearing like a saucer in the sky then disappearing, leaving behind sonic traces and exotic stories. His death turned death itself into a cunning Shahrazade, who lived in and through the stories of him dying. One story suggested that he was killed by a Tamil guerrilla, hired by the Buddhist Sri Lankan government. Apparently, the government was annoyed by his statement that their beloved piece of land was a dribble off the geographical longnose of the subcontinent. Another story was more allegorical. It was said that because the author stopped telling stories his tongue grew thicker day by day, and that the inside of his mouth was unable to hold it straight. One fateful night while he was sleeping, the tongue grew over his windpipe and choked him to death.

Now, you must surely know that these are only stories. Stories about stories about his death. Nothing more.

MOSES AARON

Born in 1944, Aaron migrated to Australia from Calcutta's Jewish community in 1952. He has written a number of novels for children, his first being *Lily and Me* (1996), which told the story of a man in his forties and his unlikely friendship with a ten-year-old girl. Other works include *Crow Puzzles* (1997), *Man Dragon* (1997) and *Doomchild* (1999), all published by Random House, and *Elijah Greenface,* published by Hodder Headline in 2000.

He draws on storytelling traditions and styles from his family, from Hasidic Judaism, Nikos Kazantzakis—a Greek writer nominated nine times for the Nobel Prize, and Lafcadio Hearn—a writer known for his work on Japan. 'King Solomon's Ring' is taken from *The Eye of Paradise: A Book of Stories,* released by Brandl & Schlesinger in 1998.

King Solomon's Ring

My grandmother ... told me many King Solomon stories.

One was about a talking ant who told King Solomon not to be proud because she was more powerful than he was.

Another was about a snake that wanted to kill the man who saved his life. King Solomon tricked the ungrateful snake and the man killed it with his stick.

A third story was about a two-headed man who wanted a double part of his father's inheritance. King Solomon said that if one head knew what was happening to the other, they were one man. Otherwise they were two men. He poured boiling water on one head. Both heads screamed in pain. So the two-headed man only got a single part of the inheritance.

I do not remember all the details of these stories. The two stories I most clearly remember are 'King Solomon's Ring' and 'The Magic Mirror'.

'King Solomon caught Asmodeus, king of the demons and put him in chains in his dungeon.'

'How did he do that?'

'With his ring. It was made of gold. On it was carved the magic name of God.'

I immediately had an image of King Solomon pointing his God ring at Asmodeus and 'zapping' him with it.

Years later I found out it wasn't King Solomon who 'zapped' Asmodeus. It was his faithful servant, Benaiah.

'There was an insect called the shamir which could cut through stone. King Solomon needed it to carve the stone for the altar in his temple. Asmodeus was the only one who knew where the shamir was to be found. King Solomon gave Benaiah his magic ring and told him to capture Asmodeus.

Now Asmodeus only drank water from a water pit at the top of a mountain that was covered by a huge stone with his seal on it. Benaiah came to the top of the mountain, made a hole in the side of the water pit, drained off some of the water and plugged the hole with wool. He made another hole higher up, poured a skinful of wine into the water pit and plugged this hole with wool.

When Asmodeus returned he examined the seal, saw that it was untouched, lifted the great stone and drank. Immediately he fell into a drunken sleep.

Benaiah put a chain through King Solomon's ring and tied it around Asmodeus's neck.

When Asmodeus awoke, he tried to break the chain but couldn't because the ring had the magic name of God on it. Benaiah brought Asmodeus to King Solomon.'

It was on their way back to King Solomon that Asmodeus 'laughed till he wept' in the marketplace. However even though Asmodeus told King Solomon where to find the shamir, King Solomon didn't let him go but kept him a prisoner in his dungeon.

'One day King Solomon visited him in the dungeon. Asmodeus told King Solomon that if he took off his chains and gave him his ring, he would show him something no one had ever seen before. King Solomon unchained him and gave him his ring.

Immediately, Asmodeus picked King Solomon up and threw him a thousand miles away.'

I gasped. 'Was he killed?'

'Of course not. He was King Solomon. He landed unhurt in a desert.'

'Asmodeus put on King Solomon's crown and sat on his throne. No one knew he wasn't the real King Solomon.'

'Why not?'

'Because he changed his shape so that he looked just like King Solomon.'

'How did he do that?'

'He was a demon. Demons can change themselves into any shape they want.'

'What happened to King Solomon?'

'First he got out of the desert. He came to a big city. He had no money. So he became a beggar. He told everyone he met that he was King Solomon. Everyone laughed at him.'

'Why?'

'Because they thought he was mad.'

'One day King Solomon came to a faraway kingdom. He became a cook in the king's palace. The king's daughter fell in love with him. The king did not want his daughter to marry a poor cook, so they ran away. They came to the seashore. They were very hungry. They saw a man selling fish. Solomon bought one of the fishes. The princess cut it open. Inside was his ring with the magic name of God.'

'How did it get there?'

'Asmodeus threw it into the sea and the fish swallowed it.'

'If it had the magic name of God, why did he throw it away?'

'Because he was a demon. Demons cannot wear rings with the magic name of God.'

'King Solomon put on his ring. Immediately he was back in Jerusalem.'

'Did he put Asmodeus back into the dungeon?'

'No. Asmodeus saw him and ran away.'

In the Haggadic version, Asmodeus didn't just run away. Once again it was Benaiah who 'zapped' him.

'He forced his way into the palace, lifted up the king's robe and saw that he had the legs of a rooster. Immediately Benaiah uttered the name of God. Asmodeus shrieked and vanished through the palace ceiling.'

One day, my grandmother was frying hilsa fish for our lunch. Hilsa is a long, narrow fish with a big, cigar-shaped roe. It must have been a Sunday because I wasn't at school and Orthodox Jews don't cook on the Sabbath.

'Why don't you let Itzhak cook it?' I asked. (Itzhak was the cook my grandmother was always abusing.)

My grandmother snorted. 'If he cooked it, when you opened its belly, you wouldn't find the roe. You would find a stick of charcoal. That's why. Now sit down while I finish frying and I'll tell you a story about a fish's belly.'

'There was a king who was very, very rich.'

'What was his name?'

'I don't know.'

'One day his friend, the King of India, visited him. He told him that he must throw his most precious jewel into the sea.'

'Why?'

'To avoid the evil eye.'

'Didn't he have a "seven eyes"?' (A 'seven eyes' is a round amulet of bright-blue Egyptian paste with seven holes in it. It is a charm against the evil eye.)

'No.'

'Why not?'

'I don't know.'

'The king's most precious jewel was a huge emerald ring. He threw it into the sea. That night they had a fish for dinner. The king cut it open. Inside was his emerald ring. The King of India was terrified. "The gods have rejected your gift. The evil eye will get you."'

'Did it?'

'Yes.'

'What happened to him?'

'I don't know.'

'Then how do you know the evil eye got him?'

My grandmother gave me one of her upside-down answers. 'The gods did not accept his emerald ring. He didn't have a "seven eyes" to protect him. So the evil eye must have got him. Now go and tell Itzhak to lay the table. The fish will be cooked in three minutes.'

Many years later, I found out the king's name. It was Polycrates. I also found out what happened to him.

'A few months after the visit of the King of India, Polycrates was overthrown in a palace coup and crucified.'

'Would a "seven eyes" really have protected him from such a horrible death?'

'Of course. If you own one, even if you don't wear it on your body, the evil eye cannot get you.'

One day I read a Sufi parable.

'Three pilgrims brought gifts to a master. The first gift was a bottle of perfume; the second was a bag of gold coins; the third gift was a box of spices.

The master put some of the perfume on his hands; he gave the bag of gold to a passing beggar and he gave the box of spices back to the third pilgrim without opening it.

The master's disciplines thought that he had accepted the perfume because the first pilgrim was worthy to become his disciple; he had given away the gold coins to show that money meant nothing to him and he had returned the box of spices unopened because the third pilgrim was unworthy to be his disciple.

The true explanation of the master's actions was this: He put some of the perfume on his hands to please the first pilgrim because he still needed worldly rewards; he gave away the gold coins to teach the second pilgrim what real generosity was and he returned the box of spices unopened to teach the third pilgrim that possessing the box of spices was nothing. What really mattered was the effort which the third pilgrim had put in to get them.

It was this effort that had transformed him and made him worthy to use the spices in some other way.'

What if Polycrates' ring was like the box of spices? What if the gods didn't reject his ring but accepted it and then returned it in the fish's belly?

My grandmother shook her head. 'That's not possible. If they had accepted his offer, why was he crucified?'

I have no answer to my grandmother's upside-down question.

There is one story about a magic ring that I don't remember my grandmother telling me.

'One day King Solomon called his faithful servant, Benaiah to his throne room.

"There is a ring, a magic ring. If a happy person looks at it, he will weep tears of sorrow. If an unhappy person looks at it, he will laugh for joy. I want that ring."

Benaiah immediately went in search of the magic ring. When he was gone, King Solomon sat on his throne and laughed because the magic ring did not exist.'

Is it really King Solomon who plays this nasty trick on his faithful servant Benaiah? Or is it Asmodeus Rooster-Legs masquerading as King Solomon and getting back at Benaiah for capturing him with King Solomon's magic ring?

'Benaiah travelled throughout the kingdom. He asked everyone he met about the magic ring. No one knew anything about it.

One day he came to a jeweller's shop.

"Do you have the magic ring?" he asked.

"No," replied the jeweller, "but I'll ask my grandfather."

A little while later an old man came out. "I have the ring you are looking for."

The old man took a plain ring and carved something on it. Benaiah looked at the ring and immediately he began to laugh. He paid the old man and returned to King Solomon's palace.

"Have you got the magic ring?" King Solomon asked with a mocking smile on his face.

"Yes, I have the ring," replied Benaiah. He kneeled before King Solomon and gave him the ring.

King Solomon looked at the ring. Immediately his smile froze on his face and he began to weep.

Carved on the ring were the words: "THIS TOO WILL PASS".'

This is a story with an exemplary moral. My grandmother knew all the King Solomon stories. So why didn't she tell it to me? She wasn't alive when I found this story, so I had a posthumous dialogue with her. I imagine her sitting in her rocking chair smoking her ill-smelling hookah.

'Why didn't you tell me the story about the magic ring with the writing on it?'

'I did tell it to you.'

'Why don't I remember it?'

'Because you forgot it.'

'How do you know I forgot it?'

'Because I remember telling it to you.'

'What if you didn't tell it to me? What if you "remember" telling it to me even though you didn't tell it to me?'

'That is not possible.'

'Why not?'

'Because I am dead. The dead remember everything that happened to them when they were alive. I remember the very first time I told you the story about the magic ring.'

'Where was it?'

I was expecting my grandmother to say it was in the sitting room in her house in Calcutta where she told me most of her stories. Her answer surprised me.

'In a barber's shop. The barber had a ring on his finger. You asked me to tell you a story about a ring, so I told you the story about the magic ring. Now do you remember?'

I shook my head. 'No, all I remember is the painting of Adam and Eve on the wall.'

'There was no painting of Adam and Eve on the wall.'

'But I remember it. The snake was bright green and it was coiled all around the tree.'

'Why would a Hindu barber have a painting of the garden of Eden on the wall of his barber shop?'

I shrugged my shoulders. 'I don't know.'

My grandmother laughed. 'What a strange memory you have. You remember an imaginary painting and you forgot a real story.'

Dead or alive, my grandmother's upside-down logic is unanswerable.

Even though I cannot remember my grandmother telling me 'The Magic Ring', I will never forget the first time she told me the story of 'The Magic Mirror'.

I must have been about six. Someone told me that when you close your eyes, you become invisible and nobody can see you until you open your eyes.

That afternoon, I went into my parent's bedroom, stood in front of the oval dressing-table mirror and closed my eyes.

'Why are you looking into the mirror with your eyes closed?'

I opened my eyes. My grandmother's reflection was in the mirror behind me.

'I'm trying to find out if I'm invisible when I close my eyes.'

My grandmother shook her head. 'Who told you such nonsense? Was it your father?'

'No it was one of the girls at school.'

She laughed. 'Sit down on the bed. I'll tell you a story about a magic mirror.'

'King Solomon invited the Queen of Sheba to visit him. Three days before she arrived, King Solomon called his magician. "Look into your magic mirror. Tell me what the Queen of Sheba looks like."

The magician looked into his magic mirror. "Great King, I cannot see the Queen of Sheba."

"Look again," ordered King Solomon.

The magician looked into his magic mirror. "Great King, I cannot see her."

"Look one more time," ordered King Solomon.

The magician looked into the mirror a third time.

"Great King, I see the Queen of Sheba. She is the most beautiful woman in the world. But she has hairy legs and the cloven hoofs of a goat."'

'That's impossible.'

'No, it isn't. If she was the child of a human and a jinn, a desert demon, she would have hairy legs and cloven hoofs.'

'Who was the jinn, her mother or her father?'

'I don't know.'

'King Solomon removed the carpet in his throne room and in its place he put a carpet of mirrors.'

(In one version of the story, the demons make King Solomon a glass palace with a transparent glass courtyard that looks like water. Underneath it are the likenesses of the creatures in the sea. This is an exquisite counterpoint to King Solomon's carpet into which are woven the likenesses of the creatures on earth and in the air.)

I looked at my reflection in the bedroom mirror. 'Why a carpet of mirrors?'

'The Queen of Sheba didn't know what a mirror was. So when she saw her reflection, she thought it must be water on the floor of the throne-room. She lifted her long skirt to stop it getting wet and King Solomon saw that she didn't have hairy legs or the cloven hoofs of a goat.'

I laughed. 'That was a good trick. But what would he have done if she had hairy legs and goat hoofs?'

'I don't know but she didn't. So it doesn't matter.'

Years later, I found out that my grandmother was only half right. The Queen of Sheba didn't have cloven hoofs but she had hairy legs.

What did King Solomon do?

He told Queen Sheba that her hairy legs were a blemish to a woman and made her depilate her legs with a mixture of arsenic and unslaked lime.

Now I don't doubt that King Solomon didn't like hairy legs on a woman. However, it is absurd that the Queen of Sheba got rid of her hairy legs to please him. Why? Because the Queen of Sheba is the incarnation of Lilith, the first woman and the first feminist.

'God made Lilith and Adam at the same time.'

According to a misogynistic commentary, God made Adam of pure earth from the four corners of the world and Lilith out of muck and filth.

'Immediately they began to quarrel.

"I will lie on top of you," said Adam.

"Why should I lie underneath you?" asked Lilith.

"You are a woman. A man's place is on top. A woman's place is at the bottom."

"I will not lie underneath you," Lilith replied. "We are equal because we are both made of earth."

Adam tried to make Lilith lie underneath him.

Lilith uttered the magic name of God. She rose up into the air and flew away to the Red Sea. God sent three angels to send Lilith back to Adam. Lilith refused.'

Whenever I tell the story of the Queen of Sheba's hairy legs, I tell it with the traditional ending. Then I tell the story of Lilith and invite the audience to make up a 'hairy legs' ending to the story. Here are two hairy legs' endings.

'King Solomon comes to the Queen of Sheba with a pot of arsenic and unslaked lime and tries to persuade her to put it on her hairy legs. The Queen of Sheba agrees on condition that he puts it on his legs because hairy legs are as much a blemish to a man as to a woman. King Solomon looks at the disgusting concoction in the pot, smells it and judiciously decides that hairy legs are not a blemish to a man or to a woman.

King Solomon calls his guards and orders them to hold the Queen of Sheba down by force while he puts the hair-remover on her legs. The Queen of Sheba snatches it out of King Solomon's hands, utters the magic name of God, rises into the air and tips the hair-remover all over King Solomon's head and body.'

There is a very strange story about the Queen of Sheba's genealogy. It answers the question I asked my grandmother when she first told me 'the Magic Mirror'. Who was the jinn, her mother or father?

'One day a King was hunting. He saw two serpents fighting. The black serpent was about to kill the white one. The king took pity on the white snake and killed the black one.

That night a handsome man appeared in the king's chamber. He told the king that he was the white snake and offered him wealth or the knowledge of medicine for saving his life.

The king replied that he had no need of money or the knowledge of medicine but that he wanted to marry his daughter if he had one.

The jinn agreed on condition that the king promise never to question anything she did. If he broke the promise, she would leave him.

The king married the jinn's daughter. She gave birth to a boy whom she immediately threw into the fire. The king was horrified but didn't say anything.

His wife next gave birth to a girl. She threw it to a passing dog who ran away with it. Again the king said nothing.

Sometime later the king was on an expedition. His wife was with him. In the middle of the desert he discovered that all the water skins were leaking and all the food was contaminated with filth. Without food and water they would all die. The soldiers said that his wife was responsible.

This time the king forgot his promise. He asked his wife why she had done this terrible thing. She told him that his chief minister had poisoned the food and the water. The king ordered him to eat and drink. The chief minister refused, so the king killed him.

His wife then guided them to a place in the desert where they found food and water. She told the king that she sent their son to a nurse but he died. However, their daughter was still alive. At her words, a little girl came out of the ground. However, because the king broke his promise, his wife left him and he brought up his daughter alone. Her name was Bilqis and when her father died she became the Queen of Sheba.'

According to my grandmother, the child of a human and a jinn has hairy legs and the cloven hoofs of a goat. The Queen of Sheba has hairy legs but what about the cloven hoofs? They seem to be as phantasmagoric as the goat-image of her in King Solomon's magic mirror. The only story I know in which the Queen of Sheba doesn't have human feet is the medieval legend of Sheba Goose-Foot.

'The Queen of Sheba had one goose foot.'

Why a goose foot? Why not a goat foot? And why only one goose foot? The story does not say.

'When she visited King Solomon, they came to a pond. Across the pond was a tree trunk. It was a tree that grew on Adam's grave. When Adam was dying, his third son, Seth, came to Paradise to find a cure for him. He was given a branch from the Tree of Knowledge. He returned to find Adam dead and planted the branch on his grave.

Not knowing what it was, King Solomon's workmen cut the tree down to use in the building of his temple. However, it kept changing its size. Sometimes it was too long, sometimes it was too short. So they threw it across the pond.

The Queen of Sheba refused to walk on the tree trunk. Being a sibyl, she knew that it was the tree upon which Jesus would one day be crucified. So she piously waded across the pond. Immediately her goose foot was cured.'

I love this medieval 'wonder' tale. However, I find the metamorphosis of the Queen of Sheba into a pious woman as absurd as her getting rid of her hairy legs to please King Solomon.

So presumably did the nineteenth-century writer Gustave Flaubert. In his hallucinatory novel, *The Temptation of Saint Anthony*, the Queen of Sheba reappears Lilith-like as a voluptuous temptress.

'She comes to the saint's cell, sitting cross-legged on a pure white elephant. Her gold brocade robe was decorated with rows of pearls and sapphires, a tightly fitting dress painted with the signs of the zodiac reveals her ravishingly beautiful body, her fingers are covered with rings, two great pearls are in her ears, and a diamond scorpion stretches out its tongue between her breasts. She offers the saint extraordinary treasures: embroideries of Assur, powdered gold of Baasa, a shield made of seven dragon skins; a palace of black marble; islands covered with pearls; a pavilion in the middle of an isthmus between two oceans. The saint withstands these temptations.

Last of all she offers him her body.

"I am not a woman. I am a world. If thou were to lose thyself under my hair, near my breasts, thou wouldst be astonished at my limbs and burn by the light of my eyes, between my arms, in a whirlpool of ecstasy …"

She approaches to kiss him. The saint makes the sign of the cross.

"Thou disdains! Adieu."

She departed weeping, then returned.

"Are you sure? A woman so beautiful!"

She laughed and the ape that held the end of her robe upraised it.

"Thou repents, beautiful hermit, and groans! Thou wearies but I mock at it. Oh! Oh!"

She went with a dancing step …'

What exactly did Saint Anthony see when the ape lifted the Queen of Sheba's skirt? Was it a pair of exquisitely hairless woman's legs? A goose foot? The hairy legs and cloven hoofs of a goat? Or what?

The book does not say.

I read it aloud to my grandmother. 'Why doesn't it say what he saw?'

Her answer surprised me. 'It doesn't say what he saw because he saw nothing.'

'How do you know that?'

'Because like you in front of the mirror in your parent's bedroom, he shut his eyes. If he had looked on her naked flesh, he would have done what she wanted him to do to her and she would have killed him.'

'Why would she kill him?'

'Because she is Lilith and after a man does what Lilith wants him to do to her, she kills him.'

'But if she had hairy legs and goat hoofs, he would have been so disgusted he wouldn't have done anything to her.'

'He wouldn't see that. He would see what she wanted him to see and afterwards she would kill him.'

'How?'

'I don't know.'

One day, again in my father's library, I found out exactly how Lilith kills a man.

'She removes her ornaments and turns into a menacing figure. She stands before him clothed in garments of flaming fire, inspiring terror and making body and soul tremble, full of frightening eyes, in her hand a drawn sword, dripping bitter drops. And she kills that fool and casts his body into hell.'

If this is what the Queen of Sheba would have done to Saint Anthony, it is a very good thing that he kept his eyes shut and, in my grandmother's quaintly euphemistic words, 'didn't do what she wanted him to do to her.'

BERNADETTE INEZ EARLE

Bernadette Inez Earle was born in the mid-1940s in India during the declining years of the Raj. She attended Sacred Heart Convent, New Delhi, worked for a British engineering company and married an air-force fighter pilot in 1954. They migrated to Australia in 1969. She has worked in administration and teaching, and co-owned a Canberra events management and tourism business. She writes essays, poems, stories and life-writing pieces and edited *The Indian Summer: Australian Anglo-Indian Stories,* published by Ginninderra Press in 1999. This story-memoir first appeared in that collection and typifies personal accounts of migration and resettlement.

Leaving: 1969

'The measure of love is what one is willing to give up for it.'
– *The Flying Dutchman*

The land beneath us defined itself perfectly. Its serrated outline wound around the swamps of the Sundarbans, pointing like dripping fingers into the Bay of Bengal. Growing fainter, it stretched towards Burma, fading from sight as the aircraft climbed into the clouds.

Earlier, at midnight, our taxi had sped down the dismal streets of Calcutta. The once great capital of Bengal, the city of our forebears, for almost two centuries the hub of the Raj. Now, as we passed, I saw shrouded pavements of sprawling bodies, the destitute, each staking their nocturnal claim while the city slept.

The aeroplane stood half hidden and solitary on the tarmac. The pain of the impending parting was almost too great to bear.

'It won't be long before we're together again,' Pat promised. 'As soon as I get my clearance. You be good children and look after your mother … *Remember*: don't stay overnight anywhere,' he warned me before we kissed goodbye.

Through the small window, we watched till his figure turned into a speck then disappeared. Engines roared, as I fumbled with the buckle, easing the belt over my thickening waist. This was the last time we were to see him in his uniform with the wings he was so proud of, the ribbon for bravery pinned just above. The citation had read, 'That in complete disregard to his own safety, he had brought his burning jet fighter home over the border.'

'Easier than landing in enemy territory,' had been his laconic reply.

Well, we're on our own now, I thought, looking at the three solemn faces of our young daughters.

'Are you all right?' I asked.

'Yes, mum,' they lied, blinking back their tears.

The questions had started some years before ... 'So you're kangaroo hopping as well?' we were asked, as rumours circulated that we were leaving.

'Yes, after almost twenty years in the Air Force, I want to leave.'

His request for release had stated the reasons. Both our families were overseas. We wanted our children to grow up knowing them. Two mothers waited, one aged. We had other reasons as well: the future of our children.

Two long years later, the reply carried a sentence: 'Release accepted ... *no* benefits ... *no* pension or gratuity.'

The car was the first to go, then the household effects ... curtains ... carpets ... electrical appliances ... even my Queen Anne stool. We continued with our dream while our friends told us we were crazy to leave everything behind. I now reflected with secret pride, hadn't even the vicar in Sunday cited us as an example of faith, by believing in the unknown and trusting in the Almighty?

I also hadn't forgotten the inflated rate he had charged us for a few day's accommodation. Money ... My fingers felt for my small purse. Reassuring myself, I stroked the crisp neatly folded Australian notes—two tens, one five, and two dollar notes—the fifty-cent coins felt cold to the touch. The permitted foreign currency for the four of us.

❖

I remembered back to when the exodus from the country had first started. I was twelve years old then, and history was about to disrupt all our lives. Thousands of us, East India Company descendants, had forebears who had forebears who had, as far back as the seventeenth and eighteenth century, arrived in India. British and European settlers, army officers, soldiers and adventurers. We children now stood at the convent on that hot August afternoon in 1947, clutching an Indian Independence Day commemoration medal and singing, with gusto, the unfamiliar Hindi words of the new national anthem.

After Independence, riots and bloodshed tore the country apart. Partition brought with it heartache and disintegration. One morning, I heard shots being fired. I rushed to the window and saw looters running from the shops with bales of cloth, tins of food and whatever they could lay their hands on. One man was struck by a bullet while running with a sewing machine on his shoulders.

'My puppy,' I thought in terror, and dashed to the front veranda, scooping him up in my arms. A shout from my frenzied mother brought me to my senses. I crouched behind the low wall and crept back inside.

'Your head is an easier target for a stray bullet than the puppy on the floor,' she screamed in fear.

Shops and schools were shut. Groceries were sold in secret wherever they could be … on the terraces of tall buildings at nightfall or in quiet corners. With displaced persons pouring in from over the border, squatting was rampant and accommodation impossible to find. Whole families were living together in a single room.

Shiploads of family and friends had started leaving by every P&O liner for either the UK or Australia. Others chose to remain.

❖

'Below us is the Vietnam war.' The pilot's announcement brought me to the present. He continued his announcement. 'Our estimated time of arrival in Hong Kong will be 4 p.m.'

I felt relief but it was to be short-lived.

'Sorry, madam, you will have to make a stopover for the night in Hong Kong due to engine trouble,' an airport official announced after we had landed.

'I can't. We have to leave tonight.' I remembered my husband's caution.

'Qantas might have a few seats—but you'll have to wait six hours. We'll transport you to and back from a hotel in the city, for a rest and some refreshments.'

'Thank you,' I mumbled with resignation.

Tall skyscrapers and spotless streets—a sharp contrast to the ones I had left behind. After a rest, we walked to the nearby Chinese markets. I had a tight hold on my purse. But my six-year-old had other ideas. She had fallen in love with a doll with long blonde hair. It came with a tiny brush. I remembered the Shirley Temple doll I had been given when I was her age and hesitantly opened my purse, parting with, to me, the vast amount of $5. It wasn't till many years later that my son enlightened me to the fact that the $5 would have been Hong Kong dollars and not the Australian ones that I had mistakenly paid. I didn't need to calculate what the kitty now held.

On returning to the airport, an official demanded in Chinese English, 'You have to pay $28 airport tax.'

Stunned, I replied calmly, 'I don't have it.' Were they going to toss a visibly pregnant woman and three small girls into prison? After patient explanation about the engine trouble and the six-hour wait, we found ourselves seated safely in a Qantas aeroplane sucking on the first Minties[1] of our lives.

'We'll be in Sydney in the morning,' I promised the girls cheerfully.

After a short midnight stop in muggy Darwin, Sydney ... the Harbour Bridge ... and the brightest blue sky and sea I had ever seen.

'Customs won't take long,' I said to the impatient children. The two suitcases held a few new clothes.

'What's this?' a blustering red-faced officer grunted, holding up a bulging brown paper bag.

1 Minties is a brand of chewy, white, peppermint-flavoured sweets that attained the status of national icon. Its advertising featured people in difficult situations all with the caption, 'It's moments like these you need Minties.'

'Oh! Those are some fresh green chillies for my sister. She hasn't tasted one in a whole year!' I begged for leniency.[2]

Plunging his big fist into the depths of the bag, he growled, 'Neither have I!' With a swift movement he stuffed a fistful of plump green chillies into his pocket and handed me the bag.

Grateful to have escaped the lockup once more, I fled with the girls through the nearest exit.

'Look out for uncle and aunty,' I said, exhausted. A sea of strange faces stretched before us ... Search as we did, our hopes gradually faded.

'They couldn't have received my telex,' I wailed.

The lady at the desk nodded in sympathy.

While the girls sat in a huddle, I searched frantically for a telephone number.

'Hello?' ... a crackle over the line, then ... my sister's voice! 'We've just returned home. Wait there, don't move, we're coming back,' she promised.

At last a tiny Volkswagen drew up alongside the kerb. Amidst hugs and tears of relief, it was loaded with two suitcases, three children and a large lady to make the trip through Sydney for the fourth time that day.

Today, almost thirty years later, I can still remember the joy of our reunion as my mother opened her arms and welcomed us to our new country.

2 Anyone who has flown into Australia will be familiar with the strict import controls on any vegetable matter so as to protect a relatively disease-free island continent.

RIHANA SULTAN

Born in 1977, Rihana Sultan has a degree in Communications. She lives in Sydney and works in the public service sector.

'Not a House but a Home' first appeared in *Waiting in Space: An Anthology of Australian Writing,* edited by Paula Abood, Barry Gamba and Michelle Kotevski and published by Pluto Press in 1999.

Not a House but a Home

'This has ruined the whole décor scheme,' my mother sighed. She was not looking forward to the next time we had visitors.

'Now people will refer to us as The People With The Whiteboard,' she said, laughing into her mug of tea.

As a result of my father's best friend owning a used furniture shop, we were often surprised by strange new purchases which would suddenly arrive at our house. But now with the latest purchase, the tone of, 'did you seriously pay good money for that?' had reached, 'what the hell were you thinking?!' proportions.

One afternoon not long ago I came home, walked into the lounge room, and there it was. Leaning lengthways against one pastel pink lounge-room wall, its sleek white surface shrouded in new-smelling thick clear plastic, was the newest addition to our family's eclectic collection of household furniture: a whiteboard.

There has never been any real explanation from my father as to why, of all things, we suddenly needed a whiteboard as big as a bay window.

'As if we are opening a seminar centre,' my mother had muttered sarcastically when she first saw it.

When one of my sisters worked up the courage to ask why, other than a vague suggestion that we 'write something—anything,' my father revealed nothing. Instead, he just sat in his dark brown armchair with the fraying arms and ignored, or perhaps pretended to ignore, our confusion over the whiteboard.

Of course, deep down, we all knew what our father wanted us to do: write Arabic. Being a late-sixties immigrant from Jordan, my father wanted his half-Indian children to learn his language. When I was about five years old, he made me go to Arabic Sunday school.[1] I hated it. The other kids teased me because I didn't look like them and because I didn't already know how to speak Arabic. The only good thing about going to Arabic school was that I could eat as much junk food as I could carry. Of course now I realise that my parents used chocolate as blackmail.

Since my parents didn't own a car, I went to Arabic school with some Lebanese kids who lived in our street. The man who drove us only had one-and-a-half legs. I never found out what happened to the other half, but it was his left leg that had been amputated, so he could still drive. Then one Sunday, I realised that he had two whole legs again. Not knowing anything about the miracle of prosthetic limbs, I had just assumed, with a kindergarten mentality, that his leg had grown back, foot and all.

For a couple of months the whiteboard remained in its plastic outfit, its pristine perfume fading fast. Then it was moved to a different room with a different shade of pink. Now suspended precariously by two screws at the top, it is the first thing you see upon walking through the front door.

I was livid when I first saw it perched there. Barely a month before, I had spent an entire day painting the front room and now, thanks to the whiteboard-hanging-man's shoddy workmanship, not only was there a humungous whiteboard gracing the main wall, but there were scratches in my once-immaculate paintwork.

'I am never doing anything in this house again,' I yelled at my father who, knowing full well that he had made a huge decorating faux pas, said nothing.

1 Australian schooling is almost universally in English. A few 'community' and 'foreign' languages are included in some curricula, but most migrant communities provide language classes for their children on weekends. The phrase used here is ironic since Sunday School is historically what Christian children attend as a junior alternative to church.

Occasionally, my sisters and I do make use of the whiteboard. But to my mother's dismay, it is usually only to put in ink the insults and smart-arse comments which we are so fond of hurling at each other. Inevitably, there are incidents when we have to greet people at the front door with one arm struggling to unlock the screen door[2] while the other frantically erases inappropriate messages. I did, however, learn the prayer that my father wrote on one quarter of the board.

Of course the whiteboard is not the only curio to be found in our house. Other items include a sextet of oversized waiting room chairs. With skins of dried blood red leather, the square-backed chairs had legs of rust-spotted, highly reflective silver metal and arm rests equipped with built-in ashtrays. But in a house full of non-smokers, this feature is put to use as a cup holder.

Heavy as they are to move, and with their ghost auras of stale cigarette smoke, my mother hates the waiting room chairs. The main lounge room is home to three members of the much-resented leather clan. The one near the yet-to-be painted grungy yellow side door is a resting place for many a prayer mat and a string of rosary beads, while another squats conspicuously by the stairs. Completing this trio is the most cursed one of all—it sits right in the path of the midnight visits to the second bathroom at the other end of the house. To reach the other bathroom, you have to journey through the study, and it is there that you encounter the final pair of the waiting room rejects.

Waiting room chairs and whiteboards aside, a more recent acquisition from A&D Sadi New and Used Furniture is a battered upright fan. For now it has found a home in the corner next to my father's armchair. As a result, watching late-night movies has taken on an air of the unnerving. Peripherally, the fan can be downright eerie. Although the enamel on the protective cage around the fan rotors was once probably slick and eye-blindingly white, it now oscillates like a giant mechanical sunflower, jerking and nodding in all manner of directions.

Another curious contraption adopted by my father was the portable dust collector, a fairly nondescript plastic box, about the size and shape

2 A modern version of the wire 'flyscreen' door, with a metal grille that can be locked as a security measure.

of a VCR box. People not accustomed to the concept of air cleansing usually ask, 'So what is it for?' We sometimes explain that one of my sisters has mild respiratory problems, so perhaps this purchase was justifiable. But after minimal usage during the customary period of a gadget being a novelty, which in a house full of novel gadgets lasts little more than two days, the dust collector now sits in the hallway. Looking new, unlike the fan, and still encased in its foam packaging, it earns its keep as a full-time door-holder-opener and a casual wet towel rest.

Being the reluctant recipients of another man's trash, which has come to be perceived as treasure by my father, it all comes down to the fact that while these items are strange or even useless, they make our house a home.

A fan is a fan is a fan after all, and come an especially hot day, it may well prove to be a welcome, although disturbing, piece of equipment. The waiting room chairs, too, are chairs all the same, and have been known to come in handy. And there are those windy days when the dust collector does its best work both in collecting stray dust and ensuring that the hallway door doesn't slam with every aggressive breeze.

Which leaves the whiteboard. Letting optimism prevail, it could possibly assist in deterring overzealous Jehovah's Witnesses,[3] though my father invariably invites such missionaries in for a drink, and then proceeds to lecture them on the teachings of the Koran.

3 Jehovah's Witnesses are members of an exclusive sect of Christianity which believes in a literal interpretation of the Bible. They are famous for knocking on doors to convert people to their religion.

BRIJ LAL

Emeritus Professor Lal taught Pacific History for many years at the Australian National University, Canberra. Born in 1952 and originally from Fiji, he played a major role in constitutional reform but was expelled from the country in 2009 following the third coup against parliamentary rule. His distinguished career was recognised in his being made both an Officer of the Order of Fiji and a Member of the Order of Australia. He has written poetry, critical studies of the Indian diasporic community in Fiji, and a number of personal memoirs, most notably those in *Mr Tulsi's Store* (2001), published by Pandanus Books.

'Kismet' is one such story from that collection. It is framed by the transportation of contracted labour from India to Fiji by the British, resulting in a unique but not always harmonious mixing of races, castes and religions. Note, in Fijian names, *b* is sounded *mb*, *q* is *ngg* and *c* is *th*.

Kismet

'The bond between us
Is chimerical surely
Yet I cannot break it.'
– *W. H. Auden, 'You'*

Class of 1969. There is for me something very special about my first group of students at the Labasa Secondary School, unforgettable, like the first kiss, the first dizzying puff of a cigarette or the first taste of beer. The students seemed innocent and full of promise, and I was fresh out of college. A cultural desert, my Viti Levu friends had said about Labasa, a dry, dusty, one-street sugar town, at the edge of everything. A haven for misfits and missionaries, someone else had remarked. But scholarship boys like me had no say about where we were posted. At least the school had a fine reputation, and I saw my time there as a limited sentence, a starting point for an eventual career in the Education Department, hopefully as an Inspector of Schools. In the end, I remained at Labasa Secondary for only one year. What a year it turned out to be.

I have often wondered where my students are now. They were such a likeable lot, respectful of teachers and full of earnest ambition. I remember them well: Satish, Mahend, Liaquat, Vinod, Radha, Sambhu, Mustafa. Some of them went on to university, but many left school midstream to join government service, the local bank or the field staff of the Colonial Sugar Refining Company.[1] And the girls: so deferential and delectable in their white dresses. They had such magical names: Gyan, Daya, Maya, Naz, Saira, Sushila, Feroza, Priya. The boys were at school to prepare for jobs but most of the girls, or their parents, had a good marriage and a secure domestic life uppermost in their minds. If husbands agreed, a minor career as a bank officer or as a typist might be possible, but no more. Such a waste, I always thought, beautiful promise lost forever to children, husbands and mindless domesticity.

Of all the girls, Mumtaz stood out for me. I fell in love with her the moment I set eyes on her. Love at first sight, you could say. Something about her marked her out as special, proclaiming rare defiance and playfulness. Darker skinned and taller than most, she had an exquisitely chiselled face: liquid brown eyes, sad and haunting, sensuous, well-formed lips, and long, dark, wavy hair. She was smart but erratic, often daydreaming and invariably late with homework, the first one out of the room at recess and lunch and the last one in. She was the leader of a pack who promised adventure to her friends. Yet there was also a hint of sadness about her that seemed to hide a deeper pain. It was that curious mixture of daring and sadness, of pain and playfulness—or play acting—that I found most attractive. I looked forward to my morning class, knowing that Mumtaz would be there, in the last row, sitting neatly behind the wooden desk, pony-tailed.

1 The Labasa district was given over to sugarcane farming. Imported Indian workers were originally housed in barracks and developed as a community insulated from the indigenous Fijian population—hence the almost completely 'Indian' context of this story. This artificial division in colonial society eventually led to political conflicts in an independent Fiji.

I used to miss her whenever she was absent. I did not know if she had any boyfriends. Probably not, for Labasa was notorious as a murderous place where cane knives had lopped off a few unsuspecting lovers' heads. I did not want to find out.

My feelings for Mumtaz grew with time, causing heartache and anguish I had not experienced before, did not know was possible. Whenever we met in the corridor, I felt self-conscious and awkward. Mumtaz would avert her eyes, smile and say, 'Good morning, Mr Akash.' A few paces down, the girls would break out into a giggle. Once or twice, I caught them looking back at me teasingly. Was I making my feelings *that* obvious, I sometimes wondered, anxious and vaguely embarrassed, but also helpless. I often wondered whether Mumtaz understood how much I was in love with her. Hopeful signs came at the end of the first term. A few times I caught her looking straight into my eyes, unblinking, searching. Not a word passed between us, just silent glances, perhaps suggesting a deeper longing. Whatever it was, it was delicious.

In the second term, I began to look for opportunities to be alone with Mumtaz. Knowing that my colleagues preferred the Staff Room at lunch—where they talked, ate, smoked and played cards—to library duties at the same hour, I volunteered to fill in for them. Typical of me, they thought, the earnest, studious 'professor'. I played along. In return, they shouted me drinks and drove me around to weddings and parties on weekends. Mumtaz followed me to the library, often the only one, with a novel or exercise book in hand. I felt immensely happy to be alone with her. We communicated with each other through an awkward smile. I relished the joyful anxieties of these surreptitious moments together. Mumtaz was an avid reader of Mills and Boon. Once or twice she asked me if I approved of her taste. Did I like romantic stories? I did, I replied, but not Mills and Boon!

That year we 'did' *Wuthering Heights* for the School Certificate. That book remains one of my favourites to this day, its haunting tale resonating with twists and turns in my own life. Sometimes, I imagined myself as Heathcliff, plagued by a deep inner turmoil and a fierce, raging love for a woman he could never have, but who never gave up trying. I roamed the windswept moors in my mind as I paced the room. Mumtaz seemed genuinely intrigued by the novel.

How could a woman know the deepest feelings of a man's heart, she once asked. A good question to which I still don't have an answer. Was it ever possible to love someone so madly? Heathcliff's madness of the heart defied description. 'The heart has a mind of its own,' I replied, fending off further questions. 'Does the mind have a heart of its own, too, Sir?', she asked, not missing a beat. Her quickness surprised and pleased me.

One day during library duty, I asked Mumtaz whether she liked music. She did, especially songs played over the radio late at night: *Farmaish,* Requests, and *Bhoole Bhikhre Nagme,* 'Songs of Yesteryear'. Songs by Rafi, Talat, and of course, Lata Mangeshkar. I knew these programs, which featured sad romantic songs that often tore at the heart in the unlit stillness of the night. As you listened to the names of the people requesting sad numbers, you realised just how many lonely hearts were out there. Mumtaz sometimes asked if I shared her taste. When I mentioned something about reality, she interrupted me abruptly. 'Love is not about reality, Sir. It is about dreams. When the hope of true love burns bright, all difficulties dissolve.' Probably a mangled quote from something she had read somewhere. Why wasn't I like the other teachers, playful, relaxed? Why did I read so much? What secrets did I hope to discover from books? Some questions have no answers. '*Kismet,*' I replied, fate, and left it at that.

From songs to films. Mumtaz, like most girls of her age, was intensely curious about them. What did Waheeda Rehman look like on screen? And Dilip Kumar? What was that much-talked-about film *Admi* all about? And the tragic triangular love story *Sangam*? Indian films are long and syrupy, their plots mindless, meandering, but that was the only entertainment available in town. So one day I asked her whether she would like to see a movie with me. Mumtaz shot a glance that needed no answer. And then she turned her head away towards the window. 'Oh you need not worry about that. There will be something for you in the book that I am lending you.' I meant a five dollar note for her bus fare and the movie ticket. Mumtaz remained silent. After a long pause she said, 'They wouldn't allow me to come to town on Saturday alone.' Her family, she meant. 'Good girls' stayed home and helped with housework. 'Then bring your mother along.' 'Thank you,

Sir,' Mumtaz smiled as she sprinted out of the library. Mother or no mother, all I wanted was to be with Mumtaz.

We usually went to the morning matinee at one of the town's two theatres, the Majestic and the Elite, such improbable names for this rustic place. I would stand discreetly near the entrance, taking the seat next to Mumtaz just when the lights were beginning to be dimmed. All week, I lived for this moment of darkened bliss: the songs, the casual touching of hands, the soft sighs, the gentle rhythmic tapping of the floor, a smiling glance, sweet squeeze of the forearm. With time, we got more adventurous. Mumtaz would send her mother to the vegetable market while she escaped to the municipal library next to the river near the fire station. Except she never went there. Instead, we sneaked behind the building to the huge tree on the bank of the river. There, sitting against the knotted trunk, with our backs to the world, we talked about everything and nothing, the way people in love do, revelling in the feeling of gradually increasing affection between the two of us.

Teacher-student love affairs are not common, I know, and rarely condoned by society. They are seen as unnatural, immoral, a breach of some unspoken understanding and trust. Teachers not only teach but are also expected to act as the guardians and enforcers of society's morals. They are substitute parents. I knew what was expected of me, but there was nothing I could do about how I felt about Mumtaz. The head has no control over matters of the heart. I was also aware of another hurdle, religion. In Labasa, Hindus and Muslims never intermarried. Even Sanatanis and Arya Samajis, orthodox and reformist sects of Hinduism, North Indians and South Indians rarely intermarried, because of ancient prejudices about colour and caste. The Hindu-Muslim relationship, however, was beyond contemplation. How this hardening of attitude came about, despite the common levelling of experience of indenture and later village life, was beyond me. The line drawn in the sand was firm, not to be crossed. But I was not daunted by such difficulties. I knew that at the end of the year, or soon afterwards, come what may, I would marry Mumtaz.

Towards the end of the second term, just before the school break, Mumtaz asked to see me for a couple of hours on that weekend. I didn't ask why, but borrowed Krishna's battered blue Falcon and waited for her at the river at the end of the market. Then we drove across the Vumika flats towards Malau, the nearest picnic spot in town, once pristine but now made filthy from the smoke and sawdust from the timber mills. We walked gingerly on the pebbles, holding hands for the first time. Mumtaz was quieter than usual, as we sat at the edge of the jetty, legs dangling, casting bits and pieces of wood into the water below. 'I am afraid, Mr Akash,' she said at long last. 'Of what?' 'About you and me and the future. About us together.' 'Nothing to be afraid of,' I said, waiting for more. *'Jab Pyar Kiya to Darna Kya,'* I somewhat flippantly quoted a favourite Lata song, 'Why be afraid of being in love.' *'Chup Chup Ahen Bharna Kya,'* 'Why sigh in silence?' Mumtaz was unimpressed.

'You don't understand, Sir. I am a Muslim.' I did. 'But what's that got to do with you and me,' I said, struggling not to betray my emotion too much, vaguely sensing what was coming. Looking into the distance, Mumtaz replied, 'My brothers will kill me rather than let me marry a Hindu. You don't know them, Sir. My own mother will disown me. That's the worst thing that can happen to a daughter. We have a saying in our language that the road to heaven is through service to one's mother. No one will come to our *Milad* and *Daras,* invite us to *Eid*. No *Salaam Dua,* no place at the mosque. We will be treated worse than lepers.'

Mumtaz had chosen her words carefully. Having thought about all this for a long time, she was now confronting the truth. Trapped and helpless, she spoke with touching earnestness. Words failed me. After a long silence, all I managed was, 'Love should have nothing to do with one's faith.' 'I know, I know,' Mumtaz mumbled, 'But life is not like that, is it, Sir?' She meant with her family. 'They will never understand. You should meet my brothers,' she continued, and I got the hint of terror and violence. Big and burly, they guarded their sister like bull terriers, threatening to smash anyone's head who dared as much as look in the direction of their compound. Mumtaz herself was frequently beaten for looking towards the road when men, even neighbours, passed by.

'Sir, will you do *nikah* with me?' Mumtaz pleaded. Without that Muslim ceremony, the marriage would be *haram*, impure, cursed. The children would be outcasts. Poverty had already put the family on the fringe; marriage to a non-Muslin would put them beyond the pale. I knew that family honour, especially the chastity of unmarried girls, weighed heavily with the rural folk of Labasa. And was the reason for many headless or mutilated bodies floating in Qawa river. But I had to be true to myself. I am not a religious person in the ordinary, temple-going sense. Spiritual yes, but not religious. One's faith was a private matter, and God should not police matters of the heart. I would never ask Mumtaz to change her faith. Mumtaz burst into tears as she leaned on my shoulders. She said she often prayed for Allah's guidance, beseeching Him to see things her way, 'Wasn't I [Akash], too, God's son?' she would ask. Didn't her father always say, '*Ram-Rahim*, all the same?' '*Ya Khuda*,' she said despairingly.

I was too drained for words as we drove back to Labasa, riddled with doubt, confused. Was I being stubborn? I was angry, too angry at the world for erecting and policing barriers that compartmentalised us into our racial and religious identities that negated our common humanity. Why does one have to choose between one's faith and one's love? Before she left the car, Mumtaz handed me a small brown envelope. 'Goodbye, Mr Akash,' she said quietly, as she disappeared into the dusty market crowd. I was afraid to open the envelope straight away. When I did at night in bed, I found ruled note paper containing the lines of a haunting Rafi song:

Who dur ke musafir, hum ko bhi saathlele, hum rahe gaye akele
Tu ne jo de diya gum, be maut mar gaye hum,
Charo taraf lage hain udasiyon ke mele
Hum ko bhi swath lele, hum rahe gaye akele.

The words and emotions they conjure are untranslatable. The singer is pleading with her beloved to take her away with him to some faraway place, away from all the cares of the world. He is her everything. Without him, her world is engulfed in unbearable sadness, unendurable. I felt immensely helpless and uncomfortable throughout that long, drizzly night, torn and pulled in different directions.

A few days later, I received a call from Nausori saying that Ramu kaka had died. I had to go and decided to combine my trip with the coming term's holidays. I wanted to tell Mumtaz about my plans, but how? I did not know her address. I also remembered Mumtaz's brothers and what they might do to me if they found out. I would be back soon, I thought, and Mumtaz would understand.

I returned three weeks later, expecting to find Mumtaz at the Saturday matinee. She was not there. I would see her on Monday, I told myself. It turned out to be some Monday. I knew the moment I entered the school compound that something was not right. Colleagues avoided direct eye contact, walking past me with a pretended busyness. Then, when the head boy came to fetch me, I knew it was all over. John Sharan, the Principal, shut the door, seated me on a chair in front of his paper-strewn table, and asked me to start from the beginning. How did it start? How long had it been going on? How far had it gone? Did the teachers know about what was going on? I told him the truth and my desire to marry Mumtaz and to seek another posting somewhere in Viti Levu.

John Sharan exploded after I had finished. I had let him, and the entire school down, he fumed. How could I? He had such high expectations of me, and I had such a bright future. Why was I so stupid to think that my affair would remain hidden? This was Labasa, not Wellington: everything was everyone's business. I couldn't stay at the school, he said after a long harangue; I had to go, for my own safety. Sooner or later they would come for me with their sharpened cane knives. I told the principal that I will go at the end of the term. I had to leave immediately, he insisted. I resigned from the school but stayed in Labasa for a few months.

I left the principal's office knowing that my career as a teacher was over. My reputation damaged beyond repair. Colleagues sympathised. Krishna, my best friend, was distraught at the thought of losing me, but he knew that in Labasa I would not be forgiven or forgotten, He was right; he was from Labasa. But I couldn't leave without first finding out what happened to Mumtaz. My heart cried at the thought of the terrible, merciless beating she must have endured at the hands of her brothers. For all I knew, she might have been murdered to protect the family's reputation.

I was determined to find out before I finally left Labasa. I even dreamed of plans to take Mumtaz with me. On the pretence of returning her books and papers, I borrowed Krishna's car again and drove to

Tabia, about nine miles out of Labasa. Someone there would know her address because there were so few Muslims in the settlement. When I enquired at Mr Tulsi's store, people pointed me to Mr Shamsher Ali. He was a man of substance, a big cane grower with a solid iron-roofed house and owner of the village's only Bedford truck. His Haj skull-cap and stylish beard and handsome body belied his 60 years. After a customary cup of sweet black tea, he asked me the usual Indian questions about my parents, where I came from. I lied about myself: I was Krishna, the friend of the disgraced teacher. I began calling him '*Chacha*', 'Uncle'. That broke the ice. It is the polite Indian thing to do, to treat older people as relatives. We talked about how Akash had resigned and left the school. Mr Shamsher was surprisingly understanding, saying the government was heartless posting young unmarried men to strange places. As I left, he asked, me—instructed, actually, in the old-fashioned village way—to visit him regularly. 'Treat this as your own home, *masterji*.' I readily agreed.

Over the next few weeks, Mumtaz's story revealed itself. Mahmood, Khalid Hussein's son, was the one who had spilled the beans. Apparently, Mahmood himself, a Sangam High student, was interested in Mumtaz, and his family had even thought of making a formal proposal to Mr Shamsher. Mumtaz's indifference to his assertive overtures had enraged Mahmood, who then told his family about Mumtaz's romantic involvement with me. In no time, the story spread like wildfire, and heads of Muslim families descended on Mr Shamsher to do something about the affair which threatened to bring disrepute to their community. Mr Shamsher had no choice but to act. He saw Mr Rahiman, chairman of the school's Board of Governors. It was Mr Rahiman who told the principal that my resignation was the only acceptable price for peace.

I wanted to know about Mumtaz's family, and this is what Mr Shamsher told me. Mumtaz was the youngest daughter of Mr Ibrahim. A Tamil Muslim married to a Malayali, he had come to Tabi from Ba. Why or when, no one knew, or cared to ask. After a few years, Labasa had turned sour for him. Mr Shamsher took pity and hired him as his field hand, housing him and his family in a rough, rusty lean-to structure at the edge of the farm across the road. Everyone seemed to like Mr Ibrahim. He was not fastidious about his faith.

He drank yaqona,[2] smoked and attended Hindu functions. He even sang *bhajans*, which surprised the village folk. The more I learnt about him, the more I realised that Mumtaz was her father's daughter. Mr Shamsher said that Mr Ibrahim was planning to lease a sugarcane farm in Seaqaqa across the mountain range from Tabia. But one day he died, just like that, of a heart attack, and his family disintegrated. The two boys, never much good, drifted away, leaving Mumtaz and her mother to fend for herself.

Mr Shamsher decided to 'keep' the family on the side, more out of pity and concern, he said. I believed him. Mumtaz's mother worked as a domestic help, washing clothes, planting rice, minding young children and infants. They got by. Then, things began to change. It was rumoured that Mrs Ibrahim was seeing other men in the village to make ends meet. At first, Mr Shamsher was not forthcoming, only saying things like a poor man's wife being everyone's sister-in-law, fair game for the village men. The gossip about Mumtaz's affair with the Hindu teacher broke the camel's back. Any affair for an unmarried girl was bad enough, but an affair with a Hindu was unforgivable. 'But *Chacha*, what has religion got to do with love?' I asked. 'It's Allah's will, *masterji*,' he said with the authority and conviction of a community leader. 'Everything has a purpose and a place. People are born in a faith and must die in it. Giving up one's faith is a thousand times worse than death.' Reason has no business interrogating faith, I realised. And Mr Shamsher's mind was made up anyway. '*Khandaan ki barbaadi*,' is how Mr Shamsher described the whole thing, disaster for the family. The Ibrahim family had to leave. Mrs Ibrahim pleaded for more time. They had nowhere to go. But Mr Shamsher's heart had turned to stone.

No one knew precisely where in Ba Mrs Ibrahim had gone to. '*Udhre kahin gain hai*.' People said, she has gone 'somewhere around there.' That Christmas holiday—and for several years afterwards—I went to Ba, spending days at the town market next to the river, hoping to find Mumtaz. But to no avail. Once or twice, I was so full of despair

2 Yaqona, pronounced 'yanggona', is kava, a liquid based on the ground root of a pepper-related Pacific plant. It is important in Fijian ceremonies but is also drunk socially for its mildly intoxicating effect.

that I thought of killing myself, but that would not bring Mumtaz to me. At least alive, I had a chance of one day finding her. That thought kept me going.

I left Labasa vowing never to return to that wretched place. I was not only unemployed, I was unemployable as a teacher. 'Cradle snatchers' have no place in the classroom, people said. But my heart had also gone out of teaching, knowing that I would always be looking for Mumtaz among my students, haunted by her memory. I returned to Nausori, broken and dispirited, a social leper, a huge embarrassment to family and friends. I moved to the town, rented a small room at the back of Makanji and Sons warehouse Rewa and took casual jobs as a salesman for Court's Hardware Store, as a driver for Patel and Company, as a bookkeeper at Burns Philp.[3] To keep my sanity, I attended evening History and Literature classes at the University of the South Pacific. And when troubles began in 1987, I applied for a migrant visa to Australia. For reasons that I still do not know, I was successful. I arrived in Australia in 1990 to live in Liverpool.[4]

Liverpool was a natural choice for me. It is a mini-Fiji, with its temples, mosques, churches; its spice and grocery shops, video outlets, fashion houses selling sari and salwar kamiz, restaurants and takeaway joints. A variety of social and cultural organisations, cacophonous and competing with each other for membership and funds, serves the community. Cultural evenings of song, music and dance, the celebration of festivals such as Holi, Diwali and Eid, are regular fare there. Newspapers proliferate, disseminating news about forthcoming events, soliciting contributions for this cause or that, announcing news of deaths, births and marriages. Pettiness and bickering, the bane of our community, are alive and well there, causing fissures and frictions which enliven the mindless suburban life.

The Liverpool shopping centre in the heart of Northumberland Street is my favourite place to gauge the ebb and flow of our community. I go there every Saturday. I see people in bright floral clothes, marvelling at the range of goods displayed in the cheap

[3] Burns Philp was a major trading company in the Pacific and operated the major department stores in several island countries.

[4] Liverpool, here, refers to a suburb which was then on the outskirts of Sydney.

shop windows, women haggling over the price of gaudy clothes, men bunching up around key street corners, surveying the passing human, especially female, traffic in a quintessentially Fiji way, leering. Keeping up with the Joneses, people compare notes about what they have, what they want to buy: which brand of car or refrigerator or furniture. I also hear sadly of young people on drugs who clog the local court. And I occasionally see boys with knotted hair, trendily torn jeans affecting the Rastafarian gait, and wonder how and why they have lost their way.

I was walking along Northumberland Street one day about a year ago when I saw a figure that looked vaguely familiar. She was assessing a salwar in one of the clothes shops. I instinctively stopped to take a discreet sidelong glance. Could it be Mumtaz? I could not be absolutely certain after the long passage of time. I wanted to find out, but thought it inappropriate at the time. Cultural protocol, even in Australia, discourages directness, especially with Indian women; and I am not exactly the extrovert type. Still, the figure—golden brown skin, hair stylishly knotted back, a slight flare of the hips from children—remained with me as I headed for my apartment, bringing back memories of a past I had nearly forgotten, the smell and touch of village life, of friends who had dispersed to various corners of the globe, the heartache of Labasa. I knew, as the week went by, that I wanted to find out if it was indeed Mumtaz I had glimpsed.

I returned to Northumberland Street early the following Saturday morning and went straight to the shop where our people go to buy their bhindi, dhal, atta and spices. In the local parlance, it is the shop for all reasons and all seasons. Time flew as I paced the pavement smoking incessantly, feeling slightly awkward and nervous, like a person preparing for an interview. Then just before midday, she appeared around the bend and headed inside the shop. It had to be Mumtaz. I followed her, weaving my way through the narrow space between the shelves, pretending to buy things myself. Getting close to her, picking up a packet of dhal, I asked gently, 'Mumtaz?' She looked at my eyes for what seemed a very long time. 'Mr Akash?' she said tentatively. My smile answered her question as we embraced.

'It is so good to see you, Sir,' she said as she pressed my forearm with both her hands. 'I am no longer your teacher, Mumtaz,' I said, as we headed to a coffee shop across the street. 'So just plain Akash will do.' 'Playing with words again, are we?' she shot back laughing. *Akash* means sky in Hindi. We talked for hours like two excited children. Mumtaz looked graceful, at ease with herself; conversation came naturally to her. But I was all nerves, stuttering, unable to hold my coffee cup steady. I felt awkward, after the passage of so much time. Obviously, Mumtaz was married. Her clothes and stylish manners gave her away. She must have married a European, I reckoned; Indian men would not 'allow' their women the freedom Mumtaz evidently enjoyed. I was bursting to find out more, but common sense and courtesy dictated a more delicate approach. We exchanged phone numbers and promised to keep in touch. Mumtaz was genuinely pleased to see me, I think, but what did she feel? Was the past forgotten? Was her pleasure simply the pleasure of meeting a man who once loved her? Did she, after all these years, recall her Labasa days with the same intense fondness as I did? I was afraid of the answers. Perhaps the past should be allowed to rest in peace. Mumtaz has a new life, I said to myself, and I have my memories. As I returned to my apartment late that day, I resolved not to re-open closed doors.

But my resolve melted when Mumtaz called early the next day inviting me to lunch. She was working as a project assistant in the inner city. 'And how is Mrs Akash?' she asked, with a mischievous twinkle in her eyes. 'You should have brought her along. I would love to meet the lucky woman.' 'There is no Mrs Akash,' I replied. 'No? Never?' 'Never married,' I ventured, 'but I have known a few women if you must know.' Mumtaz tilted her head and, with a trademark flutter of the eyelids, said, 'A pity.' 'What? Never married or the few casual encounters?' I asked. 'Nothing much has changed, has it Mr Akash?' she said, laughing. It certainly brought back the old memories. Mumtaz herself was married, to an Australian of German descent. But her tone discouraged further probing. She was so pleased she had met me, she kept repeating. She dreaded and despised Indian men, she said emphatically. 'I haven't met anyone like you, Mr Akash,' adding, 'And I don't want to anymore, either.'

Over the next few months of regular meetings over coffee and lunch, we re-established the old closeness of the Labasa years. But there was no physical intimacy. Both of us wanted it that way. I wanted to know how she had ended up in Australia, when. Mumtaz deflected my questions. She had come to Australia as a babysitter for her uncle's children. That sounded unconvincing. I persisted; I wanted to know her true story. 'That past has a place of its own, sir. It is now, this moment, that matters. And the future.' But she read my mind, and agreed to talk. 'Just this once. Promise me never to ask about my past again.' I did.

Mrs Ibrahim had returned to Ba, to her elder brother's place, an unwelcome, burdensome stranger. Indian society was like that: once married, Indian women belonged somewhere else as someone else's responsibility. Mrs Ibrahim made herself useful as a domestic hand, washing, cleaning, chopping wood, weeding the garden, working in the fields. She didn't complain; it was her '*kismet*', fate. But Mumtaz was different. People resented her independence and her vibrancy. She was frequently hit for playing soccer with the boys, climbing trees, talking too much or too loudly. She was trouble waiting to happen. So when Mrs Ibrahim became a defacto wife of another man in the village, the uncle wasted little time despatching Mumtaz to a distant relative in the squatter settlement in Waiyavi Lautoka. It was a dreadful place for a young girl, exposed to endless squabbles among neighbours, open promiscuity among her own friends and relatives, scrotum-scratching men groping, making advances, an attempted rape by her own distantly related brother-in-law. Mumtaz somehow managed to escape unharmed.

Mumtaz missed her mother. She was the only constant, loving presence in her life. She was protective of her, instinctively taking over the role of her father, calm, reassuring. The pain of her mother's complete dependence on an uncaring man, bearing all the taunts and jibes reserved for '*rakhails*', 'kept' women, distressed her. She asked her mother to leave. Together they would be able to make ends meet. She could wash clothes, mind children in the neighbourhood, do anything; at least they would have their dignity intact. And they would have each other. Mrs Ibrahim refused, knowing there was no other place to go. But for Mumtaz, the hardships and humiliations only stiffened her resolve. The only solution was to leave this wretched place and migrate with her mother. The happiness of her mother had become an obsession with her. But how? Mumtaz was unskilled.

One day, Ateca, a Fijian friend of hers, mentioned the name of an Australian man she had met who wanted to marry her. She herself was not interested, but Mumtaz might be. She was. A week later, she wrote to the man: 'Sir, my name is Mumtaz Ibrahim. I am 23 years old. I want to come to Australia. I want to marry an Australian man. I will be very happy if you could help. Please write back. I hope you like my photo.' Frank—short for Frankenstein—a tailor and a casual labourer, in his early fifties, liked what he saw. He knew that Mumtaz would make a wonderful trophy for him. Within a few months, he sent the sponsorship papers along with a one-way ticket, but not his own photo. Mumtaz was anxious about the new, strange world ahead of her, but she had little choice. Her mind was made up. She left Fiji, without tears, she said, and without once looking back.

Frank was hardly the man of her dreams, Mumtaz discovered when she met him at Sydney airport. He was old enough to be her father.[5] 'I locked my heart and threw away the keys,' she said, tears welling up. But with nowhere to go and no one to turn to, she too, resigned herself to '*kismet*'. Frank lived on a farm on the fringes of suburban Sydney, making a living as a handyman. He was a man of simple, unsophisticated habits. Shooting rabbits for food and fun was among his weekend hobbies. He guarded his new bride jealously like a hawk, monitoring every movement. For Mumtaz, her new life was as far removed from rural Fiji as it could be. Everything familiar had disappeared from her life: the festivals, films, the food, the friends. Once or twice she remembered some other families in the sprawling suburbs of western Sydney who were distantly related, but she was too embarrassed to meet them. Would they want to meet her? And how would Frank react? Probably fly into a rage and abuse her in public. So she spent the next three years on the farm, trapped, vulnerable, dependant. She planted vegetables, cooked, cleaned and occasionally got into fierce fights with Frank's children, some older than her, who resented her presence among them.

5 This story shows a practice common through the 1980s and 1990s: older white men would take on younger 'mail-order' brides, mostly from Southeast Asia. Sometimes an arrangement of mutual convenience, it also tended to involve exploitation and domestic violence.

Mumtaz was nothing if not enterprising. She got her Australian passport at the earliest opportunity and, with Frank's assistance, sponsored her mother. Later other members of the family arrived through sham marriages to Mumtaz's Australian friends whose fares she paid to go to Fiji: they got their paid holiday, and her brothers got their visas. Bringing her family became an obsession for several years. Her relations with her family had later soured, embroiled in petty jealousies which hurt her deeply but that, Mumtaz said, was another story. One day, after Frank had thrown one of his regular tantrums in a supermarket and left her, almost penniless, to find her own way home, Mumtaz decided that enough was enough. She bought herself a packet of cigarettes and a lighter, which said 'I am single and I love it.' The words lodged in her mind like a rock.

The next day, she left Frank, not knowing where she would go, but she had to leave him. Frank, full of rage, followed her for several months, threatened to burn down the apartment where she had sought refuge, begged her to return, but for Mumtaz, there was no turning back. The end had come. The next few years were hell for her, without employment, without support. The Salvation Army took her in, fed and clothed her and found her casual employment. To this day, she remains grateful to them for helping her in her moment of desperate need when others had looked the other way. After about three years of an aimless anxious life, she met David, an accountant. Seven years later, they are still married.

'Happily?' I couldn't help asking. 'What is happiness, Mr Akash, what is love?' And then the thrust, 'I once loved a man whom I could not have, who never bothered to come looking for me.' If only she knew the truth. David was a good husband, understanding and supportive. She had no reason to complain, she said. Complain? 'We have our ups and downs,' she said. There was nothing wrong with David, but the closeness had gone. The routine of marriage had snuffed out the physical and emotional intimacy of the earlier years. Cross-cultural marriages can be like that,' I volunteered. 'All marriages are like that,' Mumtaz responded emphatically. What she yearned for, spontaneous picnics, dancing on the kitchen floor, all-night parties, were missing. Now she was trapped in a mortgage and a moribund marriage. David was self-contained. He loved his golf and the occasional outing, but not much else. Mumtaz wanted, more than anything else, to recover the lost years of her childhood: Hindi music, Indian food, social gossip, parties. David did what he could to oblige. He went along to social functions and entertained Mumtaz's family and friends at home, but without understanding or cultural empathy for their way of life.

I realised, as she talked, that despite her modern, westernised appearance—the smoking, the drinking, the expensive clothes, the nightclub scene—Mumtaz was essentially a traditional girl at heart. She told me of her fascination with Hindi movies. Remembering Labasa, that did not surprise me. I had lost interest in them long ago, except in the new-wave art films by Shyam Benegal and Mrinal Sen: *Nishant, Akrosh, Junoon, Manthan*. She liked the syrupy ones with long-drawn-out romantic twists and happy endings. Why? She liked them because they helped her imagine what her life might have been, what she would have liked her life to be. She, too, would have liked a proper wedding, the *mehndi* on her palms, a big feast, the traditional send-off, the sort of things most village girls dream about. She, too, would have liked to be a *dulhan*, a bride, in a big family, spoiled, with lots of children and adoring grandparents. She hankered for a world that fate had denied her. It was all a dream in her heart, though, for she knew that, in reality, she had very little time for Indian men and the male-dominated values of Indian culture.

Mumtaz's is an improbable story of willpower and survival. I know: I come from a similar background of hardship myself. But for a girl, the ordeal must have been all that more difficult. Mumtaz's journey reminded me of the indentured women, including our own grandmothers, who had rejected violence and poverty and constant taunts of intolerant in-laws and, shouldering their little bundles, had left for unknown destinations a century ago. Such courage, such determination. Mumtaz having to sleep with a lawyer, from her own community no less, to get visa papers for her family processed, recalled the rampant sexual abuse of Indian women by European overseers as well as their Indian subordinates. I understood perfectly why Mumtaz despised Indian men. Her personal tragedy, she lamented, was after they had got their visas for Australia, her family had distanced themselves from her, disapproving of her independence and superficially westernised ways. Mumtaz was not bitter, just sad at the way things had turned out, sad that all the personal and financial sacrifices she had made over the years now counted for nought with her family.

'I am a survivor,' Mumtaz kept saying. That seemed to have become her motto. I could see her sharply developed survival skills. Her sharp tongue and an incredible ability to think fast on her feet were her handiest instruments. She told me about distantly related married Indian men who rang her for a date, knowing that she was married with a child but assuming that she was—must be—fair game, a loose character, just because she had married an outsider. Most times she would ignore them or quickly change the subject. But when they persisted, she would cut them down sharply. Like the man who, trying his luck, remarked casually to Mumtaz at a wedding reception that she must be a very 'experienced' woman, having married a white man, and he would not mind learning from her. 'Yes, I am experienced,' Mumtaz replied without missing a beat. 'I have a good teacher. Send your wife to my husband. He will teach her, and then you can learn from your "experienced" wife all your life!' I couldn't hide my amazement at her quickness and my surprise that these things happened here. 'I come from the gutter,' Mumtaz said. 'I understand the gutter mentality.'

Mumtaz was more than a survivor. She had triumphed over life's petty adversities, and managed to keep her head high amidst all the betrayal and tragedy visited upon her by friends and family. She was a restless soul, though, marooned, desperately wanting to turn the clock back to her adolescence when life had been so full of promise. 'What might have been: Don't you think they are the saddest words in the English language?' she once asked me. I nodded in agreement, as we talked wistfully about the lost years. Life with Mumtaz would not be easy, I knew, as I got to know her over the months. She was strong-willed, feisty, pig-headed, touchy to the point of rudeness when she felt slighted or challenged. She could be manipulative and vindictive as well. She had an indulgent self-consciousness about her own physical attractiveness, which she flaunted frequently to taunt and torment Indian men whom she thoroughly despised. And her casual attitude to her past marital indiscretions troubled me.

But Mumtaz was also soft of heart, and to friends generous to a fault. She had an infectious zest for life, an innocent exuberance and physical vitality that promised adventure and fun. With her, there wouldn't be a dull moment. I couldn't help but be attracted to her once again, fatally, like a moth to a flame. One day during one of our regular meetings in our favourite coffee shop in a quiet corner of Northumberland Street, I asked Mumtaz somewhat diffidently if we had a future together. It was a question that had to be asked. Mumtaz looked away. 'There is nothing in the world I want more than to be with you for the rest of my life.' I couldn't resist asking why. 'Because you give me my *bachpana,*' she said, my youth. With me, she continued, 'I can imagine myself to be anything: a little girl, a woman, a friend, a soul mate.' I was what she always imagined her ideal man to be: attentive, non-judgemental, unafraid of her independence. 'But?' 'Reality, Mr Akash,' Mumtaz said with a tearful smile, recalling our conversation all those years ago. Her commitments and responsibilities to her family. She would move one day, but not now. I knew, too, that despite their present feuds and fights, Mumtaz would one day return to her extended family. She secretly hankered for the imagined emotional closeness of her childhood.

She also did not want to break our relationship hoping it might bear the fruit we both desperately wanted. 'Can we still be friends in the meantime though?' Mumtaz asked with a pleading look in her eyes. I looked away with a welling sadness in my heart, knowing how difficult that would be for me. Lovers, or people in love, cannot be just friends. It is a cliché, I know, but it is also true. It would be impossible to continue a relationship like this without physical intimacy and definite commitment. I was also running out of time. In five or ten years' time, I would not be the man I am now. I did not have the heart to tell Mumtaz this, but I had been diagnosed with diabetes, and we all know the havoc that disease can wreak on the human body.

I was overcome by a feeling of betrayal and emptiness, tortured by the thought of having to give up something I had lived for all these years. The prospect of a life with Mumtaz I had imagined for so long was vanishing before my eyes. How I wished things turned out differently. Perhaps, some things are simply not meant to be. 'Everything has its time and place,' I recalled Mr Shamsher Ali saying all those years ago, as I left the café in the gathering darkness. '*Kismet*'.

SUNEETA PERES DA COSTA

Born in 1976 in Sydney to parents from Goa, Peres da Costa is an award-winning author and playwright. During her time in New York, where she was a Fulbright Scholar and received an MFA in Writing, she completed her semi-autobiographical novel *Homework*, which was published by Bloomsbury in 1999. The novel was a tragicomedy about migrant neuroses and contained satiric vignettes on Anglo-Australian national identity. She has written many successful radio plays and has recently published poems in *Contemporary Asian Australian Poets* (2013). Her new novella, *Saudade*, was published by Giramondo in March 2018.

'Dreamless' is taken from *Fire and Shadow, HEAT 1: New Series* (2001) by Giramondo. Part autobiography, this meditative piece is also a literary evocation of diasporic anomie and a writer's notebook.

Dreamless

For a brief interval of my life, I did not dream a single dream. If I had dreamt and forgotten, it would have been another matter, but as it was I was convinced I could not dream at all. When this happened to me, I had just moved from one country to another, one continent to another. In fact, my world had literally been turned upside down because these two continents were also in different hemispheres, such that I would sometimes wonder, like Alice, as I fell into my albeit much more desolate abyss of sleep each night, 'Might I reach all the way to the other side of the earth like this, might I reach home this way?' I had been reading *Alice in Wonderland* while waiting at the real estate broker's office in the new city to which I had moved. I had bought the copy of *Alice in Wonderland* for a few dollars on the street before I went in to meet the broker; on the first pages, as she plummets towards Wonderland, Alice guilelessly remarks, 'How funny it will seem to come out amongst the people that walk with their heads downwards! The Antipathies, I think …' And as I had read her words the slip was very pregnant to me because it was with some bad feeling that I had left my own antipodean home.

Before I left, I had written a book, a book that meant a great deal to me at the time I had written it; the book was about many things, but mostly it was about madness. Sometimes while writing it, I would become so absorbed by the story's sadness, so consumed with its reality, as though in the throes of a terrible nightmare, that tears would be rolling down my face without my even being conscious of them. When I arrived in the new country, the book was about to be published, but the feelings of importance I had had for what I had written had now turned to indifference and perhaps shame.

When people questioned me as to whether the story was autobiography or fiction, I offered convoluted arguments of form, though what I really wanted point-blank to answer was that to me there was really no difference between these concepts. If there was a difference, it was as difficult to distinguish as that between my actual face, the face that I knew so well, and the angry wounded face reflected in the blurry bathroom mirror of the new apartment I had illegally leased. (As it happened, the broker who I had gone to see had told me that it was too difficult to find me a home as I did not possess an adequate 'credit history': in realtor vernacular, a euphemism for the fact that I had no finances. Actually, if I had been in serious debt, he pointed out, this at least would have constituted a history of a kind, but as it happened I had no history at all.) What I wanted to answer, when I was questioned about the reality of what I had written, was that reality could be darker than Dostoyevskian realism.

I was thinking of Dostoyevsky because as I lay down on the sofa-bed which I had bought with my last savings from a charity shop in my new neighbourhood, I was trying to read *The Brothers Karamazov*, but so insensible was I to this terrifyingly hallucinatory universe, that I found myself turning back every few pages, able to take in only little of the story. The words swam before me with little purpose or distinction; the fate of each character was numbingly predictable. Indeed, I felt bored by Dostoyevsky! I was not tired, but reading *The Brothers Karamazov* this evening—it was early dusk—on my tattered, perforated sofa bed, I fell asleep.

In the beginning, I could fall asleep at any moment. I could nod off without any trouble at all, and when I awoke after sleeping for twelve hours, I was the most tired then; not tired in my bones as though I had slept too deeply or too much, but weary with a vague feeling of disgruntlement. I should say that this weariness was something I had never known before. My whole life, I had woken in earnest and with an uncanny conceit about my place in the world. In the world, if people were distinguished by their night and morning sensibilities, I would be a 'morning person', by which I mean that I rarely hesitated about the importance of getting out of bed.

There was a writer, Jean Rhys, who lived earlier last century and whose work was so ahead of its time that she remained until her death quite unrecognised. It should cause no sadness that her fame was largely posthumous; what is remarkable is that anyone achieves fame before their life is finished. Reading her work, which speaks with honesty, with a brutal kind of candour about not feeling in place anywhere in the world, I would have the feeling that her words had no skin, no surface, and these open wounds that were her words would cause me to sigh. I thought about Jean Rhys now when I awoke, tired and disgruntled. I thought in particular about one of her late stories, 'Let Them Call It Jazz', written from the point of view of a West Indian woman who is evicted from her London flat; her destitution, her solace in alcohol. Jean Rhys was an insomniac, she was an alcoholic and, although for a long time she was forgotten by the world, she was prolific. In many of her novels, she wrote about women not wanting to get out of bed of a morning. I thought about her because in order to write as well and as much about women who did not want to get out of bed of a morning, Jean Rhys would herself have had to have risen pretty early.

At the time that I stopped dreaming, I believed the feeling of numbness that hit me in the morning when I awoke with the sun on my face—I had not bought blinds or curtains because I had very little money and many debts; I was waiting for the money for the book I had written, but the money was very late in coming—I believed the nihilism into which I woke had more to do with my forgetting my dreams than not having any at all. I was not tortured by this forgetting because I supposed that it would pass sooner or later. When I woke up,

I would not dwell on my amnesia, but remembered that I had many bureaucratic feats to perform, such as getting a bank account for the little money I did have; important purchases to make, like getting an answering machine. I would try to make the best of my ability to think about the future, but the future stood before me as a void.

When I went outside, it was strange to see the trees in full foliage in the middle of the year. The colours on the billboards and in shopfronts were so gaudy that I was at once drawn to and nauseated by them, as a child towards a fun-park ride. It was unnerving to see taxis speeding by on the opposite side of the road; it was perturbing that all the doors, except for the revolving ones, which I found absurdly existential, opened outward. I enjoyed the feeling that no one outdid me in my estrangement, that no one surpassed me in my alienation. I fancied my malaise was not dissimilar to that of the autobiographical narrator in *The Notebooks of Malte Laurids Brigge*, a book which I had in my possession and which I would read on public transport, wondering how it was possible that Rilke's poetry was so much superior to his prose; wondering how, when his verse was in formal German—a language I had to read in translation—I still found the cadences absolutely and unspeakably stirring.

And yet, it was the narrative disruptions of *The Notebooks* which I now admired. The frequent discontinuities of the prose seemed suggestive of my metaphysical state: I was moving on public transport; the subway or bus, as it happened to be, stopped to pick up other passengers and to carry us to our varied destinations; my momentum and thought were frequently interrupted and in continual renewal as the vehicle was reinhabited from the inside. This was a mimesis uncharacteristic of the Rilkean poem whose internal state is far more static, whose metaphors are always tightly sealed, whose structure is unbreachable even as its subject implores transfiguration. Rilke's prose was not perfect, my predicament was not perfect. I was not in Paris. There were children selling plastic trinkets on the subways; there were tramps and beggars all about me, but I was not in Paris; there was no one shouting a dissonant *chou-fleur*.[1]

1 This suggests the street sounds of Paris—a vegetable seller calling out in French, 'cauliflower'.

In the country to which I had moved it was hot because it was midsummer. I didn't know quite how hot because the temperature was calculated in Fahrenheit and Fahrenheit meant nothing to me. I felt giddy constantly; I wanted to drink litres upon litres of water. I took my clothes off piece by sweat-soaked piece while I cleaned my dirty apartment, for which purpose I had bought an inordinate number of bottles of pine disinfectant.

At the supermarket to which I had gone to buy the pine disinfectant, I had needed to buy a number of other things too, but as I entered the aisles, each one burgeoning with food and produce and household utensils, I became stupid and forgot the logical location of things. The simplest mental associations—that milk would be found in the same place I might find cheese—eluded me entirely. I sought cheese where the meat was kept and milk where the fruit and vegetables were. The supermarket itself appeared to me labyrinthine. My hunger was for the most basic nourishment: bread and oranges; coffee, cheese and some plain crackers; milk and fruit juice; shampoo. I searched for these items but because coffee for me meant Vittoria, and juice Sunburst and shampoo Pears, I immediately felt cheated by the fact that they weren't there; I imagined at once that the new and unfamiliar product names contained ersatz commercial goods, that I was being set up or duped.

My paranoia was fuelled by the fact that, even though I spoke the same language, some very basic things could cause bafflement and bewilderment to the people around me. One example of this was the word 'trolley'. It was difficult to believe that the word 'trolley', whose meaning I took quite for granted, could arouse such sighs of frustration and head-shaking confusion. As it took me some time to find that a 'trolley' was called a 'shopping cart', I carried the things I had wanted to buy in my hands until I turned a corner and saw the trolleys, jammed, as you find them everywhere in the world, one inside the other.

It was surfaces that were befuddling; it was the forms the groceries took, rather than the contents themselves, which appeared to me distorted. Under the garish lights of the supermarket, each object, from the packets of soap to the tins of pink salmon, was monstrous, a mirror that mocked me, a mirror in which I could not see myself reflected back without being overcome by a feeling of disquiet.

And yet, when I returned to my dingy apartment, the grocery bags lost this exaggerated quality; later, when I placed each item in the refrigerator—the light of which was broken—the groceries took on their familiar, utilitarian forms.

When I returned to my apartment, I wasted no time uncapping the pine disinfectant and scrubbing the blurry mould-mottled glass of the bathroom mirror; I wiped the grime that had become congealed with stale morsels of food on the hot-plates of the stove; I scrubbed the old, unfinished parquetry floor and the two streaky windows with a fastidiousness I did not know I possessed. I washed the bathroom tub and tiles. Finally, I sat down under the naked light globe in my kitchen. When I tore open the crackers and the cheese and began eating, I was eating to fill a hunger for which it was irrelevant what was fraudulent and what was wholesome, a hunger that came from a place more primitive than the names of the foods that would satisfy it, a hunger, I suppose you could say, without a name. And every few hours this hunger would return, for even though I may have lost my dreaming ability, I had not lost my appetite.

In order to open a bank account and buy an answering machine, the two feats which I believed would place me in the present, provide order and institute habit in my new life, I had to go out into the world, I had to come face to face with people. My trepidation was not unfounded, for everywhere I went to apply for a bank account I had to wait in a long queue to talk to the authorities. I had credentials, letters attesting to my legitimacy to be in the new country, but like Kafka's K, a stranger in the town about the Castle, I was continuously delayed and denied entry, I was continuously subjected to interrogations. Made patient to maniacal point, I felt I was losing my mind.

All of the authorities to whom I had to speak seemed impossible to locate. If I did locate someone, they seemed menacingly listless or, like the Landlady in *The Castle,* they stared at me with vacant eyes before launching into a series of impossible questions and interdictions. For the most part, I was left alone while people disappeared into nearby rooms to forage in deep filing cabinets, while someone called someone else on the telephone and spoke about me as though I were not there. At one time, someone sat before me but stared at a computer monitor without saying a word for an hour. Soon I began to wonder whether the heavy-duty air-conditioning systems—whose effect on someone like me, who had just come in from the outside, was to make them shudder with cold—had blasted the eardrums of the authorities.

I confess that part of the difficulty communicating was on my side: when I was admitted after a great wait and sat down to explain my situation, I opened my mouth to speak and my words would either pour out as volubly as water or I would speak in incomplete sentences, which would include tautology after contradiction. Sometimes a word, after it was spoken, would hover, with all the potential and poise of a new idea, then it turned soft and ineffectual, and then, before I knew it, it assumed the fragile properties of glass and promised to come crashing to the ground about me. My panic about this splintered glass would then cause me not to speak at all. Eventually, I got some answers, accomplished, as they say, the bare essentials, but these achievements seemed as much a part of chance and the indiscriminate bouts of pity that the authorities took on me, as any action I had brought about myself.

I could not dream and therefore I could not write: it took me a long time to make this deduction, but when I did I could see that good writing emerges from a sort of darkness; it requires an annihilation of space, an annihilation of time and that these annihilations have their phantasmagoric corollary in the dream which casts light on what the mind diurnally conceals. The resemblance between the dream and writing is in a sense that between what is original and what is plagiarised; there is always something inferior in the copy, something which betrays it as a copy as such, but the inferiority in time can come to be seen as an aesthetic virtue; the faults in that bastard text can make it in its own turn original.

I could not write. I could have imitated someone else. The writer Janet Frame came to mind. I was reading her novel, *Yellow Flowers in the Antipodean Room,* a novel about life-in-death and death-in-life. Frame loves in her novels to play with such juxtapositions and paradoxes; she loves to toy with dialectics of interiority and exteriority. It made me wonder, reading her novel, what part her misdiagnosis as a schizophrenic had played in her faith in language. For since her misdiagnosis as a schizophrenic Frame has written about people who, in one way or another, would rather be incarcerated than live in a world which, if not for psychiatric institutions, could be regarded as a psychiatric institution in its own right. I could not imitate Janet Frame: she was truly inimitable. When I say her literary output would not have been the same if she had not written because of what happened to her, I am trying to say that my own world, my waking world, would have had a huge hole in it too.

Now that I had invested money in an answering machine, I kept looking to see whether the answering machine was flashing at every moment. In this way, the answering machine became the only reference point for my earthly significance. I was perfectly aware that my family and friends were on the other side of the world—when I was awake they would be asleep and vice-versa—and still I made this demand of the answering machine: to account for my life, to register my gains, my losses. After a few days of seeing it blank, I began to wonder whether there might be fault with the answering machine, and so I went downstairs to a public phone booth to test it. Though the thought crossed my mind, I did not go so far as to leave a message on my own answering machine; I simply hung up, as I had on so many machines before.

Each evening as I became terrified that my sleep would be as empty as my answering machine, I would blink away my fatigue. And soon enough this took on the proportions of a kind of self-induced insomnia. Outside my tiny window I saw the moon, always waning it seemed. I looked at the clock, a wall clock so worthless it had been abandoned by the previous tenants (their leaving this particular plastic clock, repulsive to the eye, above a refrigerator whose light was broken and which leaked erratically, could only be a sign of their meanness, not of their largesse). If it was late enough, I knew I could call my family on the other side of the world. I was supposed to be asleep when they were awake; between us there were thirteen hours, which now seemed like all the time in the world to me. Now I could not see the space between us as a distance that could be calibrated. I could understand time—after all, time is the vector by which an insomniac measures her abnormality—but it was as if I had been flung into another galaxy in which, besides gobbling his fledgling children, Cronus had wolfed down space itself.

If it was not late enough to call my family and friends, I would lie flat on my back on the kitchen linoleum and go on like this, cataleptically, eyeing now the clock, now the moon, in whose expressions I was seeking, like a daughter in her mismatched parents, common guidance or a sign. The stars were seldom visible in the city to which I had moved; someone had told me that you had to squint to see them. But even when I squinted and squinted, I saw nothing but blackness and smog and skyscrapers forever. We say forever, imagining it is a time, but in fact forever is a space eternally empty of presence. It was not the calling long-distance itself but my ability to close the distance if I so wanted that comforted me more than the voices of those whom I had left and for whom I longed, because, it has to be said, I had left because they could comfort me no longer and, as for longing, one longs only for what is impossible, for what is irrecoverable.

It could be said that a person as cruel and bitter as I deserved nightmares, not dreamlessness, not a comatose-like insomnia. What I wanted was the power of choice, distinction, the right of refusal, all of them egotistical and childish desires. I had been called these things—egotistic, childish—before I left my home by a friend from whom I had become estranged. Notwithstanding our estrangement, the woman had given me as a farewell gift a book of poems by a famous poet of the country to which I had come. The poet was not a poet that I admired; his verse was imbued with an idealism I considered naïve. Although I did not believe in God, I loved poems that mourned the absence of God; I loved poems that spoke of the centre not holding. If I suspected that this sometime friend suffered a narcissism which she confused with mutual harmony, the fact that she had chosen this book of all the books she could have given me, was an innocent but telling example of her misreading of me. And yet, as I had very few books to read, one night I read from this book of poems, lines in fact about somnambulism and death, and I found them so beautiful and hypnotic that I chanted them aloud to myself: 'The wretched features of ennuyees, the white features of corpses, the livid faces of drunkards, the sick-grey faces of onanists/ . . . The new-born emerging from gates and the dying emerging from gates,/ The night pervades them and enfolds them.'[2]

2 These lines allude to a poem from Walt Whitman's *Leaves of Grass*.

So moved was I by these lines that I was overwhelmed with regret for the friendship which I had abruptly severed. I decided to call this old friend. I had her telephone number written somewhere. There was a time when I would have been able to recall it by heart, but now I had to search for it. She was a social worker and, after we had talked for some time, she told me, only half-jokingly, to see a psychoanalyst. It didn't do any good to counter that I was not depressed, only homesick. She was very good at convincing people that she knew them better than they knew themselves. She remarked that the city to which I had come was the world's psychotherapeutic capital and we both laughed and I continued laughing even when I hung up, but I was laughing at myself for my situation seemed so grotesque: I had no money to see a psychoanalyst even though there was a surplus of people who specialised in mental problems, there was a whole industry devoted to disorders.

The city to which I had moved was a monolith on a piece of land so tiny that it felt at any moment that it might disappear like Atlantis. It was clear that no one cared for anyone else; it was clear that people were dreadfully alone and empty, whether rich or poor, young or old—and the new city was full of piercing contradictions. To say that the degradation and inhumanity did not attract me would be a lie; no one had forced me to move to this new city. I had come of my own accord. The new city was extreme; its intensity delighted me because this intensity in all its manifestations, but especially when I walked its streets at night, imbued the new city with the quality of illusion.

When I was a child, there was a cliché of the city to which I had moved that said it was so energetic that people had little reason to go to bed. A cliché often has a lot of truth to it, a truth so hackneyed we forget to take notice. But in the case of this cliché there was little truth: the building in which I lived was always very quiet when I came in late, and I was sure that everyone was fast asleep. What's more, by day, the people in the elevator looked tired and irritated and, occasionally, as though they wanted to kill someone. When I looked at their faces, I had the increasing sense that their faces were my face too.

One of the first things I did when I received the money on which I was waiting was to buy a bed for myself. I had wanted to buy myself a bed on my birthday, but didn't have the money and I was worried about buying such an expensive thing on credit because until I had the money I didn't believe I would get it. This was a good principle it seemed to me at the time—to only spend what you had—but in fact it was impossible to live this way; my mother lives this way and it reduces everything to its most literal meaning. It is impossible to live this way because, living beyond one's means, not lavishly, but beyond what is easiest and most reasonable and fair, is often where love begins, despite what a psychoanalyst will tell you. And yet, this living beyond one's means, this yearning for more, is what makes us wretched and hateful.

The gift of the bed that I bought myself did not seem less important because I had bought it on any other day besides my birthday. I knew I would not have bought such a bed for myself if it was not *for* my birthday, but I did not delight in my new bed any less because it arrived more than two weeks after my birthday had come and gone. The day that I bought the bed I had gone out intending to buy only a mattress to replace the threadbare battered sofa bed on which I had been sleeping. I knew that an old man sold cheap mattresses of reasonable quality on a street corner not far from where I lived. When I went to his mattress shop, he painstakingly instructed me about the quality and texture of certain mattresses. I was so excited that I made the decision to buy a mattress very quickly. He would not accept a credit card and I had not carried my money with me because, unused as I was to having so much at once, I was concerned I might lose it. The nearest bank was about ten minutes' walk away and, while walking towards it, I caught sight of the bed that I ended up buying.

My bed, a high, Mexican sleigh bed of rosewood and wrought iron, was on display in the front window of a shop into which I would never have ventured except that the signs all about announced that a clearance sale was on. The bed was so significantly reduced that the cost of its delivery was almost as much as the bed itself. I pointed this out when I paid for it—and I paid for it on the spot because I could not help myself, with my virgin credit card—I pointed out, not stridently, but good-naturedly, that I lived very close by and that perhaps I should be eligible for a discount on the delivery of the bed.

But the sales assistant would brook no contradiction about the delivery costs, which she said were standard.

The two men who were assigned to the delivery of my bed were from the same town in the hinterland of Venezuela, a tiny town in which everyone, it was said, knew everyone, and yet they themselves had not come to know each other until they came to the city in which we all now dwelt. They had come for better opportunities, but because the degrees they both held were quite redundant in the new country, they made their living by moving furniture. They asked me what I did and, when I told them, without wincing, that I had written a novel, we began to debate whether it was possible to write without a home, how the writing about one's home is often distorted both there and away from it. One of the delivery men launched into a laudatory speech on Joyce, who, he claimed, perverted the irregularities of history, of language, irregularities by which all three of us had come to be in the world. He was so compelling in his discourse on Joyce that we got lost and once went through a red light. Now it occurs to me that I often got lost precisely because the city, laid out like a grid, was one of the most easy to navigate.

When I was able to dream again, I was happy. I didn't know what involuntary part of my psyche's impulses had set my dreaming to stop, but I was happy that my dreams had come back. In an effort to understand what had happened, I read Freud's entire *magnum opus* on the subject, but even then I could only grasp how the dream worked, not why, not why not. Since there were no condensations, no distortions or displacements to speak of, I wondered whether my dreaming insensibility mirrored my waking insensibility. If, as Freud says, the dream resembles a translation to which we must apply a waking hermeneutics, it was as though when I woke up I had never known the original language, never been a native speaker. My sleep had been more akin to a blank page, rather than an indecipherable script. When I began to dream again, it was hard for me to recall that grief I felt when I had been unable to do so. In fact, I had the impression that a joke was being played on me by the capricious gods; I had been unable to dream and could not remember what dreamlessness was like.

It was sometime after I began to dream again that I slept beside a man who had lost his family when he was young. He slept fitfully and often; soon after closing his eyes, he would cry out so plaintively that he would wake himself up. When I asked him what he had dreamt, he would say only that he had dropped something or slipped over. Sleeping beside this man, I had odd pleasant dreams which would come back to me wistfully during the day; then and there, thinking how comforting it could be to lie beside him, I would want to summon him to me again. I began to imagine that my sleeping beside him was natural and therefore imperative. My pleasure in sleeping beside him was so total that I could not think of a time when I had slept alone. It is easy to accustom oneself to what is comforting; what is difficult is to get used to what is unpleasant. This is never a revelation, yet each time it has the shape of a revelation. What is difficult is to do something with the pain that comes when you lose that to which you have, rightly or wrongly, but usually very easily, accustomed yourself.

This man was someone who, not really under the influence of any soporific, was always sleepy. During the day, if he answered the phone at all, it would be somnolently and to say that he was taking a nap. If we met in a public place, he had the habit of dropping off. While I left him for a few minutes at the entrance to a museum or requested that he wait outside a movie theatre so that I could go to the toilet, he would fall asleep leaning against a graffitied wall. He was infatuated with graffiti; graffiti was to him what hieroglyphics or ancient Greek tablets are to some curious and fanatical historians. How one could be so curious about the scripts of dead people I did not know, but I too had necrophilic predilections, I too was taken by the Dead Sea scrolls and by cuneiform. Because the meaning of what is undeciphered is yet to be revealed, always latent, it gives us hope. Illegible, unknown, it is like a disaster that is indefinitely deferred. Perhaps it is this paradox that piques our curiosity. I don't know.

All I know is that I could not understand my lover's infatuation with graffiti. The graffiti which he brought to my attention throughout the city—and it was a new city for him too—and also a new language; the language he spoke was an ancient one, guttural, full of fricatives, and he often reverted to it when we were making love, such that it had an onomatopoeic effect—the graffiti he brought to my attention was repetitive and hectic; nothing was indelible about it, not even its urgency. He tried to tell me that the graffiti amounted to an *effacement* of meaning, that the graffiti was anarchic precisely because it refused to be remembered; if it were erased by the city authorities tomorrow, this would not only be expected, but a testament to the graffiti artist's mastery. I did not refute him; I did not say that by objectifying the graffiti, by liking it, he too was missing the point. Rather, I thought, as he explicated the aesthetic principles of graffiti, that he had lost his family when he was a young man; he hated testimonies and memorials because they gave meaning to loss, exalted loss, when the hardest part of losing for him was the state of profound meaninglessness which was his life.

My favourite time to be with this man was night-time because he was most animated and alert then. Eating, to a gluttonous degree, appeared to fill him more than his actual hunger and, while watching him eat, I could forget that he would be falling asleep at any moment. One night after we had eaten dinner, he found among a pile of books on my coffee table the copy of *Alice in Wonderland* that I had bought months before when I could not dream, and we began talking about this book, a book that we had both read as children, he in the city that had been his home and from which he had exiled himself because there was too much hate, too much incivility, too little peace. I had read *Alice in Wonderland* in my home too, a place unravaged by war but a place that nonetheless caused me anxiety when I thought about it. He then gave me an improvised translation in his language, full of fricatives and gutturals, of the Jabberwocky's poem, a performance so enchanting that I asked him at the end to repeat it. There were other moments like this in which it seemed we were reconciled by something larger than the languages we did not share. I had loved enough people who did speak the same language to see that knowing someone, which often involves loving them in a hopeless capacity, has little to do with sharing a language.

I think that he could not bear to see me go away and so when he heard that I was going away for a short while he decided that he would absent himself first. The uncoupling of these two notions—parting, returning—begins at a moment when we are still helpless and quite vulnerable and it goes on and goes on quite unswayed by the arguments or muscle of our will. It does not take us our whole lives to work out there is no such thing as the beginning, no such thing as the end, often no end in sight at all. When the man who was my lover told me he wanted to end it, he drank a lot of coffee; he chain-smoked until my apartment was so full of tobacco fumes I went to the bathroom and threw up, after which I came out to find him reading the newspaper, another neurotic habit of his which caused us to argue even more. He had been a political correspondent before he left his country, a country that manufactured large-scale horror by way of a war with the people of a territory it had long ago annexed. The war was the largest industry in the country from which he had come, an industry that kept the mass media enthralled. We did not disagree on these points of argument, we did not disagree at all. Some things are irreconcilable; he wanted to end it, I did not want to end it and so it was not a question of disagreement; it was not a question of persuasion.

I was going away for a short while to promote my book and, when I was in the airplane, at an appropriate altitude to see things, I wondered whether he had read my book—he had not said anything about it—and that this was why he was leaving me. When I got off the airplane, I was taken to a convention centre where I drank a lot of alcohol. There was a party of sorts, but I spoke only to one woman who had come to promote a book that she had self-published with her husband, a how-to book for children on the subject of writing thank-you cards. I did not need to prompt this woman to tell me about her book; she did not stop for breath; and, when her husband came towards her, she continued her story with even greater élan. When they had got married, she said, they had stayed at a small coastal resort. There were such terrible storms that they had been flooded in for the first three days of their honeymoon. They were not made miserable by the rain, however; they were quite good at entertaining themselves, and one of the activities with which they entertained themselves was the writing of the three hundred and fifty thank-you notes for the wedding gifts they had received. Such was the reward for their ingenuity, resourcefulness and self-discipline: the how-to book on writing greeting cards had brought her by popular demand to a national book festival.

After I went away to promote my book, I went again, on a longer trip, a holiday. A holiday was something I had not had in a long time. I was going to holiday in the village in which my father was born.

A village is a small thing, barely a smudge on the map of the world. At the time my father was born, the village and the territory in which the village was located was part of Portugal. It was only when he was a young man that it ceased being so. On a particular day when he was a young man some soldiers from the larger land-mass which shared its borders took over the territory in which my father's village was located. There was no war, few reprisals and recriminations; very soon it was said that the territory, including the myriad villages such as the one in which my father had been born, had been 'integrated' with the larger sub-continental land-mass that adjoined it. But this integration in words amounted to very little in the minds of people such as my father.

The historical fate of each person is inexorable but varies in its degree of tragedy and comedy and farce. My father was an interpreter of the Portuguese language. Neither Portuguese nor English were his native tongues and it was a constant source of humour to me that it was by trading in these two languages—English and Portuguese, languages which had been used by colonial administrators centuries before to subjugate my father's ancestors—that my father had made his living. He did not get any exciting literary commissions. He translated birth certificates and marriage certificates. His efforts were often directed at jobs as prosaic as translating the written components of the driving test to Portuguese native speakers. The one question which would time after time floor the examinee was about blood alcohol levels. There was an irony in this because on more than one occasion, having been called upon to interpret at the trial of a Portuguese native speaker charged with drunk driving, my father had recognised the defendant as someone who had, years before, nudged him to get the answer to the blood alcohol question at the Roads and Traffic Authority.[3]

A village is barely a smudge on the map of the world but the village of my father's birth to which I was going occupied a mythic place in my imagination: its whitewashed gothic church, its green rice fields. When I thought of seeing my father's village, I wanted to capture with words my feeling of elation and sadness to be seeing it again. A place such as

[3] The RTA (Roads and Traffic Authority) is where people in New South Wales go to get their driver's licence.

the village of my father's birth which had been brought under the sway of now one impostor, now another, could hardly be said to exist except in language: the church built on the ruins of desecrated temples, the rice fields irrigated by landless aborigines—how else but by language could the violence and betrayal which was the history of the place of my father's birth be recalled? I was not taught the native tongue of my father; I was not taught Portuguese; and yet I had an intimation of *saudade*, that melancholy for lost things, often confused with nostalgia. *Saudade* is a melancholy with no object, a melancholy whose object is the insufficiency of language itself and, in this sense, it does not lose much in translation. The Italian writer Antonio Tabucchi has written novels and stories in Portuguese for the very reason that Portuguese offers him a posture of reflection and mediation he cannot find in his native language. His novel *Requiem*, which I am re-reading because I admire it so much, is the stream of consciousness of a somnambulist in Lisbon, a man who walks back in time towards his past and to the past of Portugal and indeed the whole history of Europe, all of which is staged as a wild reverie. The distinction between philosophy and fiction collapses around the autobiographical in Tabucchi's work to produce an uncanny, revelatory inventory of the possibilities of knowing oneself in an adopted language. For while language is not everything and is often nothing at all, it is all the same an entry point into the world without which we are dreamless, without which we are dispossessed.

Just before I was to go away, the post office lost a certified letter that the consulate of the country in which my father was not born but by which, by the vagaries of history, the village of his birth had come to be administered, was returning to me. The letter contained the passport of the country in which I was born, the visa enabling me to be in the country in which I now lived, as well as the visa allowing me to travel to the village in which my father had been born. The passport and visa to my father's place of birth were technically easy to obtain again, but it seemed impossible to obtain at such short notice another visa to be in the country in which I now lived. What's more, after making the necessary enquiries, I discovered that, without this visa, I would be able to exit the country in which I now lived, but I would not be able to re-enter it. This was a situation that seemed laughable at first and very serious after a few minutes thinking about it. I went to the post office, I went to the two consulates, that of the country that had issued me with the visa to travel to the village of my father's birth as well as that of my own country of birth, the country whose passport I had lost. I went to these consulates four or five times, for interviews, for questions, and after many long-distance phone calls and much currying of favour, I found a way to leave with the guarantee of returning, a guarantee that is always fantastic anyway.

The dream is not a rebus awaiting resolution; the dream, however we try to reduce it, is as incomplete as it is irresolvable. Just a few days before I left, I had the following memorable dream: the lover who had spurned me had come with me to the house in the village in which my father was born. There were many people there, many of whom I had not seen since I was a child. The many languages they were speaking at once constituted a veritable Babel. When I made to introduce my lover to them, I forgot his name and, hoping he would not notice, called him by a made-up name. Of course, he did notice the nonsensical name and, taking offence at it, went to sulk in the room where the family portraits hung. After some time, I remembered his correct name and, in order to make amends, went to address him by it, but he did not forgive me now, anyway.

When I woke up, I was crying. I knew my tears were for something else beside the certified letter, but it was the first thing that I remembered having lost. 'The dream is, as it were, centred elsewhere,' Freud writes. The recognition of the metaphoric displacement, of the condensation of my largest loss into the tangible-intangible 'certified letter', comes only now that I, too, am 'elsewhere'. To know that I had lost much more than the letter, I have had to remember what I had forgotten was gone, and that recovery is as difficult and as necessary as that of these pages which I lose every time there is a blackout here in the village of my father's birth (where I dream, where I see the stars) and where my battery-less laptop frequently dies.

SHALINI AKHIL

Born in Fiji in 1935, Shalini Akhil now resides in Melbourne. She is best known for her comic novel *The Bollywood Beauty*, published by Penguin in 2005 and made available by Momentum in 2012, which is about the trials of a young adult migrant trying to reconcile her modern urban lifestyle with traditional expectations from parents and community. Her work has appeared in various anthologies including *Growing up Asian in Australia*. She currently blogs on 'Kai India' and works as a stand-up comedian.

'Destiny' first appeared in *Meanjin* volume 63, issue 4, published in 2004, and is included here by arrangement with the licensor, Shalini Akhil, care of Curtis Brown (Australia) Proprietary Limited.

Like Mena Abdullah, Akhil uses humour and a child's viewpoint to support an assertion of racial-ethnic identity. 'Indianness' is not opposed here to an Australian hegemonic 'white' society, but rather made over into a more widespread struggle to make global 'Hollywood' culture meaningful in specific locations.

Destiny

I was very young when my obsession started; sparked by the cartoon version, it intensified with the television series. Every weekend I'd be rendered speechless from the first bars of the intro to the closing credits as I watched in awe, stretched out flat on my belly on the loungeroom floor. Every year I'd get the show bag from the Royal Easter Show,[1] and when we got home, I'd sneak up onto the garage roof and fight off make-believe villains whose faces always ended up resembling those of my brothers. They were no match for me—my

1 From the nineteenth century onwards, Australian cities put on annual public exhibitions of their state's produce, with demonstrations of rural skills, sideshows, etc. Many of the product stalls would sell bags of sample goods, or 'show bags', and these eventually proliferated to include comics, toys and so on.

reflexes were lightning fast, my aim was true and my hair flowed like streamers, dark and glossy in the sunlight. It felt right, being her. It was destiny. When I grew up, I would be Wonder Woman.

Then one day my grandmother came to stay with us. She stayed for a while, and she watched *Wonder Woman* with me. After a few sittings, I thought she was ready to hear my secret. I told her about my destiny. Though she commended me for thinking about the future, it seemed she wasn't as sure about my choice as I was. As we discussed my plans, my grandmother reminded me that I was Indian. It was then I began to realise I could never be exactly like Wonder Woman.

My skin was the wrong colour, my eyes were the wrong colour, and my legs just weren't long enough. Not that it would have made a difference if they were, because my grandmother didn't like the way Wonder Woman dressed. I tried to explain to her that what Wonder Woman wore was a costume, a special costume to fight crime in. But my grandmother kept saying that she thought it looked like she'd left the house in her underwear—like she'd forgotten to put her skirt on. 'You can fight all the crime in the world,' she said, 'but if you leave the house without putting your skirt on, no one will take you seriously.'

So we started to think about what a crime-fighting Indian girl might wear. Truth be told, I wasn't too impressed with Wonder Woman's choice of outfit either; in the cartoons her pants looked okay, but in the TV series they looked a lot like those plastic protector-pants they put over babies' nappies. Initially, I had tried to make up reasons for her to wear them: maybe she needed the extra padding just in case she fell over, or maybe the seat in her invisible jet wasn't very comfortable. But no matter how I tried to explain it to myself, I couldn't really see why they thought putting Wonder Woman in a pair of sparkly nappies would make her better at fighting crime.

My grandmother suggested that Indian Wonder Woman would wear a lungi. That way she could run and kick and squat and jump, and still keep her honour. I wasn't so sure about that, so my grandmother made me a deal. She said that Indian Wonder Woman could wear a lungi over her sparkly pants, and that way if she ever needed seven yards of fabric in an emergency, she could just unwind it from around her waist. She could use the fabric to wrap the bad guys up in and then tie them up with her rope. I thought that sounded like a good idea. We sketched a lungi over Wonder Woman's legs.

My grandmother didn't like Wonder Woman's top, either. She said that superheroes should have functional clothing, and that a strapless top just wasn't practical for a lady as active as Indian Wonder Woman would be. She liked the colours though, so we kept the basic design and added some shoulder straps. I wanted to cross them over on the back, and my grandmother said she could sew me a top like that, so we drew it into the plan. Finally we moved on to her accessories. My grandmother thought that all of her accessories should be made of 24 carat gold, and that her earrings should be more than just two red studs. Maybe they could be crafted from rubies instead; that way they'd still be red, but better than before. I didn't really mind about the accessories; all I wanted was a red Wonder Woman top with criss-crossed straps at the back.

At lunchtime my grandmother mentioned that rolling rotis was like a magic power. I didn't really believe her. But then I watched her as she rolled them one after the other, and they all turned out perfectly round. I don't know how she did it, because when I tried, they looked like blobs or squares. When my grandmother rolled her rotis, they spun slowly around and around underneath her rolling pin, and she didn't have to pick them up and stretch them out with her hands like I did. I was a little disappointed, but she said it had taken her a while to learn, and that she would train me. My grandmother said that the magic rotis were very good with superhero eggs, so I asked her if she would make some for me.

My grandmother chopped up some onions and some chillies to add to the eggs—she said they would make me run faster, and help me to see better in the dark. She fried them in a little oil and we both coughed; she said it was a sign that the power in them was very strong. She beat some eggs and poured them into the frying pan and stirred them around until they were cooked. She sprinkled some salt over the eggs and divided them between two plates. My grandmother said I could pick the chillies out into her plate if they were too hot for me, but I managed to eat some of them. The eggs tasted good with the magic rotis.

I felt sorry for the old Wonder Woman. I imagined her eating her peanut butter and jelly sandwiches alone, without a magical grandmother to suggest wearing a lungi over her embarrassing sparkly nappies. That day I decided to change my destiny. When I grew up, I was going to be Indian Wonder Woman.

SATENDRA NANDAN

For many years a Professor of Literature, Satendra Nandan became well known internationally when, as a politician, he was detained and then exiled from Fiji during the country's first military coup. He wrote about his Fijian childhood and political career in *The Wounded Sea*, published by Simon & Schuster in 1991, following it up with another autobiography, *Requiem for a Rainbow*, which was published by Pacific Indian Publications in 2001. Born in 1939, he studied in India, Britain and Australia, and taught for many years in Canberra before returning to set up a new university in Fiji, after which he retired and moved to Australia. Best known as a poet, his books are *Faces in a Village* (1977) published by Viti Publications, *Voices in the River* (1985) published by Vision International, *Lines Across Black Waters* (1997) published by Centre for Research in the New Literatures in English and *The Loneliness of Islands* (2007) published by Ivy Press International.

'At the Surgery' and 'Personal' are from Nandan's *The Loneliness of Islands: Collected Poems (1976–2006)*. 'A Remembrance' was published in *Caring Cultures: Sharing Imaginations—Australia and India*, edited by Anuragh Sharma and Pradeep Trikha and published by Sarup & Sons in 2006. 'In Between' appeared in *Mehraab* (*'The Arch'*), compiled and translated by Anuraag Sharma, published by A.R.A.W.LII Publications in 2008.

At the Surgery

All begins with the alphabet:
T was for twins
P for pumpkins or was it pigs?
Behind the Pauline girls,[1]
Van Gough's Irises on a print
Gnarled frame, snarled greetings.

1 'The Pauline Girls' refers to white women who were prejudiced against migrants. The label refers to a populist right-wing politician, Pauline Hanson, who favoured keeping Asians and Muslims out of Australia.

An AMA[2] chart for men: Check blood pressure, moles,
Cholesterol, hepatitis and prostate—
It made you sick
The clean artery next to the clogged one.

A Chinese man entered:
Trim in a floral tie
Walked right into the Doctor's door.
One of the Pauline twins
Jerked herself up:
'We here first
You must wait yeh turn in the queue.'

The Confucian forehead wrinkled
His astral eyes glittered inscrutably
Like a sliver of light
Through a winter's landscape.
But his voice was gentle, healing;
Accent Oxonian than Oriental:
'Madam, I am the doctor
You've all been waiting for.
Come in. I know, you need surgery.'
He smiled, his breath breaking
The bridge of time.

Personal

The faded photo
Like a daguerreotype
Inserted among the classifieds
The dying words of the living
For sale auctions divorces
Lost & found in memoriam
To let for rent ad nauseam

2 AMA is short for the Australia Medical Association.

A penny a word
Column after column
Such calumny of civilisation
Selling and buying we survive
On second-hand stuff
With the self-confidence
Of the second-rate.

The Personal caught my eye
The face familiar slightly suicidal
An old picture of a younger man
He was dead cremated
This is a belated acknowledgement
Of death floral tributes thanks.

I'd missed the death notices
On the radio
The nation's voice
With many a view
But not a single vision
The price now three dollars
Inflation diminishes even death
From we regret to
We've been asked
Announced crisply in cornflake accents
The words a second later
Coke is the real thing
Do it to me one more time
All said done heard
Like the flight of a frightened bird
In seconds.

Ah how a moment's eternity's
Lost between the noises of life,
We need more than stethoscopes
To hear heart's breaking
In an act of loving-living.

This a friend's face
Stared at me starkly
I'd known him since school days
We'd gone our different ways
He to a civil job on the islands
I had crossed the seas for continents.

Twenty years later
Under a dim light
On a drizzled night
I saw him in his taxi
Waiting for the last passengers
Looking a bit anxious
Things had changed
The city talked of blood
Sacrificial menstrual murderous
I waved from my car
I'd stop for him perhaps tomorrow.

Looking for green guavas
School children stumbled
On the body battered in the bush
Screaming they saw a taxi—abandoned
Not far from the scene so terribly obscene
The news I believe was on the air
Investigations were continuing
The police drove recklessly
To apprehend dangerous drivers
On the road to the cremation ground.

But for me
Tomorrow is never
I am
Once again so late
For another late friend.

A Remembrance

She comes back into my life
As wet wind on a winter's evening:
A pain I'd forgotten
In my former self—a foreign country.

My grandmother, wry and wrinkled,
Skin that holds the bones—
Crumpled bark of a tamarind tree.

I pass that gnarled life
Clutching gaunt branches
Stringy, scarred, deep sorrowed
Like veins on an old hand—
A furrowed field that lies fallow.

Some tenderness tugs
At the two tanpura strings
Of my self.
The night sings *bhajans*:
Secret sorrows that boughs knew
To make the birds sing,
As the dogs gnawed the bone
In its shade and shadow;
While the blood-tears of women
Made children grow with marigolds.

The anguish on an ancient face
Is all that remains
Of a world—half forgotten, half remembered,
So many memories then
So many embers now, burning
As I hold a palmful of prasad—
Grace that nourished the tree by mantras.

Home it is now to birds (mainly mynahs).

But once under it lay
Boys tautened by adolescence
Girls with sharpened ripening breasts
Golden in summer's heat,
Flesh upon flesh, scented by trampled *chameli* stars,
Seeds that could split stones.

We watched the sun,
Bleaching the world,
Blinded by tiny leaves
And barbed by twigs,
Make its daily round—
An old man visiting old friends.

Other trees stand like tired men
At a funeral—waiting
To cover a companion
With a handful of grim earth.

I remember only one:
The tree of my Nani's birth.

In Between

Between your voice
And your word
Is the silence:
The sky.

Between your writing
And your words
Is the radiance:
The stars.

Between your understanding
And your accent
Are the colours:
The rainbow.

Between your prayers
And your love
Are the waves:
The ocean.

Between the spaces
In your heart
Is the breath of life:
The earth.

Take care.

MANISHA ANJALI

Manisha Anjali (b. 1988) is a Fiji-born Indian writer and artist based in Melbourne, having lived for some years in New Zealand. She is the author of *Sugar Kane Woman*, published by Witchcraft Press in 2016. Manisha describes herself as a folk story writer and has had her work appear in *Blackmail Press*, *Mascara*, *Seizure*, *Flapperhouse* and *Alien She Zine*.

The story 'Fever Dreams' first appeared in the online journal *Mascara* in April 2007.

Fever Dreams

Aji has put me in a small cupboard. I am to lie here in the darkness with the hots and colds until it all goes away. My eyes are sticky. They have glue coming out of them. It hurts to keep them open. But I am afraid to close them completely in case they glue themselves shut forever. Then Aji would have to cut my eyes open with a knife. I have big red spots on my chinny-chin-chin down to my ankles. They itch like a bastard but I may not be allowed to touch. Aji will smack me if she sees me scratching. The hots and colds keep me awake and put me to sleep. I am somewhere in between real life and a scary dream. I can hear my brothers and sisters playing hide-and-seek outside among the trees; and my pussycat is scratching on the cupboard door because she is worried about me.

My oldest brother T-Rex had the spots first. He spent ten days in the cupboard. Then my sisters, Marigold and Uma, had the spots at the same time and they did their time in the cupboard together. Then it was Rita, then Dari, then our smallest brother who we called Rambo. I am the last to get it. Aji is our grandmother. She has had the spots three times. She has spent many times in cupboards and dark rooms. It is the only way to get rid of the hot spots, she says. No sun, no fun.

In the cupboard I meet Amitabh Bachchan, a hero from Aji's dreams. He wears a white suit and holds a shotgun. He has shiny hair and shiny teeth. But as he laughs, all his teeth fall out one by one, turning into little drops of blood as they hit the floor. In the shadows I hear the howls of my pussycat. She is trying to tell me something, but I cannot understand her. Amitabh's laughter shakes my eardrums and my head throbs as more glue fills my eyes and my spots are aflame.

I have had enough. I cannot lie here anymore and let this famous man bleed all over me. So I try to get out of bed. I begin walking sideways like a sea crab. I walk up the walls and onto the ceiling. I look down at myself writhing like a grub in my bed. I am sad. I miss the sun. What a small, smelly cupboard. What a bitch my Aji is.

Then I sink to the floor. The splinters in the wood hurt my body. I feel like I have broken through a sun mirror and the mirror has scarred my skin and bones. I can hear the bell on T-Rex's new bicycle, Marigold and Uma laughing under the mango trees and the cries of my poor pussycat outside my cupboard door. When I wake I am not in a mirror any more. I am wet all over and my hair is all over my face. I must look like the devil. I feel like I have just been to hell.

I feel cold on my face. It is Aji. She holds a wet sponge to my forehead.

'One day when your children get the measles, you will hide them from the sun too,' she says, then coughs into her shoulder. 'You might hate me for this now, boy, but one day you will understand.' She hums an old tune and puts the sponge on my heart. Then she holds my eyelids open with her old fingers and squirts in some cold medicine.

'The sun has gone down,' she says. 'You must come and join us for dinner.' She picks me up and carries me into the living room. All my brothers and sisters are sitting cross-legged on the floor with plates of rice, dahl and butter. They eat with their fingers.

'Your pussycat just gave birth to five little kittens. You want to see?' Aji asks. I nod. I really do want to see. Aji points to the living-room corner. My pussycat is lying on her side with her four new babies. The kittens are sticky and wet. They have glue coming out of their eyes too. Their teeth are soft and they fit perfectly into my pockets. My pussycat licks her sleeping babies. They smile.

GLENN D'CRUZ

Born in 1962 in Chennai, Glenn D'Cruz moved to Britain and then Australia in his early years. He holds a senior lectureship at Deakin University and mainly publishes his work as a theatre critic, though he has also made an academic study of racial representations in Australia, which was published as *Midnight's Orphans: Anglo-Indians in Post/colonial Literature* (2007). The piece in this collection is part of an autobiographical essay.

A longer version of the story-memoir first appeared in *Visibly Different: Face, Place and Race in Australia,* which was edited by Maureen Perkins and published by Peter Lang in 2007.

'Where are you coming from, Sir?'

The second epigraph to Joseph Heller's novel about the Jewish experience in America, *Good as Gold,* states that 'if you ever forget you are a Jew, a gentile will remind you' (Heller 1980, p. 7). This statement from a story by Bernard Malamud resonates with my experience of being an Anglo-Indian, since people remind me I am *different* in situations where I have forgotten that my skin, eyes and hair mark me as a 'wog', to use an antiquated Australian colloquialism …

Damascus on the Beach, Madras, India, 1991

On my first visit to Madras as an adult, a curious local approached me on Marina Beach and asked me a question I had answered at least twice a day since arriving in India. 'Where are you coming from, Sir?' I took a deep breath, and replied, seemingly for the thousandth time, 'I'm from Madras, I was born here.' Now, even though I have Indian features—dark skin, black eyes, and wavy black hair—my friend on the beach was unconvinced. With a characteristic shake of the head, he smiled kindly and said, 'No, Sir, where are you really from?' He was obviously an astute reader of body language, and my efforts to neutralise my Australian accent did not pass muster. In Australia, most people assume I am Indian, but in India, I am 'true blue'.[1]

This encounter changed the way I thought about my cultural identity, and it made me even more aware that geography and social context play an important role in determining how people made assumptions about my ethnicity and physical appearance ...

Actually, it's quite common to hear Indian-looking people speak with English or American accents ... In fact, I regularly encounter so-called British Asians looking for their ancestral roots in India, and Indians must be very familiar with this particular category of tourist, given the large number of British-born people with Indian parents. Today, many people use the term Anglo-Indian to refer to this rising demographic, rather than the children of colonialism ... The point I am making is that physical appearance, as a marker of racial difference, matters more in Australia than it does in India, where accent, carriage and clothes play a greater role in determining one's place in the order of things. In other words, the signifiers of racial difference are conditional.

As a 'mixed-race' Anglo-Indian, I have had to field questions about the disparity between my Indian appearance and my Western mannerisms for most of my life. However, it was only after the episode on Marina Beach that I formulated a thoughtful response to the questions 'Who are you?' and 'Where do you come from?' Today, my stock response has two parts: the first is biographical, and it remains more or less the same regardless of context; the second involves a somewhat complicated explanation of my cultural identity, and it changes, sometimes subtly and sometimes markedly, with my geographical location ...

Madras, India, 1962

I was born in Madras, India, in 1962; fifteen years after the British left the country, leaving their 'poor relations'—the Anglo-Indians—to fend for themselves ... When the British left India in 1947, many

1 A phrase which means to be genuinely, patriotically Australian. It was popularised in a country and western song and carries undertones of white Anglo normativity.

Anglo-Indians left with them, believing they had no future in the new republic. My family did not join that first wave of Anglo-Indian migration to Britain. Indeed, my father, according to family lore, wrote a letter to a community newspaper exhorting his fellow Anglo-Indians to 'stay on' and accept their status as citizens of the new republic, a directive anathema to many members of the community.

Up until his death, my father had a great deal of affection for India, and the decision to join the exodus, for economic and family reasons, must have been a difficult one. Anyway, not long after my birth, he left India for London, My mother and I joined him nine months later. She was twenty-two years old and understandably apprehensive about leaving her family back in India, but she took some solace in my father's promise that he would reunite her with her relatives someday …

Plaistow, London, 1971

Since I left India as an infant, I had no conscious memories of the country, although traces of it were visible in my new home in Plaistow, a working-class suburb of East (or should that be 'far East') London with a high percentage of migrants from the subcontinent. My father worked as a bus conductor for London Transport, and he soon saved enough money to put down a deposit for a 'two-up, two-down' terraced house (not unlike the ones immortalised in *Coronation Street*), which was located next door to a property owned by his brother, Clement. I have mostly happy memories of the house and my early childhood in London, which was shared with a plethora of rowdy cousins (my uncle had four children). However, this state of affairs changed when I enrolled in the local primary school and discovered what it meant to be visibly different in East London.

Most of my peers categorised me, along with all other 'Asian' students, as a 'Paki'. This was the era of Enoch Powell and the rise of the National Front (a fascist political party obsessed with repatriating 'blacks' and 'Asians'), so overt racism was common in my neighbourhood. And, like many of my fellow Indians, I was the occasional victim of the popular pastime of 'Paki-bashing'. Physical violence was relatively easy to deal with, compared with the mental anguish I suffered from being utterly convinced that, contrary to the evidence of my outward appearance, I was not a 'Paki'. In order to establish this fact beyond any doubt, I rejected almost every cultural artefact and practice connected with the subcontinent. I foreswore curry at the age of six and demanded that my mother cook 'English meals'. So with a single tantrum I consigned myself to a bland diet for most of my childhood. With the benefit of hindsight and more sophisticated taste buds, I find it almost impossible to believe that I once preferred fish fingers[2] and chips to a good curry or *masala dosai* …

Of course it was hard to perceive the value of such things at the time. After all, 'Pakis' were excluded from the mainstream of everyday life in Plaistow. You didn't see any 'Pakis' playing football for West Ham United, there were no 'Pakis' on *Top of the Pops,* and the only 'Pakis' you ever saw on television were ridiculous caricatures played by white actors in blackface (Spike Milligan in *Curry and Chips,* for example). The seemingly wholesale condemnation of everything Indian by British society demanded that I lead a double life of sorts. At home, I spoke with the 'sing-song' or 'chee-chee' accent of my parents. At school, I was a cockney: 'Wotcha, mate!' …

Around the age of eight or nine, I started telling people outrageous lies about my cultural background and inventing fantastically implausible stories about my ancestry. For reasons that now escape me, I remember boldly declaring that I was an Australian Aborigine (not suspecting that one day I would indeed have just cause to claim an Australian identity of sorts). In short, I wanted to be anything other than a 'Paki', a category of identity apparently reserved for the most despised members of British society. The legacy of these childhood experiences is that I have a particularly confused and conflicted sense of cultural and national identity …

Perth, Western Australia, 1973

Despite all the racist taunts I endured as a child, I was a Londoner, and I shed tears when my father, sometime in 1973, told me that we

2 Fish fingers are pieces of mashed-up fish which are crumbled and shaped into long rectangles. They can be purchased cheaply as frozen packs and then defrosted and fried.

would be moving to Australia. You see, my mother's family had finally left India, but they moved to Australia because Britain would not accept them as immigrants. My father made good on his pledge [to his wife] and we were soon on a British Caledonian flight to Singapore, where we boarded the *M. V. Eastern Queen* and sailed for Fremantle. After the rain and general gloom of London, Western Australia was a revelation. The sun and the deep blue colour of the Swan River dazzled me as we drove from Fremantle to our new home in Maylands, then a working-class suburb of Perth. After the grey skies of London, I was overwhelmed by Perth's brightness—its clear skies and sunshine. I felt as though I had traded a black-and-white world for one composed of hyper-real colours …

In Australia, I ceased to be a 'Paki'. I was relieved that I had escaped attending a large comprehensive school in East London where racial abuse was even more prevalent. This is not to say that racism did not exist in Australia. It was just that people from the Indian subcontinent were not yet a visibly minority. I noticed that it was the so-called 'wogs'—people from Italian and Greek descent—who were usually the victims of racial vilification. At high school I was occasionally called 'Milo' (after a popular chocolate drink) and sometimes even called a 'boong'[3] but these taunts were never as malicious or as spiteful as those I had experienced in London. Moreover, no one threatened me with physical violence because I looked different. Maybe I was lucky. Racist bullies regularly tortured one of my younger cousins who grew up in Melbourne in the 1980s …

The whole business of dating girls filled me with dread and trepidation, as it probably does most adolescents. However, the anxiety that accompanies the rituals of teenage dating is more intense when you have dark skin. I rarely approached girls I found attractive, not so much because I feared rejection in itself but because I feared rejection on the grounds of my race …

I managed to summon enough courage to express a tentative interest in high school girls on a few occasions. However, the girls met my timid advances with withering stares of contempt that left me heartbroken. (It's easy to feel heartbroken as a teenager, as most

3 'Boong' is a derogatory epithet for an Aboriginal.

people know.) I found little solace in the fact that Anglo-Indian girls found me as unattractive as white girls—perhaps they rejected me because I was a nerdy, weedy dork. Maybe race had little to do with my miserable teenage love life. The point is moot, however, because it was my consciousness of being a 'racial other' that undermined my confidence as a youth. Today interracial couples are common; I hope these couples do not experience the same level of hostility I encountered in the 1970s and 1980s, periods marked by race riots in Great Britain and apartheid in South Africa …

Despite enjoying a higher degree of acceptability in Australia, people still asked me, with monotonous regularity, where I was from. As I grew older, I began to take pride in what I now enthusiastically claimed as my cultural background, and I always responded to the 'Where are you from?' question in the same way: 'I'm Indian; I'm from India.' Perhaps it was because of the racial abuse I had suffered as a child, but I never identified myself as an Anglo-Indian. I did not feel particularly English, even though I had lived in that country for most of my childhood, and I had not lived in Australia long enough to feel Australian, so I dropped the 'Anglo' part of my cultural identity and became, at least in my own mind, Indian. How times change!

It was not until my trip to Madras that I fully realised that culture plays a more significant role than physical appearance in defining one's sense of self. As I have already indicated, my knowledge of Indian culture is limited to a basic acquaintance with the cuisine of South India. So, at the advanced age of twenty-five I realised that while I have a great deal of affection and respect for India, I am not an Indian. Indeed, as I have already indicated, Indians do not accept me as Indian. This is why Marina Beach was my Damascus, for the insight delivered by my friend on that stretch of sand motivated me to find a more considered reply to his question about my origins. This incident also gave me the impetus to research my ancestry formally and find out answers to questions I had not considered before: What is an Anglo-Indian? What did it mean to identify as an Anglo-Indian? What are the constituent elements of Anglo-Indian culture?

ROANNA GONSALVES

Roanna Gonsalves was born in 1974. After completing an MA in Mumbai, she moved to Australia where she undertook studies in television production and professional writing. She then obtained a PhD in Sydney where she now teaches, works in radio, co-edits the *Southern Crossings* website and writes. Her radio documentaries, *On the tip of a billion tongues,* aired by Earshot, ABC RN during November and December of 2015, are an acerbic socio-political portrayal of contemporary India through its multilingual writers. Her collection of short stories titled *The Permanent Resident* (2016) was published by University of Western Australia. She has also written a play titled 'Yet to Ascertain the Nature of the Crime' (2010) and is currently working on a novel.

What follows is a new story that is a third take on her 'Curry Muncher' story which was published by *Eureka Street* in June 2008. The first version was a response to the much-publicised assaults on Indian students in Melbourne at the time. The second version appears in her collection, *The Permanent Resident.*

Curry Muncher 3.0

Years pass. Sometimes, in the sublimating spaces of bus stops, supermarkets, and communion lines at St Mary's Church, I think of Vincent. I wish I could go back to the moment I pretended I didn't know, and respawn into Xena the Warrior Princess[1] or even St Joan of Arc or St Quiteria, perpetrating upon the perpetrators, giving like for like with battery fully charged. I would defend Vincent from his attackers, keep my sense of dignity and trustworthiness intact, and there would be none of the powdery taste of guilt on my tongue that mixes with my spit every once in a while.

And then I see the shape of his head through the gaps in the rows of Bombay sandwich chutney bottles. It's got to be him, that oiled head

[1] *Xena: Warrior Princess* was a popular television serial with a feminist slant.

slightly protruding at the back, same height as I remember, same shy curve of the side that I recall seeing through an old restaurant door doing the dishes.

A pigeon is roosting on the top shelf, cooing louder and faster by the second, like a ticking bomb that will never go off, but will just unnerve and unnerve without respite. Customers come in one by one asking for the latest Rajinikanth pirated in see-through plastic. I stop my search for dried pomegranate seeds, and gaze at the strands of oily hair stuck together on his head like relatives in a new country. Then he turns around and we see each other at one and the same time. Our eyes meet in that two-aisled Indian shop, anchored by 500-gram packets of turmeric that is the world's best anti-coagulant, and ground cardamom that excited emperors, and a freezer full of frozen parathas packaged in arctic Canada. It's too late to avert our eyes. There is no choice but to meet and greet.

'Hiiiiiiii', our voices pitched for incredulity.

I sense a mutual need to connect physically just to anchor with our bodies what we are feeling in our heads, such is the force of my, our, thrill, our need to validate each other after all these years.

But we do not hug or shake hands.

Our faces are beaming with the recollection of a shared miserable past now safely packaged into a thing to be examined in tranquillity. Except I am not tranquil. An unseen weight descends upon us.

Vincent speaks first.

'Here's my son, my wife,' he says, 'Shalini.'

To Shalini he says, 'She is my very good friend. From the restaurant. Before Sunil. Many years before.'

Obviously she has no knowledge of what transpired that night. I want to ask, 'You're still at the restaurant?' but I'm afraid my voice might betray the old condescension.

Shalini is holding their son's hand. She offers her free hand to me. I see the hesitation in her eyes, unsure about the relationship between her husband and me, our shared past like a mangrove on the other side of a deep river she cannot cross. I know she will assume we have a history, for I have assumed such things myself. She will mistake our nostalgia for a rekindled attraction. Who knows, she may be right.

'I'm still at the restaurant', he says, but with pride. 'I'm a partner, with Sunil. I also do cooking sometimes. Chef's work.'

'Oh, congratulations!'

'Thank you. I bought my own house. Near Campbelltown.[2] You know Campbelltown?'

'Oh yes I know Campbelltown. Congratulations!'

Shalini says, 'We are doing the bathroom renovations now. It is very close to the train station, police station, and gas station also.'

She is trying to be my friend, to forge an intimacy that I will not even consider. She is coming close to the mangrove but she doesn't know it. Vincent knows it. And I know it. And he knows that I know and I know that he knows.

'And you? You are well?'

'Yes. I am well.'

'You are living close by?'

'I live in Newtown.'[3]

'Oh. It's an expensive area, no?' Shalini's voice shows a new respect for me.

'I just rent. In a share house.'

'Like a paying guest,' Vincent explains to Shalini.

'Er, the landlord doesn't live in the same house, just four of us tenants.'

This moment does not warrant such shameless self-disclosure. Shalini is already losing interest. She listens because her husband and I obviously have chemistry. But I cannot help myself, cannot help drawing attention to my difference from them, marking my preference for what money can't buy: hipster cool, convenience, close enough to the city for its shine to fall upon me, cafes at my beck, street musicians outside my window.

'The four of us share the housework and the bills. We have chickens at the back. Can't imagine living anywhere else.'

'Oh, very nice,' says Shalini, like a checkout operator dying to go to the loo.

2 Campbelltown is a fast-growing settlement on the extreme fringes of Sydney.

3 Newtown is a trendy but old inner city student and dining-out district.

'Married? Children?'

'Oh no,' I say, with mock disgust, as if there could be nothing worse, as if it's a choice I have made with full awareness of the pros and cons and a SWOT Analysis[4] to back me up. As if.

'When are you going to settle down?' Vincent is asking me, only half-teasing. There is a seriousness in his eyes full of admonishment and pity; he is unable to believe that a former international-student waitress would continue to persist with an itinerant life rather than sedimenting in a backyard in the suburbs.

'You work in the city?' Shalini is asking me, judging me, daring me to say I actually don't have a job.

'I'm doing a PhD at Sydney University. I walk to work from home.'

'Work means uni?'

'Yes,' I say to her.

'Very nice. What is your PhD about? Cancer research or something?'

Nice one Shalini. But I will not take the bait.

'Studying the cinema of the 1970s and the trope of the angry young man. And making a film too. A short comedy.'

Vincent smiles. 'At the restaurant also she was always high-funda.'

But Shalini is different from her husband. She deals with me as an equal.

'You mean Amitabh Bachchan movies?'

'Yes,' I say and decide not to volunteer any further information. I decide to focus on the child, meekly holding his mother's hand, watching us, sucking it all in.

He seems fascinated with me.

'He's so cute,' I volunteer, knowing these words always open up a conversation with parents.

'Ya ya, very cute in front of you but such a *goonda* at home, doesn't sit down for one minute.'

4 SWOT stands for Strengths, Weaknesses, Opportunities, Threats, and a SWOT Analysis is a form of management-speak for assessing yourself or a situation.

This tiresome backhanded compliment to her own child is actually a compliment to herself, the mother responsible for this spark and potential. The child responds as if to validate my assumption.

'Can I play on your phone?'

'No no baba, don't ask aunty for her phone.' Shalini reprimands the child. I know this is just a performance for my benefit. She is secretly proud she has raised such a tech-savvy kid.

But the four-year-old shit is trained to see through these performances.

'I want to see Wiggles, I want to see Wiggles.'[5]

The mother continues to indulge herself.

The pigeon coos and coos.

I play my eyes to his father, largo and legato.[6]

I am surprised, yet not, that Vincent is looking at me, judging me it seems.

'So how's the restaurant?' I ask, knowing this encounter has peaked in its adolescence. Everything from this point on is a gesture towards a short goodbye.

'It's good. Business is good. You know how it is. Weekends are very packed. But these days, Mondays Tuesdays also there are many customers. We are doing lunch also now. From last six years.'

'Oh really? Lunch also? Really good. You must be super busy.'

The pigeon coos and coos, slowing down, as if ready to fly off into the world outside.

'Excuse me, can I just ask; you know about these things more than I do. What's the best way to use this, would you know?'

It's a woman in a headscarf, looks Lebanese but is unafraid to make herself vulnerable. She's holding a packet of butter chicken mix, and surprise surprise, asking Vincent this question rather than me. It's probably the smell of the restaurant still upon him that directs her gaze. I made sure I sprayed myself with Cool Water before I left home.

Vincent hesitates for a second and that is enough for Shalini to take the lead, as she has done many times before, no doubt.

5 The Wiggles are a popular music group on children's television.

6 Largo and legato are musical terms meaning softly and in a smooth flowing manner.

'It's easy, I'll tell you,' she says, and away she goes, disengaging her hand from the grip of her spawn.

It's Vincent and me all over again, under a different ceiling, pocked with the years and the shifting lithosphere that makes mountains where there was once the sea and forces women to lose their principles.

'So how do you commute to the restaurant from Campbelltown?'

What I really want to do is apologise, clear my conscience.

'I drive,' he says. 'If I leave early I don't get the traffic.'

'Nice,' I say, 'it's terrible, the traffic, almost like Bombay, especially in peak hour.'

'Ya ya, but I leave early and come back late, you know in the restaurant how it is.'

Oh I know. I do know, and only too well. I agree with my head, aware that the time for apology has long passed, the conversation going further down a road much travelled.

Shalini is behind us, teaching the woman how to cook butter chicken, taking her through the rows of spices, checking prices, pointing to the most cost-effective way to cook an Indian meal. The child is wandering around, playing the pickle bottles at eye level, like a xylophone. The pigeon is on the floor near the entrance. It pecks at the fallen grains of rice. It is said that on every grain of rice is written the name of the being who will eat it.

Outside the traffic is noisy like a family row. But a silence falls between Vincent and me. It is like an empty bookshelf demanding to be filled. I know I must keep the conversation in the non-controversial present, but the silence cannot be ignored, and after all these years I can't help myself. 'So you still get acidity?'

'Yes,' he says, his face sheepish with an old memory.

'Do you take Eno?' I ask, 'or something else?'

'No. I am managing with my diet. I don't eat spicy food. I drink water, milk. No problem.'

'That's good.'

No response.

A bus outside honks mightily at a car parked in a *No Stopping* zone.

'So anyone from the old days still works at the restaurant?'

'No. All have left. I saw Meena last month in the shopping centre.'

'Oh really? Meena? Is she still here? I thought she was going to go to America.'

'I saw her in the shopping centre. But she was on the other side. I couldn't say hello.'

The boy has moved to the fridges, peering at the tetrapacks[7] of Frooti. The pigeon walks towards the boy. He sees it and turns to follow it. The pigeon hops outside the shop, on to the footpath. The boy follows it. The pigeon hops on to the road. The boy is in its wake. Vincent's back is turned away from his son. Shalini is in the bowels of the shop, giving cooking instructions.

There is a screech and I am immediately activated.

I detach from my conversation with Vincent and run outside.

I grab the boy just before he lunges into the traffic.

He struggles against my embrace. I hold him tighter, policing him like an expert.

I carry him back to the shop.

Vincent and Shalini are at the entrance now.

'Munna you shouldn't run on the road.' Vincent admonishes his son. Then he turns to me. 'Thank you,' he says. 'Thank you so much. You saved his life.'

He stretches out to receive his son from me.

'But I was not running, daddy.'

Shalini must shape this scene with felt-tipped finality.

'He knows never to run on the road. He's very careful. Don't shout at your son in public,' she says to her husband.

The boy jumps into his mother's arms.

'He is used to crossing the road in Bombay. This traffic is nothing compared to Bombay traffic. I have trained him to be careful,' she is saying to me, telling me, with words that remain unsaid, to mind my own business.

The boy looks at me, giving away nothing.

'Thank you so much,' Vincent butts in. 'Thank God you saw him just in time.'

7 See page 31.

Shalini will not let these words go uncontested.

'I was watching him, not that I didn't know what he was doing,' she is saying to her husband.

The Lebanese lady joins us.

'Is he alright, darl?'[8]

'Yeah he's fine,' Shalini says to her. 'Don't forget to use fresh cream in the butter chicken. After it is cooked you must add it, not before.'

'Thanks, darl.'

'And when you grind the cashew nuts, grind them very fine.'

'Appreciate it, darl. Have a lovely evening.'

The shop owner watches us from behind the till.

'I really appreciate it. What a relief!' Vincent is saying to me.

'Anytime. I was so scared for a minute.'

The pigeon flies back into the shop and takes its place on a top shelf with boxes of turmeric and cardamom power, waiting to be unpacked.

'So nice to meet you,' Shalini is saying to me.

Vincent looks surprised that this meeting is being drawn to a close.

'You already got the Lahori Fish Masala?' he is asking her incredulously.

'We will get it from the Auburn shop. There's no rush.'

Shalini shakes my hand, as if she's a victor.

Vincent nods and smiles.

'I did not expect to see you here. It is so nice. After so many years. You must come to our house,' he is saying with joy, and embarrassment, and also absolution, I hope. We exchange phone numbers. They leave.

I go back into the shop. I look for a different kind of Bombay sandwich chutney, not as sour, because it upsets my tummy. But this shop only has one brand. They are also out of dried pomegranate seeds.

8. 'Darl' is short for 'Darling' and usually denotes a working-class register of speech. It also indicates how the 'Lebanese' woman has assimilated an Anglo-Australian idiom.

'What about powdered pomegranate seeds?' I ask the shop owner behind the till.

'We will get it next week,' he says. 'Why don't you try butter chicken masala instead?'

'I don't like butter chicken,' I say as haughtily as I can manage, exercising my privilege as a customer. 'It gives me acidity.'

'How come? Butter chicken is not spicy.'

'I don't know,' I say, 'it gives me terrible heartburn.'

'Eat rice,' he says, 'see there we have rice bags on special. Cheapest in all of Sydney.'

'I will,' I say, 'I'll come back another time to buy the rice.'

'Sure, madam. Have a nice day.'

Outside, the evening is flustered as the sun takes its time to set. The moon-dropped sky is lush with memory and my throat has begun to burn like a test tube being held to a flame. It must be yesterday's dinner, I tell myself, all that chilli pickle I ate coming up with a vengeance. There is nothing to soothe my oesophagus. I begin to cross the road. A car honks behind me. I take my time as I step on to the footpath. I begin the slow walk to the train that will take me home.

ADITI GOUVERNEL

Born in 1977 in Mumbai, Gouvernel grew up in Canberra. She has since been dividing her time between Mumbai, Paris and New York and is currently working on a young adult novel. Her stories have been published in anthologies and *The Sydney Morning Herald*.

'Wei-Li and Me' is taken from *Growing up Asian in Australia,* which was edited by Alice Pung and published by Black Inc. in 2008.

Wei-Li and Me

Barry West was a rude little boy with a pug nose. He had the red-stained face of Australian summers.

'Don't touch me!' he screamed.

All the kids were playing tag and I was 'it'. I was running through the playground, my pony-tail slapping my back as my feet hit the ground. My heartbeat pulsed in my head. I grazed Barry's left shoulder with the palm of my hand. He stopped. Turned around and faced me.

Anger stretched across his face and he screamed, 'I'll have to wash this shirt now—you wipe your butt with your hands.'

'No I don't,' I screamed back, startled and confused.

'Yes you do … You're Indian and I've got your Indian shit on me.' He ripped off his shirt and threw it on the ground. The other kids gathered around us, watching and listening.

❖

I was six. It was the early eighties and my parents had moved our family from the aristocratic world of Delhi, a city filled with palaces, temples, gardens and tombs. They moved me from my playground under the tower of the Qutab Minar to Canberra. The only thing that the two places had in common was they were both national capitals. Our new suburb, Melba, spread its backside up Mount Rogers, a lofty title for what was really a hill. Each night my father and I would climb the hills and watch the sunset turn Lake Ginninderra a bright pink. 'This is our chance,' he would say, as Belconnen became a small cluster of lights. 'This is a place we can make ours.'

Delhi, with its eons of history, was not a place that could be 'added to'. Australia, on the other hand, large, spacious and full of gaps, would be a place where we could create a new identity.

We became Australians in 1982. I recall very little of this ceremony, which took place in a small room in the cinder-block building of the Department of Immigration. My parents held up their palms while a man read an oath from a piece of paper. People clapped, some whistled and small flags were waved. The citizenship papers were locked in a bank vault with my mother's jewellery.

My parents met Australia when they started work and I met Australia in the school playground.

❖

The playground consisted of a large expanse of grass, at the centre of which stood a dark wooden structure rising out of a pit of tanbark. Some days it would be a fort, and we would defend ourselves from an imaginary attack. Other days it would be a ship, and we would be pirates and sailors. The days our childhood fantasy minds were tired it would just be the playground and we would hang from the monkey bars,[1] or jump off the platforms. It was fun until the day Barry told the world I wiped my butt with my hands.

That lunchtime as I climbed the fort, Barry screamed, 'She's infected. Don't touch the fort! You'll get her germs.' I watched as the kids around me jumped off it like a crew abandoning a sinking ship.

Over the next couple of days the kids stopped talking to me, as though my words, like my body, carried an infection their immune

[1] Monkey bars refer to a common item of playground equipment. Arranged in the shape of a cube of squares assembled from metal bars, they are meant for climbing.

systems couldn't fight. On the rare occasions they did pay attention to me they would combine their hatred in a human circle around me.

'She even looks like shit,' said Amy Pulawski.

'That's so gross,' added Cris Kovacic.[2]

'No I don't,' I screamed again and again at them. Once I was forced to pull my top up and bare my chest to prove I had nipples when Barry had the idea Indian girls 'have no tits'.

On these days, I would go home with tears in my eyes and wonder why we couldn't move back to Delhi. I would beg my mother not to send me back to school. 'You have to face the world,' she would say. If this was the world, I wanted nothing to do with it. I pretended to have various illnesses—flu, malaria. Once I claimed I had gout. My mother ignored all my attempts to miss school. Each day she would send me out the door with a brown paper bag and a piece of fruit and each day I hoped things would change. They did, the day Wei-Li arrived.

❖

It was a cold autumn day. I ran into the classroom and warmed my hands against the metal gas heater bordering the walls. My teacher walked in, a halo of curly hair, her arm attached to a honey-coloured boy with a smile of excitement on his face.

She wrote his name on the blackboard. 'WEI-LI,' in white chalk. The boy stood in front of the class and in a sing-song voice introduced himself.

'My name is Wee Lee.' He smiled.

Titters ran through the classroom. It took the class exactly thirty seconds to shorten his name to Wee. By morning recess he was called Piss. He lost his smile at lunchtime when, to my relief, he became the object of their attention. The kids mauled Wei-Li the way a cat would maul a toy. They pawed and prodded him and the circles that used to form around me formed around him. He was hit, spanked and kicked.

2 It is worth noting that the children who gang up on the narrator have names indicating their European migrant origins. Once, they would have been the brunt of Anglo Barry's torments.

He was spat on and forced to pull down his pants and show his penis when Barry had the idea that Chinese boys 'have no dicks'.

Wei-Li's shoulders started to stoop and after a whole week he would walk outside and avoid talking to anyone.

❖

I watched everything from an aluminium bench. It was far enough away from the kids to avoid their attention but close enough to watch their activities.

Today the bench was freezing. I was folding my legs underneath myself in a sort of a lotus position when Wei-Li walked into the playground. I saw Barry walk straight towards him, his arms behind him and his hand in a fist. As Wei-Li faced the playground, Barry made a full arc with his arm and punched Wei-Li in the head. Wei-Li fell to the ground. Barry jumped on Wei-Li, his butt on his chest and both hands pulling at Wei-Li's school tie. Wei-Li's face turned red and a strange sound escaped his mouth.

'Think you can tell on me?' Barry threatened.

Wei-Li shook his head.

Anger rose inside me. I wanted to help him. When the abuse had been directed at me, I had always wanted one of the other kids to hit Barry. I wanted someone to make it all stop, and for the first time I realised the 'someone' could be me.

To the left of the bench was a rock the size of my foot. I picked it up and walked up behind Barry, the rock firmly in my hands. I could see Wei-Li's tongue poke out between his lips. I threw my arms over my head and brought the rock down as hard as I could. It made a loud crack when it connected with Barry's head. He fell forward, lying on top of Wei-Li, who had regained his breath and was wiggling out from under him. When Barry started moving, Wei-Li and I ran in opposite directions, I could hear Barry screaming, 'You're both dead.'

The afternoon passed like a death sentence. Barry stared menacingly at me from his desk. As soon as the bell rang I leapt out of my seat and ran out of the class. I started running up Le Gallienne Street and as I was about to reach the first cross street, I saw Wei-Li standing there. He grabbed my hand, 'C'mon,' he said. I followed him up the narrow side-street and onto a footpath. On one side was a row of houses and on the other side a nature reserve. 'Let's go this way. It's longer—but we'll be alone,' he said.

❖

In Tamil, my father's native tongue, there is a word, jalrah, that means shadow. From that day on, Wei-Li became my jalrah.

That Saturday, Wei-Li stood on my doorstep and rang the bell twice. My mother was cooking and the house smelt of mixed spices. Cumin, chilli powder and garam masala floated through the air like a scented rainbow. My mother opened the door and called out my name with a smile on her face. I saw Wei-Li standing there. A second later, as he entered my house, I saw everything Indian come to the foreground as if lit by a spotlight: the wooden statue of Ganesh, the fabric birds hanging on a string, my father lounging around in a dhoti. Everything Wei-Li saw could be used as evidence for my difference. But Wei-Li didn't notice anything, or if he did he never mentioned it.

From that day on we spent every possible second together. We would ride our bikes or secretly rifle through our mothers' purses, pilfering loose change that we would then pool to buy a Mars Bar. All sugared up, we would re-enact our favourite TV show, *Monkey Magic*. Wei-Li would be Monkey and I would be Tripitaka. We would find large sticks and pretend they were swords and staffs and fight imaginary foes who looked like Barry.

❖

Hiding from Barry had become an art. At lunchtimes, Wei-Li and I would sit in the library, or jump on the Olympic size trampoline in the gym. If there was no adult supervision, we would be sent out to the playground no matter how much we pleaded. On those days we would sit on our aluminium bench and share our lunches. Wei-Li would eat my samosas and I would eat his sandwiches, filled with pork balls and grated carrots. When we were together we felt safe.

But one day, there was no lunchtime. We were going on an excursion to Parliament house. The day was divided into two sections. In the morning, half of the class would play cricket on the lawns while the other half took a guided tour. When the first tour was finished groups would swap. I was excited until I realised the teachers were filing us alphabetically into the bus. My last name was Vishwanathan and I was told to sit directly in front of Barry West. For the first time since the incident with the rock, I was alone. The bus ride lasted thirty minutes. Thirty minutes of Barry kicking the back of my seat. I didn't say anything. I just stared straight ahead.

The bus stopped and the kids pointed at the white building with small steps. I couldn't enjoy it; I was angry. It was a gut-wrenching anger that was growing each second in its volatility. Barry left his seat and walked towards mine. When he reached mine, he leant close to me and spat straight in my face. He walked off laughing, leaving me to wipe my face with my sleeve. Tears gathered in my eyes, but this time I felt I could do something—the rock had taught me that.

I walked off the bus, and as the bus driver opened the cargo hold, I waited. As the bus driver brought out the sports bags, I calculated. We-Li walked up to me. 'What's going on?'

'Nothing,' I said, my arms folded and a look of determination on my face. I waited until the bags were opened and the teachers had started organising the activities. When I was confident the teachers were distracted, I walked over to a sports bag and grabbed one of the bright yellow cricket bats, I ran over to Barry and bashed it against the back of his neck. He fell and again I held up the cricket bat; this time I bashed it against his face. I couldn't hit him anymore because the teachers had grabbed the bat and were pulling me off him.

Barry was as fine as he could be with a bloody nose, tissues and tears. While the other kids walked through the House of Representatives and the Senate, I sat on a seat, guarded by a teacher who phoned my parents.

My mother arrived, apologetic and angry. She bustled me into our red Subaru and said repeatedly, 'What's gotten into you? You can't behave like this.' I was silent until she said, 'You must apologise to that boy.'

'Never,' I said.

My parents had a meeting with the school principal and Barry's parents. I wasn't punished and neither was Barry. The next day I discovered why.

❖

It was Friday and our teacher stood in front of the class and said, 'Barry has an announcement. Come up here and tell the class your news.'

Barry walked in front of the class and stood there for a second.

'I am moving to Jakarta. I'm leaving next week,' he said.

That lunchtime Wei-Li asked, 'Do you think it's because of the cricket bat?'

'Nah,' I said, shaking my head.

Wei-Li and I counted the days, crossing them off an imaginary calendar in our minds. Barry's departure was marked with cupcakes and wide smiles.

On our first day of freedom, Wei-Li and I went home. We walked up Le Gallienne Street, now claiming it for ourselves. Wei-Li's grandmother opened the door to two beaming kids.

'Why you so happy?' she asked suspiciously.

'Barry's moving to Jakarta,' Wei-Li said.

She smiled and hugged her grandson.

❖

Things changed rapidly after that. We grew up and as our faces changed, so did Canberra. An Indian restaurant, Jehangir, opened on Swinger Hill. Canberra's Chinatown became so busy you couldn't find parking. When I was sixteen, I went to a private high school on the other side of town where people described me as 'pretty'.

Wei-Li and I gained a group of friends who we would meet at the chess-pit[3] in the centre of the city. We would sip lattes under the

3 Many cities in Australia include a large chessboard in the pavement of a square or mall where people congregate to play chess or just chat.

gas heaters at Gus's Café and dream about a better life after uni. At night we would sit on scrappy vinyl-covered chairs in a bar called The Phoenix and, after a couple of beers, rant about how we hated homogeneity and longed for difference. We had become what we never thought we would ever be: Australian.

MARIA PREETHI SRINIVASAN

Born in 1969, Maria Preethi Srinivasan currently works with the Tamil Nadu State Council for Higher Education, Government of Tamil Nadu, as a Research Officer. She won an Endeavour Award for her doctoral research titled *Australian Aboriginal, Indian Dalit and Adivasi Women's Life Writings as Sagas of Empowerment*. She received an Australia India Council Fellowship in 2008 as well. Srinivasan has written more than a hundred poems which form an unpublished collection titled *Psalms of Bethesda*.

'Explosion Contained' appeared in *Poetry Without Borders*, edited by Michelle Cahill and published by Picaro Press, 2008. 'Refugee' and 'You Need to Know, and Yet …' are from her unpublished collection.

Explosion Contained

I wish I could put my body
Through the motions of an explosion.
If you can't bear to see me dismembered,
Do appreciate
What it takes
To stay together.

Refugee

Refugees live in rooms,
In homes.
They are given wardrobes,
But they have learnt to live out of suitcases.
Refugees are of different types:
The landless,
Houseless,
Spouseless,

And unclassified.
They must remember
What they want to forget
And be thankful
For rooms
In homes
With wardrobes.

You Need to Know and Yet ...

You need to know how bad this day has been
Yet, I feel restrained—
Why complain?
Why dampen your day?

You need to know every tale of the past
Yet
My tales smell stale (even to me!)
Our friendship is a brand new story,
It's not fair to let the past spoil today.

You need to know where I come from
My country, my people, my history
Yet
It's an endless story
(Better, you make your own discovery)

You need to know
'Cause you're a friend I turn to time and again.
Though so much remains untold.
I'd rather let it be.

SUNIL BADAMI

Born in 1974 in Blacktown, Sydney, Badami has degrees in Communications and Creative Writing from Australia and Britain respectively. He is a writer, broadcaster, performer and academic. He has written for most major Australian publications, been published overseas and his work was included in *Best Australian Stories* and *Best Australian Essays*. He presented the national ABC Local Radio show *Sunday Takeaway* and his radio documentary *Riddle. Mystery. Enigma.* was nominated for the prestigious Prix Marulič. He continues to appear regularly on ABC Radio and TV and is currently editing his first novel for publication.

'Rebecca' first appeared in *New Australian Stories*, edited by Aviva Tuffield and published by Scribe Publications in 2009.

Rebecca

'Now faith is the substance of things hoped for, the evidence of things not seen.'

– *Hebrews 11.1*

'I have been a stranger in a strange land.'

– *Exodus 2.22*

Dean's handing me the joint when the phone rings. It always does.

'Wanna get that?' he guffaws. 'Don't take the roach! You can double up next round.'

Sure, like that ever happens. I walk outside before I answer, my mouth full of smoke. I can see him through a slice of door, rolling around hysterically.

It's Joan from the church. I can't help belching smoke into the mouthpiece.

'You alright?'

'Sure. What's up?'

'Your sister. Come quick.'

And that's that: party's over.

❖

The drive home, and I don't remember what happened between hanging up on Joan and walking into the hospital. Don't know how fast I drove, but I made good time. Seems too soon for the distance.

The hospital had that hollow antiseptic smell, rubber chirruping on the tiles. Joan and Mum are kneeling by a row of plastic chairs in the corridor, their hands knotted, their lips moving. As I approach, they look up, then Mum smooths her dress down as she slumps into a chair. Joan leads me away by the arm.

'What about Mum?'

'Well, she's in shock, dear, but she has her faith.' Joan's lips curdle together. I know what she's thinking. 'The Lord will find a way.'

'What happened?'

'Esther was coming home from youth camp and their bus hit a truck. Don't know all the details yet, but it was terrible.'

'How's Es?'

'Well, she's in a serious condition. Nearly every bone broken. They could identify her only by the ID near her body.'

'Geez.'

'That's a Lord word, Ruth dear,' says Joan. 'Please don't blaspheme.'

'Um, yeah, okay. It's Jodi, by the way.'

Joan doesn't blink.

'How many people were hurt?'

'Six died—Rodney, the group leader, he was a lovely fellow; Andrew and Rachel, just married, you know; Elder Patrick ... But they're with the Lord now. Esther was the only survivor. It's a miracle.'

Sure, except for the six dead. But they're with the Lord now, so it all works out neatly.

'Where's Esther?'

'She's still in theatre. We're praying for her. Come and join us; it would mean so much to your mum.'

I can feel that old sour bubble froth up and lather me in resentment. 'Look, I don't think ...'

Joan looks back at my mother, who's staring at the wall. 'Your poor mother—'

'My poor bloody sister!'

Mum looks up as though she doesn't recognise me, then gets up slowly. She pulls me to her and I can feel her fingers pressing into my back, nagging little needles.

'D'you want me to stay with you, Mum? Mum?'

'Just go home,' she says in a croaky voice. 'Jesus is with us.'

❖

I'm surprised how quiet and small the house is. Has it been that long? Seems like an old person's home: the plastic-covered sofa, the lime-green kitchen, the shag pile,[1] the chipboard. A kind of immaculate memorial to my parents' bad taste and my troubled adolescence. I feel fourteen again, creeping in from sneaking out. The twelfth stair still creaks.

I go up to my room past Jesus being whipped and scorned. Jesus being crowned with thorns, Jesus with a spear in his side. How Dad laughed when I asked if they were *Jesi*.[2]

It's like walking into a stranger's room. All the posters have been taken down, and though I haven't been in here for years, I feel burgled. Anger swells up, and I have to swallow it down hard. I fall on the bed, though I can't sleep: my feet hang out of the frilly edges, and mangled buses speed through my mind.

I get up and roll a joint. I go out back, just in case Mum comes home, and watch the moon, a fingernail in the sky, cold light eddying into the garden.

❖

Mum's busy in the kitchen when I come down.

'Um, hi,' I say, rubbing my eyes.

1 'Shag pile' refers to a hairy style of carpet which was trendy in the 1960s.

2 The joke about Jesus rests on the Latin plural of *-us* being *i*. Since Jesus is an anglicisation of a Hebrew name, the suggestion is not serious.

'Good morning. The Lord be with you.'

'And also with—' I bite my lip, can feel the blood fizz. 'How's Es?'

'She's fine. It was touch and go, and she lost a lot of blood, but Jesus saved her.'

She gives me a cup of tea. There's no sugar.

'How long's she gunna be in for?'

'The doctors don't know. She isn't out of the coma yet. But we'll pray.' She takes a can of Mr Sheen[3] out of the cupboard and starts wiping where I put the cup. I put it down, and she lifts it up, worrying the stain in tight circles.

'Geez, Mum, will you just sit down for a second?'

'That's a Lord word, Ruth. It's short for the saviour's name.'

'Christ! Will ya stop it? And it's Jodi, Mum. Jodi. Deed poll,[4] remember?'

'Ruth's your given name. You can be who you please outside, but in this house, you're Ruth. And please, Ruth, don't blaspheme in this house.'

'God! I mean, fu—jingo!'

'Forgive her, Lord. She knows not what she's doing.'

That's it, I watch my mother, her rubber gloves laced around the Mr Sheen in front of her, her lips moving. When she became a Charismatic, she'd fall to the ground, her tongue darting in and out of her mouth as she spoke Seraphim.

Thank God that didn't last long—she dislocated a knee on her way down and promptly converted to Calvinism. It was a sign from the Lord, but how it led her to Calvinism only she and the Lord would know.

I suppose people might follow a meandering spiritual path that leads them to different faiths and creeds. Not my mother: if she was anything, she was consistent. Jesus had always been her Lord, even if she'd been Lutheran, Evangelical, Charismatic, Baptist, Anabaptist,

3 Mr Sheen is a furniture polish in a spray can, popularised on TV ads by a cartoon figure of a cheery little bald man magically making everything in the home shine for the housewife, 'Mrs Sparkle'.

4 Deed poll is the legal term for the official means of changing one's name.

Pentecostalist, Calvinist, liberal and fundamental. So many isms took a lot of faith.

Esther believed too. Once, she'd come to stay at my place for some big church jamboree, and I'd spent two days trying to vacuum up the smell of my dissolute life.

I'd even got my boyfriend at the time—if you could call him that—to stay away for a few days. Not because I was worried about being judged, but I'd had enough hassles with the Bibles being left open at relevant passages throughout the house, the patient, pious looks, the reminders of God's love. I didn't need a debate on my personal life as well.

They had the Lord and I had a life. Mightn't've been the kind of life I'd hoped for myself, but it was mine nonetheless. Mostly the less, if I'm being honest.

Mum's wiping the cabinet's down. 'Who's with Es now?'

'Pastor Steve's praying over her,' says Mum, not looking up. 'With Jesus.'

'Um, Mum?' All I can hear is cleaning. 'I would've stayed. Last night, you know.'

'Yes. Anyway, have some breakfast. You must be hungry. And don't forget to say grace.'

❖

When we get to the hospital there's a commotion outside Esther's door. Joan's arguing with a nurse in an echoey whisper, her teeth whistling.

'I'm sorry ma'am, but we just can't have that many people in the room; we need to get in there in case of an emergency and there's a strict limit on visitors.'

'We're *pra-a-aying* for her,' says Joan, 'The Holy Spirit's in there. We can't just let it all out.'

The nurse looks unimpressed. 'Look, you're not even family, and we have rules.'

'Commandments,' I say.

Joan and Mum look at me sharply.

I leave them outside and walk into a mass of people, all holding hands, their eyes shut tight. There's a murmur in the room as Pastor Steve holds the Bible over Esther's bandaged face.

'Oh dear Lord Jesus, we pray to you today to save our beloved Esther. In your wisdom and love …'

I zone out. I feel a terrible anger, looking at these strangers around my sister, the women dressed in those horrible curtainy smocks the devout adore, the men with thick beards.

Pastor Steve's the odd man out: thinning blond hair and a goatee with smatterings of grey, wearing a faded sports shirt. The most important man in my mother and sister's lives since Dad died. I want to punch him. He looks up at me, his close-set green eyes shining.

'And we thank you Almighty Lord for bringing Esther's sister—'

'Jodi.'

'—Ruth, back to us, to help us pray for her deliverance. Lord, hear our prayer.'

'Um, yeah. Could I see my sister now?'

There's an uneasy silence, then one of the elders looks at Pastor Steve, who nods, and they shuffle out silently, their heads bowed. Closing the door, Pastor Steve smiles, revealing small, straight teeth, as he looks me up and down, licking his lips.

Thank God the murmuring outside's muffled by the wheezing respirator.

I look at Esther, all her limbs are trussed and plastered. I can't see her face for dressings and tubes. Only the ends of her fingers and toes, curled up and shrivelled. When did she start biting her nails?

❖

And so, the long wait by her bedside. I ring work. I can feel Mike's thick voice drip down the line. 'If there's anything we can do …'

Sure. Swap places with my sister, arsehole.

They give me three-and-a-half weeks—two weeks' compassionate plus what's left of my holidays. There goes Goa. Out of the frying pan into the flames of damnation.

I ring Dean. 'Whoa, that's heavy babe.' Yes, you could put it that way. 'So when will you be back? Like, what're you going to do about Goa?'

'Fuck, Dean, my fucking sister's in a coma! She could die!'

'Hey—it's not my fault!'

I hang up, listening to the dial tone, till the woman behind me asks how long I'll be.

❖

Mum and I alternate shifts at the hospital, so we hardly see each other, except at swap-over times. Sometimes Joan will bustle in to 'give us a break', but that's when the seriousness of it hits me: facing another silent dinner, second helpings of guilt and resentment simmering in the crockpot.

Mum and Joan are always playing awful Christian rock-pop on the portable stereo in the room: *Jesus is our only friend/he died for our sins/but rose again/and now he looks down on us/from above/with undying lo-oo-o-ove!*

There's even some creepy ones that sound like love songs, except that they're being sung to Jesus. They say it's Esther's favourite music.

'Not *my* cup of tea,' says Joan, 'but it's the kind of thing you young people find "groupie", right?'

I know what they're doing. I turn it off as soon as I'm sure they're gone. And though I don't want to, I turn it back on when they return.

She looks so peaceful, though her face is shrouded by dressings. Even though she's unconscious, it's more time than we've spent together for ages.

❖

I fill the hours thinking about things, sitting amidst the hum of the respirator and the heart monitor and everything else around us. About her, us, me. Everything. How far apart we are, even though I'm by the bed stroking her arm through the plaster, feeling the clammy nubs of her fingers.

We'd always been religious, Dad too in his way, but as Mum got more and more fervent, I got more and more angry. It's easy to be faithful when you're a kid: the Bible doesn't ban tree-climbing or skipping.

But one day, everything you do is wrong, and you hate the feelings inside and start to hate yourself, and your choice is to go on hating or get away.

Oh, the faithful smile, but ever notice how tight their lips are?

I know Dad felt caught between us: me and Mum and Jesus. He'd call sometimes when Mum was out, not saying much, and we'd listen to each other's breathing.

He'd say, 'Your mother—'

And then he'd hear the door close and have to hang up, and I'd listen to the hang-up tone.

Esther wasn't like me. She was pretty. What a waste, I used to think. So beautiful, boys'd fight to sit next to her in church. But she never enjoyed it.

Nor did I much either, I suppose. I remember a dirt track to a clearing in the woods, a boy called Kane grunting over me as my arse scratched on the vinyl stitching of the back seat. Haven't had much more luck since then, I guess.

A nurse comes along to re-apply some dressings. My sister's legs are pasty and cased in chalk. And bigger than I remember.

'Do people put on weight, lying here all day?'

The nurse smiles. 'Hardly. All the muscle wastes in the plaster—they end up looking like skeletons. With veins showing.'

❖

I see Joan as I'm walking out of the shops. I can feel the stares, the unspoken words, drumming on my back. I'm running low on pot and it's making me jittery.

'Hallo, dear,' she says kindly. 'How are you? How's your mum?'

'Fine. Es's fine too.'

'Yes, the Lord won't leave a single lamb.'

'Joan, who else was on the bus when it crashed?'

'Why?'

'I guess ...' I bite my cheek, it's flooded red. 'I guess I wanted to pray for them too, you know?'

'Oh, that's wonderful! Your mother'll be so—'

'Um, yeah, I wanted to keep it quiet. I don't want to, you know—*charity vaunteth not.*'

'Yes, you're so right. *Corinthians* 13. Such a wonderful epistle.'

'Yes it is.' My tongue's metallic. 'So, anyway. You mentioned the group leader—'

'Rodney'

'Yes. And Elder Patrick, was it? And—'

'Andrew and Rachel. *That* was a terrible shame. Just married, you know. Of course, they're with the Lord now, but it'll be hard for your sister, them being so close and everything … They did everything together—they were like sisters—' Joan puts her hand to her mouth. 'I didn't mean it like that, dear, I just meant …'

'No, that's fine, don't worry about it. We hadn't been close these past few years, you know, with my job and being so far away and everything.'

Joan tilts her head. 'So we'll see you at the memorial?

'I don't know.'

'It'd mean so much to your mother.'

'Uh, I don't know. Anyway, thanks Joan. Thanks a lot.'

❖

I go home, walking down streets I'd hoped never to see again. The streets still smell sappy and cloying. I wonder what Dean's doing. I wonder what Goa smells like this time of year.

'Hey, Ruth, isn't it?'

'Um, yeah. Actually my name's Jodi now.'

'Ruth Fullbright. Wow! Thought we'd never see you again.'

'Yeah, well my sister …'

'A real tragedy. How's she doing?'

'Fine. Um, who are you?'

'Kenny. Remember? Kenny Callander?'

Great. Kenny Callander. The one guy I *didn't* fuck. That was the way it was: you lost your virginity and became Jezebel. A hand job behind the shelter sheds for a cigarette and soon you were doing the whole team. Apparently.

Kenny stands on his parents' lawn, looking at me, rubbing his belly. He licks his lips.

'So great to see you, uh, Kenny. Gotta go.'

'What's the rush? Wanna beer?'

Well yeah, sure. Why not? There's none at home.

I walk into Kenny's parents' house. Got married young, he tells me. That's what you do here, once you leave school. Take a girl to the dance and you're practically married anyway. Divorced a couple of years back. 'Whore,' he says, grinning as he hands me a beer.

I drink it fast and he hands me another. I gulp that down too, and before I know it, he asks me if I'd like a joint. I nearly spray beer all over him. *The Lord giveth …*

Funny how, wherever you are in the world, you'll always find someone who likes to get stoned.

'Sure,' I say, and he rolls a monster joint, using three normal papers.

Licking it slowly, he hands it to me, wet at the seam. His room starts closing in. He sits next to me on the bed, staring as I suck on the joint.

'This is good,' I say, as the smoke condenses inside me, making my limbs heavy. He giggles, He's alright, Kenny Callander. Who'd've known. Still wouldn't fuck him though.

'Have you got any to spare?'

'What do you mean?'

'You know, to sell. A twenty?'

He goes over to a door. Inside the closet ten plants shiver under the green light. He pulls out a big zip-lock bag and tosses me a big plug. I reach into my pocket to pull out the money, but suddenly he's beside me, grabbing my hand, 'Don't worry about it.'

Then he puts my hand on his crotch, and I feel his cock pressing against his shorts. It sits there for too long.

'What do you think you're doing?'

'Come on, we both know why you're here.'

I look at him, the faint sweaty fuzz on his lip, and feel something sour and bilious roiling.

I get up, stuffing the pot in my pocket, leaving the money next to him on the bed. His face is churned into greedy anticipation, and he takes off his tank top. I look at him, lying back on the chintz bedspread.

My tongue sticks to the roof of my mouth, and my lips open and shut like a goldfish's, gagging for air. Then I heave, hospital food and beer fizzing on his chest, trickling into his pants.

As I walk out, I can hear him yelling. *Whore! Fucken whore!*

❖

When I wake, an oily sadness coats my tongue, seeping out of my skin. My head's ringing. I get up, stash the pot, and have a long shower, the water washing almost everything away.

Then I go into Esther's room. As it always was: neat and pink and covered in Jesus. Despite Mum's best efforts, my room was unsalvageable: in the end, she just gave up on it, merely Mr Sheening the door from the outside.

I feel bad going through her stuff, but what would she have to hide? The Gnostic Gospels?[5]

In the desk drawer, a packet of photographs. All the usual suspects: Joan and my mother with starchy smiles; the youth group, everyone's faces stretched into impossible happiness; Pastor Steve, his right arm tight around her waist.

And her, with another girl, smiling in church. They look like sisters: same straight blonde hair; wide, earnest smiles; sparkling blue eyes. More like sisters than we look; I have uncontrollable hair and dumpy legs, thanks to Dad's side.

It must be Rachel. I feel something sink inside me, a small Esther-shaped hole. I don't have a picture of us like that together. The last photo I remember is before I left, Mum and Dad and us girls at yet another church picnic, and I look like I've swallowed a bee. Esther and Dad smile innocently, while Mum looks at me, her face wrung with disapproval.

Faith, hope, charity, these three. 'The Corinthians', Dad called us. Mum's unquestioning faith, my foolish hope . . . and Esther. It wasn't just

5 The Gnostic Gospels are early Christian esoteric texts regarded as heretical by orthodox theology.

her looking after any poor hurt animal that ended up in the backyard, or sitting with me in church rather than with the supplicant boys, or using her pocket money to sponsor an African child while I blew it on smokes and beer.

When Dad died, Mum fasted for a month, praying and weeping, weeping and praying. I thought I'd go mad. I shut the bedroom door and didn't speak to her that whole time. How I hated her then—how I hated God.

But Esther prayed with Mum all night, every night, after she'd cooked and cleaned and done her homework. She'd come in and sit with me and listen to me raging, and then she'd go into Mum's room and they'd kneel by the bed, their eyes shut, till their knees were raw and Mum's tears gone. Every night for a month. She must have been twelve.

The congregation was always small: whoever Mum was talking to that week, whoever I was talking to that week. There was always an outsider: Dad, or me, or both. But Esther was always there, always in the light, always trying to make everyone happy. As though she could.

I suppose I've got what I came for. I suppose I know what I needed to know. I shouldn't keep looking. And yet, the more I find—exercise books filled with Bible verses, souvenirs from church, excursions, half-written letters to God—the more it seems I have a collection of pieces that seem to fit yet which still let the uncertain light splinter through the gaps. Little Esther-shaped holes.

I look up, and see a face in the pink dresser mirror, dripping tears. A face like Mum's.

❖

That evening, while Mum's at Rachel's funeral, I drive to the crash site. Don't know why. They've already established it was the truck driver's fault: unregistered, and his brakes were shot. That and thirty caps of pseudoephedrine. The church bus didn't stand a chance. Not even God could've saved them. Could He?

It's on a stretch of highway just out of town. The skid marks come to a jagged scribble.

There's flowers and a teddy bear tied with yellow ribbons around a tree near the road, condolences from people I've never heard of. The flowers are starting to wither and fade, and crows have pecked out the bear's eyes. A cross nailed to the tree.

Funny how you see those strange little shrines and never think: someone died here, someone loved. Until you look at the poor remains someone else left for someone you loved, and wish you could stop the traffic and cry: *This is my sister! Remember her!*

But the cars keep speeding on.

Now, Mum's with Rachel's parents and a million people from church, mourning a girl like her daughter's sister. And Esther's in the isolation ward, surrounded by machines. And I'm here. I wonder who'd come to my funeral.

The police have cleared up all the evidence: there's nothing left, not even glass. I look up and see a dirt track turning off a few yards away. It's a road I've been down many times. I get back in the car and drive home. I don't look back. Can't.

❖

Mum's sitting by the lounge-room door in the darkness, the Bible open on the couch arm. Just like old times.

'Just went for a drive, in case you wanted to know.'

'That's fine. You're an adult now, I can hardly tell you what to do anymore, can I? Not that I ever—'

'Yeah, okay. How was the service? Mum? Okay. Fine. Night.' I start up the stairs.

'Ruth? Your father chose that name, you know. It reminds me of him.'

My foot stops, hung above a stair. I can't breathe.

'I know you don't believe, and that's your concern. But I pray for you every day. We both do. Esther and me. Especially Esther. And we—with the Lord—love you very much.'

My foot sinks. The stair squeaks.

❖

She's not my sister. I'm sure of it. Well, not sure. But pretty sure. The bitten nails, the chunky legs. And other stuff—just a feeling. I can't explain why, but I think there's been a terrible mistake.

I can't say who the person swaddled in bandages and plaster actually is, but it's not Esther. I know it. Must be going crazy. I smoke joint after joint to make the doubt dissolve, but it's no good. My mind careens, picking up more and more speed until out of nowhere, I corner Mum in the kitchen.

'Mum, we need to talk.' She's cleaning the oven. 'I don't know how to say this, but … but I don't think that's Esther in hospital.'

Mum stops. The oven echoes. She looks up at me, an expression on her face I've never seen before. 'Why would you say such a thing?'

'It's just … I …' I'm fourteen again. I look down on the hard, spotless floor.

'Have you been smoking the Devil's weed again? The mary-jawana?'

'What? No—I mean, I'm just trying to …'

'I don't know where I went wrong with you,' she says. 'I always tried my best, always followed the Lord.' She looks up at the whining ventilation fan. *Why, Lord? Why have you let this child do evil in Your sight?*

'Mum!'

'You may have made your life as it is. You may have wasted it on sin. But why envy your sister? Your sister, who didn't forsake me, or the Lord? Who's hurt no one! Why do you want to hurt her? And—and me? *Forgive her, Lord—*'

'Fucking hell!'

Mum blinks, too shocked to speak, to move, to breathe.

'It's always the same fucken thing, isn't it? If she lives, it's God's mercy. If she dies, it's God's will. It's always so fucken easy for you. You can't have it both ways. What do *you* think? What do *you* feel? I'm trying to tell you what I feel and you … you—'

Mum walks out of the kitchen, closing the door behind her. I hear the hallway clock tick, tick, ticking away. I feel evil and stupid. Fourteen again.

❖

We talk even less over the next few days, if that's possible. She can't even look at me, and I can't say I blame her. Maybe I *am* wrong. Maybe it *is* the pot. Maybe.

All she has now is Jesus and her faith. And all I have now is maybe. Who am I to—?

Whenever I expressed doubt growing up, Mum'd sit me up in the bath into the night until she was sure she'd scrubbed the sin out of me.

I remember once in Sunday school, asking why if God was all-powerful, all-seeing, all-present, all-good, he could allow bad things to happen. *The Devil's wiles!* Cried the teacher, and cast me out. I sat on the verandah crushing ants.

Dad sat me down when we got home. 'I know it's hard,' he said in his soft voice, glancing upstairs over his shoulder. 'But consider this: if you're right and I'm wrong, I'll've still lived a good, pure life, won't I? But what if you're wrong?'

What if I am wrong?

That night, when Mum comes home, I'm waiting for her by the lounge-room door.

'Mum, we need to talk.'

'I think you've said enough.' She sounds tired in the dark.

'Look, I'm sorry about the other day, I really am. Please forgive me.' I can hear the silence glowering. The Lord *demands* forgiveness.

'Fine. You're forgiven.'

'Thanks. I just wanted to say this: if I'm wrong, and I'm not saying I'm not, and it *is* Esther, then I'm prepared to acknowledge my sins and give my life to the Lord.'

I can't believe I just said that. Did I?

'Are you high?'

'No. Promise. If it's Esther—'

'Faith isn't a game, Ruth. You can't bargain with the Lord.'

'I know, Mum. I'm not. I'm just saying I've been thinking and I realise I've been wrong about a lot of things. I want to come into the light.'

'Well, why don't you do that anyway?'

'I just need proof, Mum. I need the Lord to wash my doubts away.'

'You can't test the Lord's love.'

'The loaves and the fishes. The spirits in the swine. The leper. Lazarus.'[6]

The hallway light comes on. Mum's eyes are shining, her voice trembling. 'What are you doing? Don't play games. Please don't—'

'I'm not.'

'The Lord most loves the repentant sinner! Oh, my daughter! For this my child was dead, and is alive again, was lost and now is found.'

Amen. My mother comes to me, smiling, her arms brittle and awkward. She hugs me, really hugs me, kissing me on my neck, and for a moment, there's no one else in the room, just us. Not even Jesus.

❖

And so, things get a little better. The doctors say Esther's making a slow but sure recovery. My mother and Joan are solicitous and sweet, clucking every time they see me. I promise Mum not to tell anyone else my doubts. For now.

Part of me's uncomfortable. I wouldn't have struck the deal if I didn't think, well, I was going to get away with it. Would I?

Anyway, the deal's struck now. Don't want to think about it if I'm wrong. What else have I got to risk?

And then, in the middle of the night, I judder awake by her bed, T-shirt sour with drool. What if I'm right? What if it isn't Esther, and she's really dead? Jesus.

In the fluorescent quiet, I kneel by the bed. The lino's[7] hard and my knees protest, but I keep kneeling, my head buried in the blanket.

Oh Lord Jesus, please save my sister. I haven't been a good Christian, but I promise to be. I promise to give my life to You in exchange for hers. She doesn't deserve to die. She's never hurt anybody. Oh merciful God, please let her live. I'll do anything.

6 These are all various miracles performed by Jesus, who was constantly being challenged to prove his claims to divinity.

7 'Lino' is short for 'Linoleum', a rubberised/plasticised floor covering popular through most of the last century.

For one long second, the heart monitor stops. My breath catches in my heart. *Please, Father, anything.*

Ping! The respirator jerks back into life. She starts coughing and I press the buzzer over and over. I rush to the door and scream. Nurses scramble down the corridor, snapping on rubber gloves. She retches as they pull the feeding tube from her throat. Sticky green phlegm spatters across the floor.

She's talking. Oh, sweet Jesus, she's talking! Only a whisper, but it's a—

I put my ear to her mouth. Her voice is dry as reeds, like somebody else's.

'R-Rebecca?'

Who the hell's Rebecca?

Nurses swarm round the bed, pulling away the sheet and disconnecting tubes. I fall back on the chair, nibbled fingers slipping out of my grasp.

POOJA MITTAL

Pooja Mittal (b. 1983) was born in Nigeria, has lived in India and New Zealand, and now lives in Sydney. She has been published in numerous literary journals including *Meanjin, Poetry Niedern Gasse, Jacket* and *Hecate*. In 2001 she was the featured poet for *Poetry New Zealand* and her work was translated into Russian and performed at the Moscow International Poetry Festival. She is the author of four books: *Musings* (1996), *Diaries of a Marked Man* (2006), *Musings on Poetry* (2006) and *Subliminal Dust* (2010). Her poetry was also selected for *The Best Australian Poetry 2007,* which was edited by John Tranter, and *The Best Australian Poems 2007,* edited by Peter Rose.

The selection here is from her collection *Subliminal Dust,* published by Odyssey Books.

too fond

you're too fond of reason to be a poet.
too fond of articles. conjunctions. misused
commas. they find you in public toilets,
playing with your mind, & arrest you
for indecency. oranges & dusk paint
still lifes of you by the sidewalk. abandoned
by your art, your cigarette burns out
in the hole that used to be the moon.

where are you? where are you?
the stones ask. (silence greets them.)
you answer only to the sky, which has
the audacity to imitate the sand's night-glitter.
are you a traffic light, forgotten in your longing
for dawn? are you lost in the vacuum
of love? what emptied you out, what gathered
you in the deep, dark belly of moss?

spit out by the minds of children, poetry
gathers on the pavement. skating rinks
echo the light, their sickled backs sharp
beneath the sun. you squint into the clouds.
perhaps you were holding knives, gently,
in the hand that forgot how to write. in any
case, you've murdered the silence now,
& they'll arrest you again. too late.

the veil

'on a morning like any other,' they say
          but they mean *in* a morning
because you're always
                    in a morning
          aren't you?

& so, *in* a morning like any other
          it occurred to me
                    quite suddenly
                              that I was opaque
& that a body was merely a curtain
between two voids, both of which
          were unknown   & remained uncharted.
(the hearts of uncarved birds.)

this morning, you see, was so
          gloriously ordinary, ordinary as an orange
& speckled as one, built of infinite pores
          that breathed in air
                    & breathed out
                              fog.
          a citrus   tinge
colored the sky & rendered it finite, gave
the pock-marked canvas a certain
                    three

dimensionality. (birds, distant as freckles,
                    marring otherwise smooth
          skin.)

there are skies & then there are *skies*,
if you catch my meaning—there are skies
that gleam like boiled eggs
          or bald pates,
that crack themselves open
on the horizon & other inconsiderately
                    sharp
          landmarks. (trees, telegraph poles,
                    raised hands.) there are skies
that open up & keep on opening, blue lotuses
          almost vehement
                    in their surrender.
there are skies that should know better,
          that cloak themselves despite fair weather,
                    suspicious
as high-collared detectives, goggled
          as disgruntled pilots. & there are skies
that nestle, kept animals, fur bristle-smooth
          under the broad bright palm
                    of the sun. but *this*,
this morning, was terribly unremarkable
          especially after the rain.

there was nothing to it. soggy as a child's
sock, a sky filled with pebbles
          each cloud rounder than the one before it
& gleaming
                    stubborn
          as a delinquent's eye. in the long spaces
between them, the sky rippled (citrus) & the birds
drifted downwards (bits of ash).

          & on this morning
the earth was somehow oblivious:

a heavy sleeper, turning
wide-hipped (hills, townships)
under the pale, shaggy coverlet
of dawn. I nestled in its lap, a cuckoo's child
in a nest not rightfully its own,
but still warm, so warm, the feathered weight
of mother-bosom upon me.

I was a body.   smaller than
more exquisite than
more delicious than
the citrus morning itself. I was
a little knot, a pulsing clot, a clenched fist
of flesh (slowly relaxing),
pursed as a mouth
or a rosebud is, incongruous, solid, primeval,
infantile. I was a child. I was a body.
I was the body of a child. I was punctuation.

between two great spaces, two great sentences,
what absurd curlicue
was I?
what pause did I give the vast churning
of the world? (inexorable as a garbage truck,
making mulch of what was once dead.)
this trundle & gurgle & silent heave
of a million infinitesimal things,
& I a million times *more* infinitesimal,
crouched between the dew-moist thighs
of a sleeping, adoptive mother:
looking up at a sky whose mere freckles
were far vaster than I. starburst, cellular,
photogenic. a face too small
to be noticed
without a grand
gasping
microscope. (sun-mirror burnished,
angled upon me in a sudden blaze of heat.)

oh, microscopic things. oh, living things.
oh, dead things
& carried things
& given things
& birds in foreign skies. come down,
with your scent
of old cigarettes
& fresh scandal, of new blood
& ancient fossils. my bones mark the carbon
lines that will mark the stones
that will mark the place
the hidden space
where you grow.

oh, living things.
we are opaque,
our bodies merely a curtain
between two voids, both of which
are unknown & remained uncharted.
(the hearts of uncarved
birds.)

turandot[1]

my palms green with shavings of hospital paint.

& still you say: *I'll wait.* oh, really? what for?

chipping away, layer by layer, at the skin of these walls—

for even walls have skins—eyes—ears. our gods in tiny

red parcels. gold cloth. you bring them to me, unwrap them,

as if they were parcels of food. gods for the devouring.

1 *Turandot* is an opera by Puccini based on a Persian story but set in China. It deals with lovers undergoing tests to win each other's affections.

I pity them. their wide eyes, black-rimmed, fixed forever
as if in death. their eternal ferocity. their paw-like hands
carved into their abdomens. fingers twined. meditating,
of course. are they calm? are they at the center
of their universe? my schizophrenia, you say, is a lack of
faith. if only I were to gather myself. grains of rice.
my mind is starved. my faith, a perforated stomach. *come*
back to us, you say. *why do you live in fear?* why, indeed?
good question. psychosis is such a pale

gift.

forever

unravelled.

christmas for non-christians. the horror of a stolen past.
when you unwrap our gods for me, your hands warm
& not-quite-trembling—when you unwrap them, you open
a maw of despair, not unlike blue glass, in my mouth.
I speak, but only marbles emerge. my words roll
uselessly across the floor. we watch them together. the gods
watch them. *they are the gods,* I say. *my words.* you don't
believe me.

who believes

a thief? not I.

thought-stealer. your own thoughts, spidery with hope, crawl
about & about the truth. there is a truth. you believe that. who is
this soothsayer you trust? you leave the gods for me—to listen

to, you say. but I have enough to listen to. don't you know, sister?
when you're gone, I play with our gods
as if they were dolls. they're so gentle
in my hands. not cruel at all. even the fierce trident-holder
does nothing more than prick my fingers. the goddess of song
remains stubbornly silent. are the gods deaf to me? no. I'm deaf.
selective hearing is the privilege of the new. over time, all voices
converge, into this great teeming river

salmon

kind nightmares

froth.

disconnected always. the radio doesn't work. then again, I am
the radio. long antennae extended. when you touch them
with your believer's palms, perhaps
a bit of your belief

will transfer to me.

does confinement work, as a form of therapy?
of course. the city's infested with fleas. it's a stray
I'd rather stay away from. rabies. causes madness, you know.
my disbelief is no more criminal than yours. you don't
believe me. I don't believe your gods. *our gods,* you say.
you're right. the embroidered battle-axe
may be silken to the touch, but surely, its blade
slaughters souls. your god-doll in my hand. a strange
reverse voodoo. with time, you will visit me
less & less. I know this. you too will abandon me, sister. like

our gods. the elephant head, the lotus feet, the never-ending
chatter of love. for gods talk
            in the language
                        of love. it is
vast & terrifying. their love is as indifferent
as light. falling upon everything, baring everything. merciless.
& you ask me why I'm afraid. when I talk to them, only
a piercing silence
greets my voice. they are indifferent. I am indifferent. my worship
your hand
            our cloth.
skin bound & unbound. the walls coalesce.
your gifts, our gods, my commonplace. in this playground,
paint shavings stain my feet, not grass. sister, will you
not play with me? you'll be gone soon, as they say. last phantom,
last riddle, last curse. you & your slippers. your gods
wandering footless. leave me your little dolls. so precious to me,
your vocabulary of storms. unshakeable faith. blue marbles.
I wrap & unwrap our gods for you. *won't you come back to us?*
you speak from the walls. every echo of your call
sheds more green shavings. they fall at my feet, soft moss.
silence, shaped by agony, becomes smooth. like a flute.
our blue-skinned god plays a tune on it. the eternal
                        disappears, a magicked
            glove. perhaps you were

the goddess of song. but you won't

          any longer.

                    visit

me.

rehabilitation

the long abyss:
so slender, so solitary.
dawn's pale fruit ripens
in your mouth.

preferring the calm of despair
to the excitement of grief—
was that what you said?
long abyss, indeed.

where did your ship sail,
its white tongue raised
in mockery against the waves?
you who were so indignant,
pared down to the bones
of your thoughts.
I pick at them distractedly.

are the walls clean, where you are?
amphetamine in little pockets.
latitude & longitude,
untruths mapped in marble inches.
your ink on my palm, my skin
still warm. but you've left, now.
taken your shadow, too.

your letters do find me
in good health. my abyss

is brighter than yours, & thinner,
a knife's edge
sparkling with cocaine.
I remember to wash my hands.
I remember to sleep.

sunset's bright orange
still startles me, bringing out
the dark veins of trees
for a fresh blood-letting.
closed eyes. silhouettes.
cars in molten drops of steel
clinging to the tarmac.

no distant road, here.
everything too near.

you needn't worry, wind-sailor.
the birds become the waves,
blue-winged. or perhaps it is the ocean
itself that takes flight, on spumed feathers,
to perch on the fading light.

dawn, noon, dusk, night.
four pieces on the board.
bishop to E6.

another day gone.
another page, you'd say.
no words written.

when will I write back to you?

when the sea is emptied.

but you needn't worry. neatly watched
& pocketed as I am, they take
good care of me. I scavenge their smiles.
your memories.

purification. my slate being
so carefully erased. will your name
be gone, too? the lights of your shore
blinking out, one by one.

a long abyss.

but the walls are clean.

pilgrim

the beauty of abandoned gloves
rests gently beside your table-lamp.
your glass of wine, pitch-black: your voice
ragged with loss. you walked so long,
you tell me, to find the open road of
tomorrow. snake-like, the scales of asphalt
glittering, it followed you

with the tenaciousness of death.
wild bees lit the sky in a haze of hot fury.
here, the flask of silence broken, you drink
from the night's blue cup. how tired your eyes
as they recall your journey. the companions
that left you, one by one, to walk alone.
your gloves, empty. your hands, curled.

MICHELLE CAHILL

Michelle Cahill (b. 1969) is the author of a collection of short fiction titled *Letter to Pessoa,* published by Giramondo in 2016. She has also written essays and two collections of poetry, the most recent of which, *Vishvarupa,* published by Five Islands Press in 2011, was shortlisted for the Victorian Premier's Literary Award. Born in Kenya and of Goan ancestry, she attended primary school in London before migrating to Sydney, where she graduated in Medicine and Arts. She is editor of the online literary magazine *Mascara* and co-editor of the anthology *Contemporary Asian Australian Poets,* published by Puncher & Wattmann in 2013. Her story 'Duende' won the 2014 Hilary Mantel International Short Story Award and she was shortlisted for the 2015 Elizabeth Jolley Prize.

'Beauty Tips' is from her poetry collection *Night Birds,* published by Vagabond Press in 2012. 'Five Sijo for My Raider' first appeared online in *Cordite Poetry Review* volume 35, issue 1, in 2011. Her short story 'The Sadhu' was published online in *Transnational Literatures* volume 3, issue 1, in 2010.

Beauty Tips

for my mother

What words to fill the day? How to resist sentiment,
balancing dream and the recklessly blue sky?

Spring arrives with its allegro swell of trees, pollen,
a novel open on the kitchen bench, breakfast aromas.

Outside, the garden languors in laundry, agapanthus,
a swimming pool in need of chlorine turns emerald green

with insect wings, serrated jacaranda. What colour is truth?
I dip the soft sable in powder to dust away speckles,

cover shadows on my face, and yesterday's mascara.
Cleanse, tone, exfoliate. At all times, brush downwards.

I've disregarded my mother's beauty tips, her lessons
in permanence or grace. Her body slow, involuntary,

her eyes widened by Parkinson's, a fine tremor in the jaw
while the heart arranges, steady with belief and forgetting.

I take comfort in this. Mother, show me the other way back.
How the gravel is imprinted by the wind, by human steps.

Walk with me this evening, the sky crepuscular, rose-tinted,
the drifting scent of wild freesias like something strange,

half-known. You shuffle, sight weakened, wanting
you observe the fallen shingles, twigs, and the scarcity of birds.

Five Sijo For My Raider[1]

A sound of hooves over the dry stones of my sheets at night

My arms are withered, my bones rise to the quivering world

In the space between our thoughts are three aching syllables

....

My almost lover, no photographs of you, no good-bye note

Enemy, you have raided my country, your handwriting floats

Downstream through the forest to the far walls of my kingdom

....

Your decrees are impulse, you enter without courtesy

And I become your dynasty, not knowing when to discern

Death, by the penitence of leaves, by the haloes of traffic

....

1 The poem first appeared in a journal issue featuring Korean writing, and adopts the tone and form of sijo—a common Korean poetic mode.

From the far east, when the river broke, came rumours of a tribe

I was alone that dawn, milking the soybeans, harvesting rice

With a bronze arrow you annexed my body to this design

....

Which of us abandoned the other? We cannot answer

How quiet the apartment: wind stirs, stars begin to shatter

Snow is a scherzo dancing over the words I've lost for snow

The Sadhu

Sundeep's real name was James. He was from Dublin, but he'd spent two years backpacking through Asia.

His room adjoined Sarita's at the Hotel Buddha in Kathmandu. They met on the terrace one evening, the sky a luculia pink. Sarita had stepped out to witness the view as clouds dissolved to unveil the distant snow-covered Himalayas. Black crows wheeled above. They perched on the railings while Sundeep and Sarita spoke.

Below them was the colourful activity of the street with its organic blend of bicycles, rickshaws and pedestrians, its maze of alleys and medieval arches, framing views of buildings that had collapsed into piles of rubble during the earthquake. Still in almost every direction Tibetan flags criss-crossed the skies. These windhorses reminded Sarita of childhood. Faded by rain, their primary colours left a Buddhist insignia on the landscape. She was momentarily empty of the past, or the memory of Logan. She was completely absorbed by the impressions and presences of this ancient city.

The door to Sundeep's room was open. Inside there was a dispersal of books, clothes, boxes, empty soft drink bottles, a waterjug, a teapot, and other bric-a-brac. Sundeep had offered to make chai. He rummaged about, whistling a tune. Sarita sat down on one of the deck chairs, trying not to seem too obvious as she observed him.

Presently he emerged carrying an iPod.

'Would you like to listen to some music while I make the chai?' he asked.

Though it was nothing flash, she accepted the offer of Sundeep's iPod.

Sundeep's body floated in a loose crumpled shirt. He kept a small fold-out portable gas stove in his room. Sarita could hear the hiss of the gas flame as the tea boiled.

When he served the chai perhaps a quarter of an hour later it was thick and milky. He'd used a concoction of spices: cardamom, cinnamon, ginger, aniseed star. The tea had a spicy tang. He threaded his fingers through the handle of a teacup, wrapping them to warm his hands.

'So where do you come from?' he asked, leaning forward from his lotus squat.

She'd been asked this question by most of the local shopkeepers. Some thought she was a Nepali. Others guessed locations varying from India to America. Being of mixed ancestry, Sarita was hard to label. She was an outsider returning to explore her grandfather's home. In the streets of Kathmandu the touts tested her nerves. But Sundeep had nothing to sell her.

As she spoke about Dee Why,[2] Sarita began to feel homesick. She missed the beach, the surf. She missed her friends.

'I've heard Sydney's a beautiful city,' Sundeep said.

Their gaze touched briefly.

That evening they ventured out through the slinky streets of Thamel. They ate in one of the vegetarian restaurants recommended in the Lonely Planet guidebook. As they sipped their mango lassis, the conversation turned to spirituality. Sarita described her retreat at Kopan monastery, aware that it might have sounded like a New Age cliché. Asia was replete with dreamy-eyed itinerants on some quest to find a haven from the havoc of the past, or from the responsibilities of the present. Sarita was trying her best to forget Logan. He was her addiction, a drug she desperately swallowed at nightclubs and dance parties. But what had Sundeep been escaping? He'd lived in a Hare Krishna ashram for two years. During this time he'd lost contact with friends

2 A beachside suburb north of Sydney.

and relatives, and with his life in the first world. But the community disintegrated when the guru was imprisoned for sex offences.

'He was sitting on an incredible amount of energy. It was a pity, really.' Sundeep said.

'What do you mean?'

'I saw what he could do for people, the way that he could influence their lives.'

'And what about you?'

'I admired him. But I never really felt accepted. In the end it was quite estranging. But that's another story,' he said, with a laugh.

'Do you think too much power was his undoing?'

'I'm not sure really.' He looked at her squarely, 'It's such a fine line to walk.'

She was interested in the Buddha's teachings. At university she'd stopped going to the temple with her family. She had a healthy scepticism when it came to gurus, swamis or cults, yet she could fall for someone like Logan, surrendering like a hostage to his selfish priorities. It took her strenuous effort and endless time to love him, and even longer to heal. That he should even enter her thoughts was a source of annoyance. She had come to this damaged city to recover; to refashion the soft clay of her heart in meditation. Every day she tried to observe the many hindrances to happiness within herself, slowly unhinging the past. The crumbled stupas and temples were supported with bamboo scaffolding. At the monastery the visitor accommodation was being restored. Sarita was trying with the rhythm of prayer rounds to undo her rigidity and shape new habits of mind. She observed the temporary and random nature of feelings, thoughts, opinions, judgements. Whatever emotions were roiling about this was a process that appealed to her reason.

There was something gracefully roguish about Sundeep's demeanour. He combed his fingers through his hair and swivelled his body towards her.

'Did you get your name in the ashram, then?' Sarita asked.

She watched how the smooth skin around Sundeep's eyes puckered at the mention of his past.

Sarita had lost her orientation as they walked back to the guesthouse through a scrawl of alleys, dimly lit by gas lamps. Sundeep spoke of visiting Baba, a sadhu who lived by the river; someone whom he believed was enlightened. By now the buzz of the day's tourist stream had settled. The locals welcomed volunteers and aid workers arriving into the city, but even the shoe-string budget tourists brought hope and a flow of currency. Young boys loitered about, talking in Newari dialect. The smog was cloaked with a darkness in which the shape of a boar could be traced as it sank in rubbish near an ancient shrine. Sarita and Sundeep stepped through the shadows cast by dogs, rickshaws and tardy pedestrians.

❖

Early the next day Sarita left the hotel to get breakfast and browse through the bookstores. On the dusty, noisy chaos of the street, with its construction sites, its beggars and peddlers, she ran into Sundeep. Straddling a motorbike he appeared out of nowhere, his anaemic stare quite inscrutable.

'You surprised me,' she admitted.

'I'm going to visit the sadhu, my friend,' he said blandly. 'You're welcome to come along. Maybe you should meet him, especially with your interest in meditation.'

She'd seen sadhus covered in ash, with their hair matted like Shiva, wandering about in temples and bus stops. Not the saintly milk drinkers, or the legendary babas who wore chastity belts and *langotis* for almost a lifetime, the ones she'd seen were smoking hash by the banks of rivers polluted with human and animal faeces. Still, to be introduced to a holy man, a *jivanmukta*, was something that roused her curiosity.

Steadying herself on the back of Sundeep's bike, Sarita clutched the bar beneath the passenger seat and they set off, zig-zagging through the cracked, narrow streets. It was easy to dodge the rickshaws and pedestrians but they were stalled for a good five minutes by a cow. The cow was at liberty to wander the streets because she no longer produced milk. Someone had made her an offering, adorned her with bright yellow garlands. While she sifted through small mounds of trash, Sundeep spoke of how Lord Krishna was the first *bala-gopala*, 'the child who protects cows.' Krishna he proselytised, was the first teacher, in the *guru-shishya* tradition. Sarita had read *The Bhagavad-Gītā*. There was nothing special about Sundeep's observation. Still, she placed her arms around his waist while they waited.

They took a route which passed the Royal Palace, several parks, and colourful markets on the outskirts of the city. From here the road led to a more industrial zone, to half-constructed building sites. Dark, muscular women dressed in dusty sarees, wearing sandals, carried heavy loads of bricks in cane baskets. The housing estates became sparser as they journeyed further beyond the city. Sundeep stopped at last, to park his bike. Crossing a reserve, they approached a narrow bend in the river, the water a murky sepia. The opposite bank formed an island overcrowded with monkeys.

'Where are we?' Sarita asked.

They were downstream from Pashupatinath. Sundeep pointed north in the direction of the temple, explaining their bearings as they walked.

It looked more like a dug-out on the side of a cliff. Even by Nepalese standards it ought to have been condemned. The facing wall sloped as if the footings had slipped badly and the roofing was rusted through.

Sundeep knocked on the wooden door. There was no response. He craned his neck towards a window and called out. When the door opened a beautiful young girl, perhaps sixteen or seventeen years of age, stood gracing the entrance. Thin-boned and fine-skinned, she introduced herself as Gabriella. A slender ray of light caught her blonde, tousled dreadlocks and the gold nose ring she wore, but there was something about her that lacked vibrancy. She greeted Sundeep in Nepali, bowing politely.

Sarita exchanged smiles with Gabriella who beckoned them inside. From the narrow, dark hallway, they climbed a spiral staircase up to the main abode. Sarita had no idea what to expect from this encounter with the sadhu. As a child she remembered sadhus lying in the midday heat on the cool verandahs of *mandirs* while their perpetual fires to Agni or Shiva burned. Pilgrims came with their offerings for the devas, leaving the holy men to their solitude.

The room upstairs had a low roof held in place by timber lintels. Baba sat between bronze *murtis* of Shiva and Ganpati, behind a pyre of smouldering coals and incense. The space was flagged by a three-pronged spear and traced out in red resin, the kind used in Hindu temples. The sadhu was young and handsome. Half-naked, his oiled body was magnificent, his hair or *jata* the consistency of coir. It was tied in dreadlocks and wrapped in an elaborate heap above his head. Vermillion paste was brushed thickly over his brow. Sarita thought his eyes were like water.

She knelt by the window overlooking the river while Sundeep spoke to Baba. Her interest turned to a series of drawings that decorated the wall. Geometric designs and whirling spirals were etched in charcoal in a kind of spiritual notation that invited her curiosity. She sensed intuitively that these were the work of the girl. Gabriella remained silently attentive to Baba the whole time. Sarita asked her if she spoke English.

'A little.' Gabriella said, with a brief smile. 'And of course I'm learning Nepali since I've been with Baba.'

'Where are you from?'

'Italy.'

Gabriella was from Rome. She was a recluse in the dugout, though once a week she would leave to buy provisions at the market.

'Have you been here long?' Sarita asked.

'For nine months now I've been here,' she replied with an air of vacancy.

The opposite side of the room served as a kitchen, which opened out to a landing. A tribe of monkeys were scratching, wrestling, and peering curiously inside. Their raucous noise interrupted the conversation. Baba soon turned his attention to Sarita. Where had she been travelling, he asked. She spoke of her meditation retreat at Kopan monastery.

'We, too, learn from the Buddha.'

It was a gentle reminder that the Buddha was a reincarnation.

'That is what we all are,' he said, 'We are born and we die.' He spoke quietly, with measured calmness, and Sarita felt herself drawn, even against resistance, into his aura, by something difficult to overcome.

'All we need do is let go of everything.'

If she could have let go of Logan, months ago, when she was caught—if it was that easy. She asked Baba if he was referring to desire.

'Yes, but that does not mean we should always be passive. It is also good to be daring.'

Baba's eyes widened. Sarita sensed the magnetism of his body, relaxed and strong from the yoga prana.

'But doesn't that flare our desire?'

'Desire is always there,' he said '... just let it be.'

When he spoke, he scarcely moved or gesticulated, as if he had nothing to qualify or compare. Sarita felt as if he could see right through her and he was addressing her fear.

'I sit here by the river, everything comes to me. I have no need to go to the town, to have a car or drive. People come. I am always here. Lord Shiva teaches us to be bold ... but never be afraid of desire,' he paused. 'Be full of Love ... that is everything.'

She listened thoughtfully.

The sadhu seemed to forestall her doubts. He opened an album of photographs from his annual pilgrimage to Mt Kailash in Tibet. The journey through north-eastern Nepal was taken by bus and by truck to Nyalamu, and thence to Barga from where he'd travelled arduously for weeks on foot. She could see how visibly gaunt and ethereal he appeared in these mountain photographs, standing alone by the lake. A phantasm of his present self, he was spiritually realised. There were photographs too, of his teacher, an Indian guru who'd taught him in Haridwar.

'Will you be going to Kailash this year?' Sundeep asked.

'Maybe not this year, because of the child.' Baba placed his hand on Gabriella's belly.

The girl had not, for one moment, taken her eyes off the sadhu.

Outside, the monkeys were making a racket. One had stepped into the room shaking its head and bouncing about. Gabriella stood up and threw them some bananas.

'The female is pregnant,' Baba explained. 'It makes them more irritable. But I like to see that we are having a family around us. It is good. It is nature.'

When Gabriella returned to her cushion on the floor, Baba craned towards her, whispering in her ear. She brought him a small clay pipe, which he packed with ganja and smoked. He passed it to Sundeep and the girl who reluctantly drew back a few times. Sarita declined.

She'd felt a benefit from the sobriety of not drinking or smoking. In the monastery, she'd tried to quit all her habits and addictions.

By now, Baba had tired of counselling. Like many sadhus, he was a devotee of the smoking Shiva, the Lord of the Yogas and the Lord of the Hash, forever intoxicated. Sundeep and Sarita took their blessings. Gabriella accompanied them downstairs and farewelled them formally, her face expressionless.

❖

On their way back to the hotel, Sundeep and Sarita stopped at a teahouse for chai, and to share their impressions of this meeting with Baba. Sarita felt an urge to see him again. She was concerned for the girl, Gabriella.

'It's as if she's stranded there, alone.'

Sundeep wasn't perturbed in the slightest.

'From what I know of the story, she came to Nepal with an Italian guru from the sect in Rome, and decided to stay with Baba. She's had some problems, of course, with her visa, but if she has a child to Baba, then I think it's no problem for her to stay indefinitely in Kathmandu.'

It was noisy and hot in the tea room with its low ceilings, its crowded benches. At a nearby table a group of novice monks were chatting boisterously. Sarita snacked on a momo. She was musing about the girl.

'How can she be confined in that small space, constantly with him? Remember how Baba said she only leaves once a week to do shopping? She's like a slave. I think she's depressed. And besides, what about the pregnancy … does she ever get to see a doctor? '

'Well, that's her choice. No, I don't pity her, Sarita. I'm sure they have a loving, healing relationship. It's something I'd wish for myself. Besides most sadhus like Baba would practice tantric sex.'

Sarita had to admit he would be well rehearsed.

'He has an incredible energy about him, it just sucks you in.'

'Yes, and I forgot to warn you not to look into his eyes.'

'Why?' Sarita asked.

'They say with sadhus that if you look at them directly you can fall into their power.'

She smiled facetiously, 'You don't believe all that crap, Sundeep, do you?'

Sundeep seemed to lose his usual air of grace.

'It's not crap,' he protested. 'All that time spent in meditation does take them to a higher plane.' His eyes rolled upwards, as if he were thinking aloud.

'I'd say it would be an amazing experience. I've never been there before myself, but I've seen the maps ...'

She strained to hear as his voice lowered.

'I know it's possible to cross that boundary, to reach that territory.'

She barely grasped his meaning; a shared confidence of something visionary and tender. What could she do, about the girl? The whole worship thing was complicated, risky. Gabriella was as vulnerable to Baba as Sarita had been with Logan, the politics and faith dangerously entangled.

❖

That evening Sarita and Sundeep strolled through the gardens of Pashupatinath. Leaning against a stone wall, they overlooked the river where children swam naked. Sundeep pointed out the body of a woman. She was being dressed in a white saree in preparation for her pyre. Her flesh and bones would combust with flowers, sandalwood, with rice and butter. Fig trees formed a giant tapestry with their twisted, hanging vines and their buttressed roots. Monkeys swung from the shutters of temple windows. Sarita thought of the pilgrims worshipping in those candle-lit rooms as they had done for centuries. She thought of their families and the villages they'd left behind. She thought of the journeys they'd taken by rail or bus or on foot. A breeze carried tabla rhythms, and the sound of rickshaws to her foreign ears.

The day's pollution had washed the sky. Away from the noise and squalor of the city it was possible to enter something nameless; a human stream of worship that flowed from the temple to another space.

CHRISTOPHER RAJA

Raja was born in 1975 and came to Australia from Calcutta in 1986. He studied and taught in schools in Melbourne, then moved to Alice Springs where he taught English and History and has since written journalistic and autobiographical pieces for a range of publications. With Natasha Raja he wrote a play, *The First Garden*, released by Currency Press in 2012. His young adult book *The Burning Elephant* was published by Giramondo in 2015.

What follows is an edited compilation of 'White Boots' from *Meanjin* volume 62, issue 1, published in 2003, and 'Rupert and Me' from *Quadrant*, the January-February 2011 issue.

Warwick, Rupert and Me

When I was eleven, even twelve, I didn't know who Warwick Capper was, in fact, I didn't know what a mark was nor did I understand Aussie Rules,[1] which at the time made little sense to me and my parents, as we had just emigrated to Australia. But I learnt quickly.

'Dad, what are the sticks?'

'Son, goals.'

'Dad, what are the side sticks?'

'I don't know, son.'

By this time Mum would get involved: 'What is this game? What are you both watching?' And invariably she would get absorbed and not leave the television until the game was over. 'Look at that, he just caught and flung that player in the air. What, no foul? Hey, he looks hurt. This game is wild. What are the rules? Are there rules?'

1 Melbourne is the beating heart of the Australian Football League (AFL). 'Aussie Rules' dictate that there are four goalposts—the two inner and central posts are for goals worth six points, the two outer posts framing kicks (or 'points') and are worth only one point. Warwick Capper and Rupert Betheras are real people revered for their prowess as footballers.

No one explained to us the rudiments of the game. We learnt by watching and listening to Channel 7's commentary team.

We left India before Rupert Murdoch had taken over the airwaves, before Fox, and Sky and Star and CNN. And certainly pre-internet! Until then, my eleven-year-old Indian brain had been fed the local state-run TV channel with non-English black-and white programs. The few movies I had ever seen were shown at the local club we frequented: the Dalhousie Institute. This was an old remnant of the British Raj where English elites used to hobnob over sundowners, cocktails and aperitifs. After Independence it was left to middle-income professionals such as my mum and dad, who took me swimming at the pool while they socialised with friends over drinks and Chinese food or played billiards and tennis or simply browsed in the library. One by one these friends left to live overseas. This was 'brain drain' I heard someone once explain: 'The best brains of this country are leaving.'

My eleven-year-old brain tried to grasp the reality of being in Australia, of living in Australia for the rest of my life. I hadn't even been to an Australian school yet but I still managed to understand that this strange television football, the roughness, the secret hidden rules, would be useful currency. I was lonely and the football on television occupied me. But it was more the sport than the personalities that captivated me until I saw a match with the Sydney Swans, featuring Warwick Capper.

Capper was athletic and loved to be flamboyant. He won games single-handedly, taking a flying mark[2] over all opponents and then turning around, picking himself up and kicking a goal. Most important, he brought out such strong emotions from different sections of the audience. His tight shorts got tut-tuts from the older male commentators while most of the girls seemed to fancy him (some, admittedly, seemed to be repulsed). His white boots[3] made him stand out and made me want to wear white boots just like he did. Somehow, Capper, his boots and his fantastic entourage made my vision of Australia as a land of heroes and outlaws come alive. This idiosyncratic footballer,

2 AFL is a fast game in which a 'mark' (catching the ball in full flight) involves a high leap and earns a free kick.

3 The standard football boot is black.

in a strange and alien land, taught me the importance of being an individual and trusting in myself.

This was important. At school I was made to feel different: 'What is your name?' 'Have you ever got on with someone?'[4] 'You speak funny.' It was only after Darren Carter became my friend that I slowly began to feel accepted.

Darren was caught and thrown by a ferocious Gavin Harvey one day after school. 'It's on. It's on,' the boys cried. Darren was struggling and groaning as Gavin kept punching and kicking him. When I stepped in and grabbed Gavin by the scruff of the neck and threw him, the boys yelled, 'All in, all in.' Some boys closed around and punched and kicked. But it all amounted to little as the teachers soon came and stopped the fight. Some weeks later Darren invited me to attend football training with him, and I did. Dad bought me white Adidas boots, which I wore with pride.

❖

I first met Rupert when he was fourteen. I was fifteen, tall and still feeling displaced. Rupert Betheras, a bunch of friends and I made a movie about racism called *Wrong Colour*. I was chosen for the lead role, being the only brown-skinned person in our group. At the time Rupert was already an enigmatic character who showed an interest in graffiti, hip-hop and surfing. He was a little guy with blond hair and the last person I would have expected to play in the AFL, and certainly not in the grand final for Collingwood, which he did in 2002. But then life is full of tricks. Who could have predicted then that twenty-one years after we met we would be driving together in the remote Western Desert of this ancient continent, in a blue Jeep Cherokee?

This year wet weather and bad roads prevented many people from going to the Yuendumu sports weekend, but together we are on the scenic 300-kilometre track north-west of Alice Springs. On the drive we talk about the past and our friendship and about sport and art.

4 'To get on with someone' is to have a relationship with someone if not also to have sex.

Both of us lost loved ones early. He lost a brother and I a father. Our lives were indelibly marked by these events. He talks about his blessed life and football and his career as an artist.

For Rupe, football is a metaphor for his art. Indeed he is part of a long line of Australian artists as diverse as Sidney Nolan, Albert Tucker, Russell Drysdale, John Brack and Ginger Riley who all found a place for sport, whether as part of the everyday scene or as a larger symbol of national character and aspiration. Rupe doesn't like making distinctions between sport and art and life.

'They are all one,' he says. 'It's a tribal thing.'

As we near Tilmouth Well, on the edge of Napperby station,[5] the road is wet and soggy. Rupe is chatting about his heroes, the Swiss sculptor, painter, draftsman and printmaker Alberto Giacometti, and the iconic Russian colorist Kandinsky, and I'm asking him about whether he likes the illustrator Ralph Steadman's work. As I drive further on the treacherous Tanami Track I realise that much of Rupert's painting reminds me of a chronicle. There is the Collingwood footballer with his face smeared out; the tribal simplicity of the Yuendumu Magpies; the large and wild series he did in Paris. Or *Broadford Hold Up*; and then there are all the paintings he did around Alice Springs.

He paints the way he played football; quick, intense and with obvious passion. His effort, as it was when he was playing, is to be admired, and his confident painting is now developing into something durable. He documents how he feels, where he has been and where he is going. His paintings portray his travels and experiences from Kew to Mumbai.

To understand Rupe and his art you must recognise him as a traveller. With a pair of football boots, linen and acrylic paint, you never know where he will end up. As he wanders he collects knowledge and touches people's lives. In 2009, for example, he nominated Liam Jurrah from Yuendumu in the national draft. Rupert had played with Liam in Alice Springs. When the nomination was declared invalid for lack of a signature, Betheras went bush and got a signature. Today Liam is playing for Melbourne Football Club.

5 A 'station' is a farm encompassing a large acreage of land for grazing sheep and/or cattle.

At the same time I was hanging out with Rupert, who was constantly looking for a space to paint. And when he does paint, he hovers around the canvas as if it's a hot football. If the painting isn't working, he moves it, constantly looking for an advantage, a new light, a better angle, rather like a footballer seeking the best advantage over his opponent, deciding whether to handpass or kick the ball. There has always been a sense of urgency about Rupert: his commitment and focus whether he applies them to football or art are undeniable. Since leaving football he has thrown himself wholeheartedly into his career as an artist.

As we approach the red desert oval we see Rupert's Warlpiri friends. After a brief hello, and even before Rupert and I get out of the jeep, he is asked if he is playing. 'You wanna play?' asks the coach, Casman. 'Put on football boots.' Rupe hasn't had a game in ages and he feels tense, but there is no time to think about it now. Casman hurries him up, 'We need players. You got boots and shorts?'

Rupe borrows shorts. He has boots. A few locals urge him on. Next he's in the changing rooms, rubbing on the Deep Heat[6] and doing stretches, trying to limber up after the three-hour drive from Alice Springs.

Casman tells him he is in the forward line. He nods slowly, trying to take it all in. The rest of the team are talking in Warlpiri, which Rupe clearly doesn't understand. He follows it intuitively without really knowing if he is doing the right thing. He gets into the huddle. The team stands in formation. At no point does he look awkward. They run onto the ground. He makes sure he bunches up with the rest of the players. As they run onto the field I notice a few familiar faces. Ned Hargraves, Brett Badger, Bruce Hearn Mackinnon and Harry Nelson cheer the team on. As the ball is bounced in the centre Rupe runs around the forward line followed closely by his sturdy opponent. He marks one. I am thrilled. Later in the afternoon Rupert kicks a goal. It's good fun.

After the game we visit our friends Harry Nelson, Brett Badger and Bruce Hearn Mackinnon and his wife Ria who are part of a group

6 A brand of pungent liniment rubbed in to assuage muscle pain.

called the Industrial Magpies. We also visit Liam Jurrah's grandfather and grandmother. My Indian friend Dilip, who works at Yuendumu, invites us to sleep at his place. He cooks a memorable fish curry, and this was the talking point of the next day. As the games continue everyone wants to know when Dilip will cook them a fish curry. It is a terrific thing to see old and new Australians sharing ideas, laughing, and respecting one another.

At the same time I notice Rupert is getting restless. 'What's up, Rupe?' I say.

'I just need to get back to my painting,' he replies.

A few days later, I catch up with Rupe. He's painting in Ilparpa, among the MacDonnell Ranges, wrestling with large canvases, moving around, seeking an advantage. At the same time he's mentoring two young men who have the potential to play Aussie Rules. Quietly, he tells me he will be having an exhibition at the Depot Gallery in Sydney in October.

RASHIDA MURPHY

Rashida Murphy (b. 1960) is from Jabalpur, India. She moved to Australia in 1985, where she has written short stories and poems broadly dealing with migration and cross-cultural experiences. She has had a novella, *On Equal Terms*, published by Equilibrium Press in 2002. She has taught ESL and Writing and now edits for *Westerly* and *Dissensus*. University of Western Australia Publishing put out her novel, *The Historian's Daughter*, in 2015. This came out of her doctorate in Creative Writing and was shortlisted for the Dundee International Book Prize. She lives in Perth.

'The Moon Still Speaks' was first published in *Westerly*, volume 59, issue 2, in 2014.

The Moon Still Speaks

His name was Sohrab and he came from Shiraz. He had never heard of a wine called Shiraz because his religion forbade him to drink wine. But a few months in the company of my brothers and cousins changed that.

Sohrab spoke of his hometown with its blue domes and tiled arches and large squares and tree-lined avenues. The moon-patterned courtyards of his beloved Shiraz were so different from the dusty little village he found us in.

'Town,' I reminded him. 'This is a town. Officially. Soon we will be a city.'

'Town, huh! This is a village and you are all villagers. And soon I will go to Amrika and study at Stanford.' But that was later, once he'd learned sufficient English to insult us.

When he first came he was just a curly-haired boy with thick spectacles and a funny accent. He wore stiff white shirts and round brown moccasins that were too big for him. His eyes were huge behind those glasses. The heavy frames left dents on either side of his nose when he took them off. He polished those glasses constantly. He was blind without them and he put them on as soon as he got up in the morning. Once I found him fast asleep, after a night out with my brothers, with his glasses on. I teased him about it the next morning and he said, 'I can see my dreams better if I sleep with my glasses on,' with such seriousness I didn't know if he was pulling my leg. It was hard to tell with Sohrab.

Then there was the moon. He had a relationship with it. Even sober, he behaved strangely when the moon was full. He giggled and sat on the verandah with a cigarette so he could look at the moon and talk to it.

'Cancer,' my sister said. 'He was born in July, under the sign of Cancer. That's why he's a bit loony.' And we looked at him sitting on the roof with a bottle of London Pilsner beside him, blowing smoke rings into the air. My father threatened to shoot him with an air gun if he didn't come down.

Another time, he lay down on the dark gravel path outside our house and my brother nearly ran him over with his blue Lambretta.[1] 'What's the matter with you, you idiot,' my brother yelled when Sohrab lay motionless on the dirt, looking upwards, as if hypnotised.

Sohrab patted the ground beside him and invited my brother to lie down. 'Look,' he said. 'Just look. It's moving. It's getting closer to us and if we keep looking, it will come for us. And we can go to it. Don't you see?'

My brother didn't want to share a room with him after that and my father said, 'Well, he can't sleep with the girls, can he now? You know what foreigners are like. This one's a little mad. So what? Just ignore him.'

My mother tried to feed him constantly, especially after the revolution, when she knew he had lost his family. Lost. Like Hansel. And all he had to do was follow the breadcrumbs to find them. Lost. As if they were misplaced or hiding somewhere and would come out after the Ayatollahs won the battle against Saddam. Sohrab cried at night in his sleep and his glasses were streaked in the morning. My mother hired holy men to exorcise the evil that surrounded him and instructed us all to say prayers in a language we didn't understand.

1 Lambretta is a brand of Italian motor scooters.

Afterwards I held Sohrab in my fifteen-year-old arms and he cried some more, trembling and lighting one cigarette after another and promising me he would look after me like a brother. We had just heard that his sister Roohi was also dead, along with his *Baba* and *Maman jun* and three younger brothers. One of those brothers and his friend, who would later become President of the Islamic Republic, had been hostage takers at the American Embassy in Tehran.

'Reza and Mahmud will kill us all. My country in the hands of savages—we will all die now.' said Sohrab. 'Reza is *shaitoon*—he is devil. And Amrika is even bigger *shaitoon*!' And that was the first time I heard an Iranian call America the great Satan.

There were many places Sohrab and I could go to escape the chaos of the household. Our favourite was the pond where the turtles swam slowly between the hyacinths. Occasionally we would lift a turtle out just to watch him freeze instantly into a motionless ball where seconds earlier he had been weaving through purple haze, eyeing us as he popped his head above the water near our feet. Once Sohrab tossed his cigarette butt in the pond and I made him climb inside and fish it out.

'And you call me mad,' he said, dripping, slimy and smelly, his hand holding the offending butt. 'You take that animal out of the water to torture him every day and you think one cigarette is going to kill him?' He squelched away without looking back and didn't talk to me for a week. He didn't get angry often, but wading in the green pool upset him and he walked away from me with his back hunched and his head down.

And then everything changed. Mothers ran away, fathers emigrated, girls married, boys drank excessively, the revolution became a fixed point in history and a generation became homeless. We scooped out a large hole in the ground and laid childhood to rest along with the family cat and a torn picture of a beautiful Persian girl in a wedding dress. Sohrab and I didn't see each other for six years and I wished I hadn't made him angry that last time.

My brother found him and brought him carefully to the tiny flat in that frantic city, where I sat nursing my infant daughter. Silently, my brother led him to me, guiding him towards the soft couch, untangling my hand from my daughter's fist and placing it into Sohrab's. This friend of my youth, the one we had laughed at and called blind so often, spoke first. 'What is her name? Your daughter. What did you call her? What does she look like?'

'Roohi,' I said. 'I called her Roohi after your sister. And she has green eyes.' I didn't ask him how he was.

The specialist came to our house and shone a torch in his eyes and asked him a hundred questions. After nearly an hour the doctor gestured that I follow him out to the balcony where we could talk above the roar of traffic, away from Sohrab.

'He doesn't *want* to see,' said the doctor. 'I've come across cases of trauma like his before. I can fix everything else, you know, the diabetes, the malnutrition, the stoop. But there's no physical reason he can't see. He doesn't want to. My advice; keep him comfortable.'

Comfortable. Cover him with a warm blanket and drip feed him, like you did with the kitten you found freezing outside the door when you were small. Check every hour to see if he breathes. Wipe his eyes and mouth. Let him hold your baby girl and guide his claw hand to rest on her head. Cry when he can't hear you. Don't talk about his dead sister and mother or his father and brothers. Don't remind him of his domed city with rubble in its squares and guns in its mosques. Don't speak his language. Don't tell him that he will die far from home, among people who cannot purify his spirit forty days after his body has been buried on an alien shore. Ask him if his dreams are blurred. Ask him if the moon still speaks to him. Ask him if he would like a Shiraz. Light him a cigarette. Take him to the balcony so he can feel the moist evening air on his face. Read him the line from Matthew Arnold that first occurred to you when he said he was Sohrab and you wondered if his father was Rustom. 'Who art thou then that canst so touch my soul?' Make him a platter of saffron rice and chelo kebabs—and remember that rice makes his tummy hurt.

AASHISH KAUL

Born in 1980, Aashish Kaul is a writer whose stories have been published internationally and collected in *A Dream of Horses*, put out by Roundfire Books in 2014. He completed a doctorate in Writing in Sydney after publishing *The Ascension* with Writers' Workshop, Calcutta in 2008, and has recently published a novel, *The Queen's Play*, released by Roundfire Books in 2015.

'Load Shedding' is an original story first published in this collection.

Load Shedding

They carried me into the room, unknown hands clasping my arms and legs, taut under the pull of my bulk that swayed like a hammock, nearly a carcass, and left me on the cot, my head aslant, and in my eyes the day, pale and shivery, sinking into the night, and in my heart this soundless lament, empty chants meant for no ear, and in my mouth the taste of blood, and in my throat a desert, and in my gut a slow explosion of pain and nothingness, what else could it be, this unsayable feeling, spreading like a fever and suspending for the moment the softly cruel touch of time and fate, and perhaps because of this a searing vertigo, like an axe-blow splintering the last of the will, and then the fall, swishing past faces and catastrophes, faces both twisted and gentle, of broken defeated creatures and tigers on prowl and hyenas on watch, of snakes that hiss but do not bite, all joined to one another and giving the finger to the universe, and then the books, covering the circular walls of the chute through which I went tumbling down, mute carriers of symbols that crumbled at a touch or a glance, all these dubious shadows now fixed in whiteness, now dissolving in the gloom of memory, when all at once I emerged at the other end sliding past the gold bulk of Shwedagon in Yangon, its spire glinting in the moonlight, piercing the heavy night mists, piercing my dream, as I delved deeper into tropical darkness, chasing an image, a silhouette really, the form of someone ahead of me, moving swiftly, skilfully, through the undergrowth, always at the edge of my vision, alternately separating from and dissolving into the trees, this bald gleaming head of a ghost luring me to the ring of some ancient rite, the head of Bernhard, that raconteur or ranter, lending to careful scrutiny in book upon book his feelings and prejudices, the author dead these past two decades and more, when suddenly the pursuer became the pursued, light and sure footsteps came in my wake, followed by a shot, the swish of the bullet in the humid air that sent splinters of rock flying through the forests of Angkor, yes, I had come this far, temples rising in layers from the ink-depth of trees, vine curling on old, weathered, patchy stone, patiently and surreptitiously strangulating the countless dancing or seated divinities in their own shapely forms and gestures, the stuff of art, nightmares, or cheap gothic cinema, then the sound of the weapon being reloaded, the spiralling bullet this time striking closer to home, parts of flesh not stone dislodged, splotches of blood shining on leaf and bush, my blood, trickling away from the wound in my side, then another shot swishing past my ear, then another and another, even as I limped on toward my destination, the tremor of drums swelling through the forest, the spectacle now faintly visible, where the one ahead was guiding me, Thomas Bernhard, my lodestar, while I failed to see the face of my attacker, until suddenly, in a small opening between the trees, the moon shone straight on his emaciated features, sharp sunken eyes, thin lips tight round a cigarette, those vowel-clipping lips, the unmistakable face of an incorrigible junky, and a shock went through me, for just as he positioned his rifle yet another time, I understood that William Burroughs had come to hunt me down from the grave, but why?, and so it was, caught between the dead, I drifted toward what seemed to promise an end to my journey, when suddenly, as if I had any dearth of problems, the fierce unending trill of a bird closed my last exit and I felt myself stumbling in the very heart of the jungle, my vision fading to a fog, and the expression of fatigue and despair in the eyes of my guide, who seemed to be washing his hands of the sorry affair, giving me up for as good as dead.

It was only a dream.

I awoke with aches in my legs, one hand wedged between them, the other gone numb under my ear on the pillow, frozen, resisting the mind's grasp, while the phone could not stop ringing, making the drops of sweat burst on my skin. Slowly, then, very slowly, almost the time it takes the winter ice to thaw, become a stream, I felt my hand warm up from the inside, felt in the fuzziness of my mind the touch of mystery hidden in the depth of things.

The ring ran out its course. Silence again. Not a sound, not a breath of wind. Not the laboured hum of the old air conditioner. The fan hanging dead from the ceiling, a film of soot bordering the blades. This was the hour of load shedding, in the peak of summer, in the middle of the day, when the heat became unbearable. Forty, forty-two, forty-five degrees on the Celsius scale. The temperature could have been anywhere. It could have been worse. After a point it failed to register. Beyond the limits of the human organism. The mild limits though, not the extreme ones.

But we had been forewarned. Every year, at the onset of summer, an appeal, the same insolent appeal down to the last letter, went out from the state department. Austerity in usage and calm in the face of storm—those fierce heat and dust storms that engulfed the Indian plains each summer.

Meanwhile, the good citizen, the guilt driven right into his soft, spongy conscience, was drinking himself silly in cool dark bars, slogging behind desks, or, what was worse, toiling away in the open air to keep the city or at least the illusion of it going, with or without the dynamo in the backyard.

The state was in bed with the supply companies. That was the talk that rose each year, like the useless appeal, with striking periodicity. But it was just that—talk. Nothing ever seemed to come of it. Sooner than later, one was bound to get bored and move on. The state was forever bullish on our boredom. This time though, there were protests in parts of the city. One man, like the Mahatma in an earlier age, was sitting on a fast unto death. It seemed excessive until you realised that he was only working to secure his constituency in the upcoming elections. Dostoyevsky had long ago sketched his type in his prison memoirs that I had been reading intermittently and that were slowly turning me inside out. There were many like him, looking to cement any social or political ground that may have been available in the name of the flimsiest of causes, and who distracted attention from the few genuine cases of personal courage against sustained oppression.

Old-world tactics in the new bad world.

Besides, as far as the government was concerned, the monsoons were never far away, always hovering on the horizon, the winds of rain and respite since the time of the first settlers. So much depended on these sea-laden winds, so many disparate needs over such a vast stretch of land, so many eyes and hearts, from luckless peasants to seasoned statesmen, that you would not have believed you had come round the millennium. This time even the Central Bank governor had joined the chorus.

To hear the wish for rain in the peak of summer, to wish it yourself many times over, was to be put in touch with the ancient mystery of the land, with the hopes and fears of the deepest past, but not with its economy, nor its humility, nor, if there had been any, its romance.

And yet this was another age. Steel and glass enclaves rising from the collapsing ruins of tiny, cluttered, still miraculously thriving colonies. Villages really, or grotesquely modern-looking villages stripped of all dignity, where just some fifty years ago were sprawling houses or, better still, only forests. Need had parcelled out land, narrowed down lanes that now bustled with ever more activity amid cramped sooty dwellings, desert coolers flaky with corrosion or old air-conditioners cramped tight any which way, large spools of live wire within arm's reach, the smell of old dirt and thwarted ambitions. The effect of that never ceasing, one-way movement of people to cities and towns from the vast countryside, men and families in search of livelihood or fleeing one or another political or social abuse, vanishing in the urban grid, sometimes finding a foothold in the city, sometimes susceptible to ever greater danger and insecurity, a kind of flotsam in that desperate rush of humanity. The urban sprawl continued to grow in all directions, congealing in places into slums and squatter colonies. Devoid of their natural physical and mental habitat, men grew petty, indifferent to easy cruelty, becoming seats of violent passions kept from flaring none knew how.

And then there were the long, cruel months of heat.

I could have been out there myself, an infinitesimal cog in the big infernal machine. But I was here, locked in a stuffy room, thinking myself fortunate to have escaped, if provisionally, the fate that could have befallen me. Here lay the real misery of one's life: no matter what the conditions, one somehow felt fortunate. It seemed always to have been the case, in times of fulfilment and in times of woe. Remember Rilke? No point in dreaming of victories, what matters most is survival.

Slowly, for this was life not dream, I went over to the basin, and thrust my head under the faucet, the water flowing over my neck and face straight from the tank on the terrace. The water came steaming hot. For cool water you would have to wait a few months or be up in the shower at dawn. I pulled out a semi-cold beer from the refrigerator, the glass bottle already sweating, and, holding it against my cheek, came back to the room, settling in the old rattan armchair in the heart of this small, box-within-a-box three-room quarter, pockmarked by hole-like grilled windows with panes that closed only with difficulty.

I took a slow, long sip from the bottle and stared out of the window shuttered against outside heat. I was looking into a mirage. And in this mirage moved wiry dark frames with yellow work helmets, shadows really, obeying orders, working against time to make the subway station functional before the big games in autumn. This had been going on for a decade now, all across the city, the laying of arterial tracks, under the earth or up in the air on narrow columns, and the almost transparent figures drifting in dust and heat round the heavy drills and cranes.

I continued to watch without a thought in my head, drank more beer, waited. The air pressed down on me its full weight, and unease grew quickly, near the skin. I glanced at the clock, took another sip. An hour more. Even the floor tiles were warm, my bare feet left fleeting prints on them.

On the edge of my desk, next to the divan, was a pile of books, handpicked to lull me to sleep. If I had to be home during the accursed hour, the trick was to pick any of them and begin reading at random. In about ten, fifteen, twenty minutes, the language running riot over the page was a certain guarantee for quick loss of consciousness. Here the French were slightly ahead of others. Or maybe it was just the collection I had within reach. Exaggerations necessary at the time to break with the past, from the long dead ways of thought, were now themselves of that set. A few assumptions turned to axioms by a mere *forcing* of the will, and a vast, baroque edifice erected around them. Creating more mystery in the name of dispelling mystery, old value plundered and remodelled for new times. The sheer effort the texts demanded was sufficient to establish their fictions as truth. More interesting than the texts themselves were the effects they wrought on their readers.

The summer being long and hard, my boredom mounting from day to day, the experiment had been unfailing save once when I had picked up a slim book by Jean-François Lyotard and had gone on reading right into the power cut, as if high theory had somehow mutated into science-fiction, if, that is, it had ever been anything else. On another day, maybe Lyotard would have worked too, but I never did find out.

At last, the phone rang. It was Gina, asking me if I'd be at the haunt in the evening.

'What's that sound?'

'They are drilling into mother earth,' I sighed. 'They are drilling everywhere.'

We hadn't met in two weeks, and in a few days she was leaving for a month of work and travel. I vaguely knew of her plans. She would ride west for a week, to the salt flats near the border, then down south to the ruins of Hampi, and finally further south to the sea.

I had first met Gina at a literary party, or an idea of a literary party, borrowed and adapted to suit the local conditions. Straight from a novel where the writer had worked a little too hard to launch a character or an encounter, the contrived idea doing service for the real thing. Reality looked long in coming to the place.

Limited minds with limitless energy, as Roth would say. Everyone brimming with ideas and plots of yet unwritten books or works in progress that were coming along at a trot, growing stupid and stupefying by the minute, vaguely Kafkaesque designs without a drop of Kafka in them, and yet others just savouring the moment, glad to belong to the lit-scene and making the most of it. How easy they made it seem! Being there you would have believed anything. It seemed the best time to be a writer, it seemed everyone was writing and publishing. And to think that only the courts were crowded.

Sheer energy and a will to write was how one became a writer, remarked one. If you dug at it long enough, it was bound to come, the thought, the idea, the voice, reflected another.

That was the solid truth. But what idea? What voice? What came out instead was gossip, schoolyard chatter, and local colour, plenty of it, and mostly all there was. Always the exact name of the café, the street, the bazaar. Art, they had learnt their lesson well, was to be found in details.

But then we were the latecomers, distanced from the projects and upheavals of the old era, distanced yet more from the neglect, the squalor, the heavy press of structures, the secret script of risk and fear written in each day, the sameness of life woven around us like the mightiest of webs, eyes bent on instinctively ignoring anything that alerted one to the malignant condition. Writing from the margins, the marginal of both thought and experience, an impoverished universe of thought, of purposive action. You felt as if you had walked out of the gilded world of the classics straight into one of cheap paperbacks or pirated bestsellers that poor kids, their naked soles melting into the hot asphalt, are forced to thrust at the so easily annoyed motorists stranded at every traffic light, every few minutes.

Immediately upon entering the house I had attached myself to the nearest group so not to appear alone and attract attention, forgetting the names as soon as I heard them, and doing my best to catch the words of the girl holding forth, of the kind who mistakes literary sensations for literature. It was to this gathering that Gina came. She was in the city to complete the fieldwork for studies she was pursuing overseas. And in the field she fitted the role perfectly as I later had the occasion to witness in a slum settlement south of the city. It was the easy manner, the sharp glance, the quick curse that came like she understood the pulse of the place and the people, the edgy negotiations and theatricality that went with it, and was as much at home in it as them.

We went out into the balcony, where she pulled out paper, filter, and tobacco from a pouch and began to roll a cigarette. We sat in the cane chairs and talked, feverishly at times, the *mise en scène* behind us swiftly forgotten.

I was at the time between jobs, and I invariably ended up meeting Gina after her near-daily beat through the settlement. Once, before our round of drinks, we went to a seller of second-hand books with whom she was familiar and from whom she had been buying books for years. His stall, if that is what it could be called, was spread under an old rotting tree with a million ants doing their brisk rounds, even in winter, coming down fast from the branches and cutting their path between the empty trunks and through the books spread out on soiled blue tarpaulin. There was no treasure here, but tireless collector that she was, Gina had in minutes picked up a few titles as she went on chatting with the man and wiping the dust off the books with her hands. In a city where dust stuck to everything, it stuck faster on books, hastening their end. But amid this literary debris, the man himself was an oddity. Tall, with a well-trimmed grey beard, a black beret at a slant on his head, he stood behind his wares with self-assurance, the thick heavy glasses emboldening his eyes. He looked as if he was dispossessed royalty and didn't care. I stood on a side scanning the decaying dog-eared books, fighting the sadness that portended and heightened the thoughts of a darkening future, merciless in judgment. No matter where I began, no matter what I wrote, it was bound to end like this, over the anthill, in decay and indifference, food for ants.

The man turned his attention to me and made some or other comment. I looked at Gina. She in turn looked at him. He ordered tea from the neighbouring stall. The wind was growing cold and dust stuck to the books thicker than on anything else. The tea came, a dense sweet concoction, three or four hot sips in a small tumbler, three or four depending on the intake. I tried to take an interest in their talk. He was collaborating with a painter friend for an exhibition opening next month at a private gallery. So the man was an artist, now it made sense. He said, 'Do you know who is the most corrupting influence on Indian writing in English?'

'Who?' asked Gina.

'Why, it's Rushdie! The man can't write straight. Others follow. They feel it's all right to write like that.'

'He has written some fine essays,' I intervened against my will.

He seemed to be making a fresh assessment of me. I was worried. I had no wish to be dragged into the conversation. But instead he posed another question. 'Do you know the writer who has influenced Arundhati Roy the most?'

'Who?' repeated Gina. We were expected to be surprised. But surprise came easily at his next words.

'Why, Joyce, of course!'

'James Joyce? By myself I wouldn't have figured that out.'

'Yes. She knows Joyce backwards. Her writing is full of it.'

'You can say that?'

'Oh it's all there. Read the book.' He was apparently finished with us. His interest wavered. He began to talk with the teashop owner. Gina paid, and we left.

Such wisdom, such discernment, here in the midst of Asia's biggest piracy market, deep in the debris of the digital age, who would have thought? 'This is turning out to be good,' I said to her. 'Stay with me yet' she said, trying to stifle a laugh.

A young, fawn-coloured lizard was coming down the wall, one slow tiny step after another, towards the pile on my desk. Something in the abstract design of the topmost book seemed to have got its attention. This heat and humidity, after all, were its territory, and the hours of power-cut were the best time for its daily frolics.

Now it was dangerously close, the tiny head angled away from the wall, its tiny outstretched feet gripping the wall firmly through equally tiny packets of air. It was either subjecting the book to scrutiny or preparing to relieve itself on those volumes of theory and philosophy. I had to do something, but I was transfixed, a part of my mind wishing a miracle.

My prayer was heard. The air conditioner came alive with a jolt that sent tremors through the walls, the fan began its first slow rotations, current had come back to our lives a full hour early, and the lizard was equally confused by it, cut across the wall in a flash and slid past a recess above the window.

With the heat in the room losing its sting, the beer began to taste better, and I continued to sit and stare out of the window, where the drills worked and dark wiry frames in yellow helmets seemed to quiver in the blazing air.

SUKHMANI KHORANA

Sukhmani Khorana (b. 1984) lectures in Media and Communication at the University of Wollongong. She has published work on diasporic cultures, transnational film, and multi-platform refugee narratives. Her creative non-fiction and commentary has appeared in *The Lifted Brow, Overland, Crikey, Kill Your Darlings, Peril,* and *The Conversation.* Her poetry has been published by *Mascara* and *Rice Paper Magazine.*

Her poem 'Under my feet' first appeared in *Mascara* in 2016.

Under my feet

For those of us with wheels under our feet
The only moments that ground us are
When the earth under our soles is moving too

Like on a train
Thirroul, Helensburgh, Sutherland, Hurstville[1]
Each repetition is like a recitation
Invoking the cult of new rhymes, every time

And on a plane
When one is amongst the ephemera of clouds
Yet tethered to seats and screens
Because one really doesn't know clouds at all
Except through the names we imagine for them

You see routes and maps, and dots and lines
All these trajectories just under your feet
Beckoning you to places you might belong

1 There are the main railway stations on the coastal line heading north to Sydney.

But you keep moving
Sometimes with a ragged guidebook tucked under your arm
And I join the ride
When you ask me to take your picture in front of the van

You see me again
In the city we both inhabit on our habitual return
Where I bike to the train station
While you walk with a swagger as you get off the bus
And we both queue for coffee

Our commutes and routines and jobs stay stubbornly constant
As we move through, and roll around them
Hoping the wheels under our feet will bind us to everywhere

Tea Estate

I visit with my sister
on a monsoonal day in
the western ghats.

As we climb the factory steps
and listen to the story of tea leaves
drying and fermenting,
she tells me she wants
a family,
but her partner is hesitant.
I speak of my dear friend
who regretted having a child
when she wasn't ready,
and yet another
who longs to have one
but cannot.

On the third floor, we are
mesmerised by the smell of
black, green, and white tea.
We fetch our wallets to buy some
lest it never makes it to
our respective shores.

CHETNA PRAKASH

Chetna was born in 1980 and worked as a journalist in Mumbai before moving to Zambia, Europe, the UK and lastly, Melbourne, where she continues to write and blog, often about the visual arts. She is a contributing writer to *The Big Smoke* (Australia). Her short story, *Searching for Saloni*, was part of the Jaipur Literature Festival hosted and celebrated in Melbourne. 'The Pop-up Linen Store' is published here for the first time.

The Pop-up[1] Linen Store

'Phsst! The plane lands in two hours. You are ready, aren't you?' Veena heard the voice behind her ask. It had taken a nasty turn now, in a bid to get her attention.

Veena cocked her head to the side, itching to cover her ears. Could she do it without Alex noticing? Alex hadn't paid any attention to her since morning. Right now, she was busy folding and restacking the hand towels that the last customer had displaced. She already thinks I am strange, Veena thought.

She looked past Alex and tried to concentrate on the street through the display window. Swan Street was the latest hip corner of Melbourne, with new restaurants, cafes, books shops, clothing and design stores popping up out of nowhere everyday. Walking from Richmond train station to the shop had been an agony for her over the last four days. Passing the slim young women, in their fashionable clothes and sunglasses, had made her more conscious than ever of her bulk and her dowdy, shapeless clothes.

She had thought working would be fun. But her self-consciousness had made her behave more awkwardly than ever, and now she was convinced that Alex regretted hiring her.

1 A 'pop-up' shop takes out short-term rental of disused office space to get quick sales on cheap goods usually remaindered from larger stores or offloaded from factories because of minor defects.

'Of course, she does,' piped the voice behind her again, reminding her that today her problems were bigger. The downward trend had already started with the morning text, and now this.

'*You* should be restacking the towels. But you are too stupid to do that, aren't you?' she heard the voice say.

Veena jumped up and rushed towards Alex. 'There, I'll stack them,' she said nearly snatching the towels from Alex's hands. Unfortunately, in her haste, Veena knocked over the porcelain soap cases stacked behind her. They came down with a loud crash.

'I'm so sorry,' whispered a horrified Veena, as she took in all the broken ceramic around her feet. 'I'll . . . I'll clean it,' she said, flapping her hands in the air.

Alex silently surveyed the scale of the damage. At least four new porcelain soap cases lay smashed on the floor. She noticed another one, seemingly undamaged, near the foot of the wooden table, and bent down and picked it up. It had chipped slightly on the left edge.

'No, it's gone,' she said, running frustrated fingers through her messy blonde hair. Then she added briskly. 'I think it is better if I clean up. We can't afford more accidents.'

Veena shuffled back to the counter feeling absolutely mortified. It was the third accident she had caused since she started four days ago. The pop-up shop was to run only for a week, and today was her last day. It had been a big opportunity for her, and Alice, her therapist, had been thrilled to hear about it. 'You are making such good progress,' she had clucked delightedly at the news. In fact, it had been Alice who had gotten her in touch with Alex, saying that the experience would do her good.

That was when Veena had decided it was time to stop taking her medication.

'Great work, champ! Wait till Daddy hears about it,' said the voice with a giggle.

Veena slowly turned around this time to see who it was. Her narrow eyes skimmed across the shelves carrying kid's linen and hosiery, and she spotted Thomas the Tank Engine. It was printed on the yellow kid's towel, and Veena instantly knew it was him. She mentally urged him to shut up. Instead, she saw the engine smile back at her ghoulishly.

She quickly turned back, and started sorting the pens before her. 'It is not real. It is not real. It is not real …' She repeated feverishly to herself as she separated the red pens from the blue and green ones. Just because she saw and heard the engine doesn't mean it was really talking to her.

'Leave her alone,' she heard another voice say, this time from the front. She looked up sharply. It was Princess Elsa on the pink towel from the girl's section this time. 'Just ignore him. He is always making trouble.'

By now, Veena was intensely aware of Alex sweeping the debris on the side. She sat rigidly, her entire being focused on ignoring the talking towels somehow. She couldn't let Alex guess anything. 'Oh God! What should I do?' she thought, feeling an intense urge to pee. Then the thought of what lay ahead struck her, and she felt the wind knock out of her. She wound her arms around her waist, wanting to buckle over.

'Are you alright?' She heard Alex ask sharply. She quickly glanced up and saw Alex staring at her alarmed.

'No, I'm … I'm ok,' Veena stammered. Straightening up, she added, 'It was just a cramp.'

'Are you sure?' Alex persisted. ''Cause I want to go out and grab a sandwich.'

Veena felt relief surge through her entire body. 'Yes, yes … I mean no … I will be fine,' she said, trying to smile brightly at her.

'Ok,' said Alex, still looking suspicious. 'Just sit at the counter. You don't have to do anything unless someone specifically asks for help. Today is our last day, and I don't think there should be many people coming in. Can you do that?'

'Sure,' said Veena stiffly. Just go now, she pleaded silently to herself.

Alex hovered unsurely for another few seconds then turned around and quickly walked out of the shop, her orange handbag swinging by her side.

As soon as Veena heard the tinkling bells of the closing door she let out a long breath in relief. Then she squared her shoulders, turned around and marched to the kid's section.

'Shut up you nasty piece of shit,' she hissed at Thomas. It didn't respond. It just stared back at her lifelessly with a benign goofy smile.

Veena stood there baffled, not knowing what to do next.

'Tut! Tut! You need to sit down, Veena,' she heard Princess Elsa say behind her. She suspiciously sounded like Alice, her motherly therapist. Veena glanced at her, and found her looking at her, sympathy oozing from her impossibly large eyes. Veena walked over to her, despite herself.

'What time is Daddy landing?' she asked, her voice a soothing balm. Veena blinked, and her fingers fiddled with her cell phone nervously. 'Three pm,' she said in a small voice.

'Daddy will be proud of you, he will be,' Elsa insisted, looking very concerned. 'You found a job. The first time in six years, you have a job. Think of that.'

'Yes, but what a mess I made of it,' Veena whispered, waving generally in the direction of the soap cases.

'Oh never mind that,' said Princess Elsa. 'Six years ago, they nearly locked you up. Today, you are twenty-six, living on your own, and you are working. You are working, Veena. Think how far you have come. You are beautiful.'

Veena felt her chest expand. Princess Elsa thought she was beautiful. Maybe she could face up to her father after all. Veena gave the Disney princess a small smile, and she smiled back encouragingly.

'Do you think he still has that brown leather belt?' asked Princess Elsa with seeming innocence.

Veena flinched in horror as if struck. She ran back to the counter and started sorting the pens madly.

Suddenly, she could smell the beautiful leather shop in Fitzroy for men's accessories from all those years ago. Her suave father had taken her there, and she remembered being mesmerised by the gazelle's head hanging from the wall above the counter. Her father was looking for a belt, and she had heard him discuss the different grades and makes as she had stared at the poor lifeless but still intensely beautiful gazelle. Her father had finally zeroed in on a smooth, hand-made, brown leather belt of American make. She vividly remembered his long pianist's fingers running lovingly over it.

Later, she had gotten to know the belt much more intimately.

A giggle brought Veena back to the linen shop. It was a little child's giggle, and it reminded her of how much she hated children and everything to do with them, the toys, the clothes, the pint-sized furniture, the scooties and cars. She hated them so much that she had once spontaneously vomited in a Toys 'R' Us.

It was toys that had caused her first real attack at the age of eleven. She was in her playroom when the fairies had started flying all around before turning into a swarm of tsetse flies and attacking her. She had run around the room screaming, upsetting everything in her way, before her father had come rushing down to grab her.

Later, they would ask her, 'Why *tsetse* flies?' As if somehow if they could figure out why an Indian child in Australia would imagine being attacked by insects from Sub-Saharan Africa, the jigsaw piece would fall into place. Who the fuck knew why she had seen tsetse flies? Least of all Veena herself.

By now her paranoia was peaking. She could feel a balloon inflating inside her, constricting her chest and lungs, making it hard to breathe.

'Let me make it through today,' she prayed over and over again. But the noises behind were getting louder. The kids' characters were all talking and fighting at once behind her.

'But she had her revenge on that belt,' said Kwazi.

'Yes, didn't she? And remember what followed after that?' retorted Dora.

Peso was shouting, 'Leave Veena alone. Leave her alone.'

'Daddy found the belt in pieces,' she heard someone else say with a giggle.

'He did not.'

'He did.'

'Shut up. Shut up. Shut up,' she turned around and screamed at them.

'Uhmm, excuse me,' she heard a voice say behind her.

Veena whirled around and shouted, 'What?'

She saw a woman in a red jacket standing near the door, clutching her little pigtailed daughter by her side. They were both staring at her agape.

The woman quickly turned back, and hustled her daughter out of the shop.

The voices instantly began bickering again behind her. But the interruption had taken the wind out of her. Veena walked back to the counter with all the effort she could muster and sat down on the chair with a thud. The voices had turned into an indistinct hum behind her.

Then, underneath it all, she heard a gravelly, throaty voice call out to her. 'Come to me, Veena. Come. You need to sleep. The bed is very soft. Come, I'll take care of you.'

Veena turned to see the single kid's bed with a blue striped sheet beckoning her. There was no cartoon character on it. It stood in the far left corner glowing underneath a softly lit lamp. 'Come sleep with me,' she heard the bed say soothingly.

Veena snapped. She scrambled open the drawer and grabbed the scissors she had seen inside before.

Then, she ran towards the bed screaming.

❖

Alex walked back to the shop apprehensively. 'I shouldn't have left her in the shop,' she thought as she took long strides back. But she had needed to get away from Veena so badly. She was freaking her out, and she needed a coffee to clear her head.

'It will be fine,' she said to herself. 'Alice had assured me she was just fine.' Besides she had been very cheap, and Alex was in a tight spot right now. If she could make a small profit over the pop-up, she would be out of the red and her credit rating would be in the safe zone.

But even before she opened the door, Alex knew her worst fears had come true.

Her linen lay in tatters all over the shop. Little pillow feathers were still floating in the air all around, giving the room a 'snowstorm-in-summer' look. The kid's section, in particular, was in a state of utter destruction. In between it all sat Veena slumped on the floor, her hands slowly snapping the scissors open and shut, open and shut, open and shut.

'I'll get you for this, Alice. I'll get you,' whispered Alex, as she ran towards the telephone.

ROBERT WOOD

Born in 1982, Robert Wood holds degrees from University of Western Australia, Australian National University and University of Pennsylvania, and has presented lectures at Peking University, Mumbai University and Berkeley University. Wood has edited for *Overland, Peril* and *Cordite Poetry Review*, and worked for Australian Poetry, The School of Life and The Centre for Stories. In 2017–18, he was an Endeavour Research Fellow and Visiting Scholar at Columbia University, and a Copyright Agency Emerging Critic with *Sydney Review of Books*.

Wood has admitted to an interest in dream, myth and language. As for identity, he believes, 'The investment in identity is an investment in the body as it participates in a world. For me, that is the feeling I get from my toes to my tongue about where my mother comes from and how the coconuts sway with their own sense of longing.' (His mother is Malayali.) The poems selected have not been previously published.

Whiskey Wheat Country

Where frost on foot

and stubble on bantam ground

where carrots and cabbages

and bore-water stained mattresses

where icebox

and cast off fibro[1] walls that haunt the world

where he remarked that

1 Fibro is a building material for cheaper houses, used in the 1950s. It is comprised of sheets of compressed asbestos fibres and cement.

the colour was always sepia and the lace-webs
touched stickiness in the corners of the shed and lounge

          where the twilight was forgotten molasses
because we lost our matches

that was where my father came from
and we knew, somewhere, that his bones and wings would be laid there
when all the world found out.

Backwater, Frontwater

As if a monsoon	or a sponge
or a pandan moon	or a mounted sculpture of a man on a horse who was not
an explorer	or a saint or a poet

as if the milk from a coconut

                    or the husk from corn

as if the gentle cinnamon in a chicken stew or char kway teow

as if the waves rolled gently and the lake was filled to the brim with lotus
and lilies and the birds that graced the water were
innocent as jewels and lead, anchors and pawns
what then will my mother say she missed when we sit down
at the break of dawn?

ANUPAMA PILBROW

Anupama Pilbrow (b. 1993) co-edits *The Suburban Review*. In 2015, she received the Dinny O'Hearn Fellowship for her manuscript-in-progress, a collection dealing with Asian diasporic experiences and with a focus on dialogue and exchange. You can find her poems and essays in Australian and international journals including *Cordite Poetry Review*, *Rabbit Poetry Journal*, *JEASA*, *Southerly* and the *Hunter Anthology of Contemporary Australian Feminist Poetry*. She occasionally performs her work around Australia.

Regarding her work, she says: 'I write poems about the body, particularly about the body as grotesque or unfamiliar. The poems here consider the body and the components of the body as soft, plastic, and unfixed. When I perform these poems, I often have audience members say, "That poem was so beautiful!" I don't really get that; "The bone is a long and solid bone" offers only temporary comfort, and much of "semiautomatic" features violent images of self-cannibalism and mutilation. I don't think of them as beautiful poems.'

The bone is a long and solid bone

The bone is a long and solid bone.
It is ripped out of the leg, or the arm,
sometimes the stomach. The cold
eats it from the inside sliding marrow
down the tunnel of mouth the
pain of flesh is relief. Hold the bone
and scrape it hard against concrete
or volcanic rock to shear away
soft and round bits until the bone is
a weapon. The bone is a long and
solid bone. The bone belongs in
the ground and in your hand
at the same time. The bone is

a tongue. The bone is a labial
consonant and some languages
lack the bone, but have seen it
introduced with English. The bone
is a long and solid bone. The morning
has not arrived and your hands are full
of blood. They cannot clench it.

semiautomatic

hunger is the opposite
of everything I eat my
way out of purgatory I ingest
everything I swallow myself
I have that fear of peanut butter sticking
to the hard palate of my mouth I eat everything
but peanut butter I am
hungry and out of work
I lay down on a conveyor
belt like Chaplin's in Modern Times and I fuck it up
and I miss
everything and get sucked into the
machinery where I am eaten
first and the gears pound me
I am cooked by a Black and Decker[1] waffle
iron my hair falls out to start with I eat only my hair and nails
then I carve bits of thigh and boil
them in water to make soup I eat
slow to make the most of it
and sometimes share it with
those I love a meal brings people
together I eat leather I make choices I
have free will and I choose

1 Black and Decker is a brand of electrical tools.

to eat it instead I eat
art when I can get it
except art eats me so it's
more like a once-in-a-while treat
I eat steel mostly hammers some
drill bits I eat a Cessna 150[2] I wrap
bacon around the barrel of my
M16 assault rifle and fire
off about 80 rounds and eat
the gun which is greasy with bacon fat
I stick my trigger finger down
my throat and eat my throat
my hand eats me I eat my hand

2 A Cessna is a small single-engine plane.

RASHMI PATEL

Rashmi Patel (b. 1980) divides her time between freelancing for Indian and Australian publications, writing her novel based on three generations of migrant women, and working as a business analyst in the IT industry. She has written on women's issues, culture, technology and art for *BuzzFeed, Mint, Scroll.in, Femina* and *Grist Media*. She has showcased her work at Bangalore Literature Festival 2012 and Melbourne Writers Festival 2016. She is also an avid urban sketcher, quilter, and amateur illustrator. She currently lives in Melbourne with her husband and daughter.

'Mercy' appears here for the first time and focuses on how Australia has an ageing population with a booming industry in nursing and homecare for the elderly. The work is mostly done by recent influxes of migrant women.

Mercy

Bahareh finished touching up her lipstick and turned to Annie. Annie sat on the bed staring straight out of the window on the opposite wall. Her unwashed brown skin shone of excess oil and sweat.

'Oh come on, go take a bath. You look like melting chocolate, and not in a good way,' said Bahareh, 'count your blessings, will you? At least you will have a room to stay. Write your masterpiece in there.'

She waited for Annie to respond. Annie didn't move. Bahareh modulated her voice and spoke in a dramatic but calm tone, stressing each word: 'It's just half-an-hour from Melbourne. You can come meet me any time. All you need to do is massage her, clean the house, do the laundry, and take out the trash. It's an old woman's home after all. For Chrissake, I am not sending you to a brothel.'

Annie looked away.

'Annie, look at me,' Bahareh said, forcing Annie's face close, 'Mercy is the best option you have. I wish I could afford to keep you here, but I can't. You know that. Remember, I am risking my job for you.'

❖

B-301, White Birch Street, Finglas.

Annie knew it was going to be a dingy unit on the third floor of a public housing complex overlooking the sea. It was no secret that White Birch Street stood for everything that had gone wrong and was still going wrong with the public housing system.

That night Annie slept on the thick carpet in Bahareh's living room clutching her mother's stained photo, wanting to slip back into her mother's arms. Years ago, when her father had wanted her to study *something practical,* her mother had solemnly defended Annie's writerly ambitions: 'She is going to be a writer. All that talent stuffed in her chest will poison her to death if she doesn't pour it out in words.'

Her mother had died after a long battle with cancer and her father had succumbed to loneliness soon thereafter. Now, sleeping on that dusty carpet, she could not bear the thought that she had failed them both without any chance of redemption. As for her unsold writing, it was poisoning her anyway.

❖

Unit B-301 on White Birch Street had been tidied to welcome Annie. Still, the cramped unit smelled of damp carpets and rotting wood. Mercy Baldwin Smith rubbed her nose and surrendered herself to the stench. She didn't want to be apologetic about it by spraying those cheap room fresheners. Chemical cocktails, she called them. She turned her attention to the walls, moist and discoloured from broken plumbing, and the two large carpets that covered the living room, stubborn in their unwelcoming appearance. Her curved spine asserted its presence by sending signals of sharp, stinging pain every time she exhaled. Trying to rub it with her bony fingers was an exercise in self-humiliation: her arm could barely reach beyond the side of her thick waist.

Her friend Rosa had promised to be there to welcome Annie. Rosa was eighty and that made it even better for her: she could barely hear, see, or smell. She said, for all she cared, they could place her in a shithole and it wouldn't bother her. Mercy smiled at the thought of ageing to be eighty. She walked over to the window and peered from a small opening in the bubble-wrap that served as a taped curtain. No sign of Rosa. She couldn't be dead. It was a bright summer day, not the kind of day one would expect a tough eighty-year-old to die. Settling on the couch, she began to repeat to herself all the advice Rosa had offered: be tough, set the rules clearly, don't give away your trust without a few tests, keep account of all food …

She drifted to sleep midway through the list. When the bell rang, she rushed to open the door only to realise there was dribble all over her cheek and on the sofa. Her hands trembled in confusion. Bahareh's impatient voice could be heard through the door.

'Coming,' said Mercy, throwing a cushion over the wet spot on the sofa and wiping her face with her sleeve.

Bahareh stormed in with Annie and spoke in a rush: 'Mercy, meet the lovely Annie. Her name is Ananya but we all call her Annie.'

'Hello, Mrs Smith,' said Annie, forcing a faint smile.

'Call me Mercy, please.'

Wanting to be pleasant, Annie muttered: 'Mercy. It's such a beautiful name.'

❖

Don't get fooled by my name. I used to be Mercy. For a long time, every time someone called me by my name, I felt vaguely proud. Now the name doesn't suit me anymore. It is difficult to be the same old Mercy when your dead husband leaves you with little more than his surname. Yes, it is difficult to be Mercy when your children call you once a year. I wish they stopped bothering me because when they call, my past comes gallivanting back to me. Oh my hazy, punishing past! It's the time I was too busy being Mercy. Now it's all vanished. Poof! And I am stuck with this name. My dead husband is a ghost. My absent children are ghosts. All of my past is a ghost. It haunts me and makes me breathless. That is why I have invited you in, Annie, not so that I can play Mercy to you but to forget that I was Mercy once. I have crossed the bridge of being Mercy. I wish I could say these words aloud but I know you won't understand. At my age, it is important not to waste energy. Now, let's get down to the business of staying alive.

❖

Mercy limped to the fridge and freed a roughly torn piece of paper from the holds of a chipped fridge-magnet in the shape of a jumping kangaroo.

'Bahareh must have told you the rules but I thought it's nice to have things in writing,' she said, handing it over to Annie. In neat cursive, the paper declared:

To Do

- Laundry once a week
- Massage whole body thrice a week
- Clean whole house once a week
- Clean kitchen daily
- Lock the door by 10:00

Not To Do

- No curry
- No men
- No pets
- No drugs or cigarettes

'Simple enough,' said Annie and pursed her lips, unable to bear the scowl on Mercy's face. Before she could tell Bahareh that she would start staying there from the next day onwards, Bahareh gently nudged her and said, 'Ok, all the best, both of you. I must leave you to your peace now. Good luck, Mercy, and call me if this woman troubles you in any way.'

Mercy nodded and stared back at Annie, refusing to smile. Then she led Annie to a room that seemed too small even for its meagre furniture. Had it not been for the large window, it would have passed as a prison cell.

Annie bolted the door, collapsed on the floor, and wept for two hours straight. Then she went out and began cleaning the house: first the kitchen, then the bathroom, and last of all, the living room. Mercy remained a mute witness throughout. When she could no longer bear to see Annie's expressionless face, she put on her shoes and went out for a walk.

Annie was still cleaning when she returned.

'You know, I still have a few more days to live. You didn't need to show off all your talent today,' she said.

'Mrs Smith, believe me, I have my own best interest in mind. I wish nothing more than to make this place conducive for daily writing.'

'Conducive,' laughed Mercy, 'by God! You are fancy. Don't work yourself to death. Good night, and again, call me Mercy.'

'Good night, Mercy.'

❖

Mercy woke up at 8:00 and looked around. The house did look different. Annie was in the bathroom humming a song in an unfamiliar language. From the half-open door of Annie's room, she saw a thick notebook lying open on the writing table. She tiptoed inside, adjusted her glasses, and began reading the page:

December 2, 2015

First day's done. Mercy seems bearable. After a few hours, even the stench became bearable. Mercy hasn't used the sun to her advantage. That bubble-wrap on the windows needs to go. In the mornings we need to let the sun sterilize the place. That should make it better, much better. The couch needs to go too. The plumbing is all falling apart. I should call Hugh. Yes, Hugh can help us.

Ha! Look at me. Excited about fixing a house. Maybe it is exciting because fixing a house is more real than writing. This feels real. Mercy. This house. Her trembling fingers and torn shoes. It wouldn't hurt to take a break from living in universes made up in my own head.

Mercy didn't feel like reading any more. She left the room and went out looking for Rosa.

❖

These girls intrigue me, these Baharehs and Annies. Look at Bahareh, that chirpy sparrow. She is the best nurse I have ever had. She told me she used to make ballet shoes and teach ballet in the basement of her parents' home in Tehran before she landed here. It seems dancing is illegal in her country. Imagine that! When the police found out about her classes they threatened to convict her with sixty lashes and seven years in prison. She escaped the next day. I asked her once if she felt better here.

'You know Mercy, I danced much more back home. Here, all I worry about is how long it will take for me to settle down. I scrimp and save to pay my rent. As for shoes, there's so much cheaper variety out in the markets, they laugh if I tell them how much my shoes cost. Freedom has its costs, Mercy.'

What can I say? Maybe she should return back home. And, here's Annie. Bahareh told me Annie is broke because her books don't sell. If your books don't sell, you pull up your sleeves and go wrestle with life. Pick cherries all day. Wash dishes at restaurants. Clean toilets at malls. What makes her hole up in my room and dream about changing my life?

That is what I tell Rosa. Girls these days are too fancy, changing countries, picking new professions, wanting to have it all. I want to pull them close and whisper: you can't have it all, honey, no matter how hard you try, no matter how hard you run.

❖

When Mercy returned, she made it clear to Annie that she had overdone the cleaning.

'If you are a writer, you must be smart. No doubt. But you don't need to turn my home upside down every time you lift a mop. Let's tone it down a little.'

❖

A pattern emerged as days passed by: on good days they prepared meagre lunches and dinners together, talked of their past, and lapsed into long monologues on how the other should live her life; on bad days, they survived on tea and bananas, fought over petty issues, and threatened to end the arrangement the very next day. This jerky rhythm showed no signs of smoothing into peaceful co-existence but they seemed to like it that way. For Annie, Mercy was just an older, weaker version of her demanding father. Reminded of her childhood, she passed her days trying to get words to paper but ended up sliding deeper into Mercy's life. As for Mercy, she felt an immediate sense of relief after each encounter with Annie. How good it felt after a shouting match! Annie, verbose and loud, exhorted her ever so often to clear it all out.

'Tell me, Mercy, what makes you so bitter? Is it the fact that I care more for you than any of your children, or the fact that you are scared of getting used to me? What I think is, Mercy, frankly, you had a rather drab marriage and now it hurts to look back and think you could have had it better. Isn't it?'

Each answer, each word seemed to unclog Mercy's weak, sluggish heart. The sediment of unvoiced emotions that had crippled her over years flowed out of her in longwinding stories told over hours, sometimes days. Despite her aching bones, she felt more alive. Annie listened on patiently, happy to have fodder for more stories. Annie's novel hardly progressed but she wrote her journal daily, not knowing that Mercy read it every morning. Initially, the entries unveiled a stubborn mix of resolve and effort, but over several entries Mercy began to notice a shift in mood.

❖

December 20, 2015

It rained today. I went for a walk and came back with lungs full of air fragrant with wet eucalyptus. I slept in the afternoon and when I woke up I felt washed with hope. I churned out pages and pages of words.

December 25, 2015

Brothers of Compassion saved the day. They hosted a barbecue in the lawns and I ate till my stomach hurt. Mercy and Rosa looked happy too. We found strings of fairy lights in Rosa's old suitcase and decorated her home. At night, it looked like fairyland for a bit.

December 27, 2015

I met old Bill by the corner. I spent all my money on buying food for him. We ate like pigs, Bill and I. Then I came home and saw Mercy sitting by the window, a ball of skin and bones. It broke my spirit, that sight of her. I couldn't sleep the whole night thinking how it all ends. It all ends likes this, in poverty and humiliation.

I miss you, mom. All hope here in White Birch Street is momentary. The permanent things here are the twin shadows of hunger and death.

December 28, 2015

Bahareh says she will go back. She is crazy. She says she can't take it anymore. All the sick patients she has to attend to, all the milky old eyes, all the pain and hopelessness make her want to die. What a fool! But then she must say the same thing about me. I am a fool too, hoping for salvation from a poor, old woman. We are both fools, condemned to die with our art in our hearts, Bahareh and I. No one will know our story. And no one will know Mercy's story.

January 2, 2016

I think Mercy is going to die on me. I think she is addicted to me. I can't support this addiction. I can feel its weight. My novel is dying too. What's worse, I am addicted to her. I couldn't leave her, even if I wanted to. Maybe all of this will end together, Mercy, my writing, and I.

January 4, 2016

All my food goes to Bill. And then what's left goes to Rosa. I must be hallucinating because of hunger because I saw someone down the street who looked just like dad. He waved at me and told me to move out of here. I swear it was dad.

January 6, 2016

Mercy's spine acted up this week. She couldn't move. Not an inch. We didn't have any money for her diapers. I was in half a mind to steal a pack but I didn't have the nerve. I massaged her and put a thick folded towel between her legs. In the morning, I found her in the bathroom, struggling to wash the bedsheet and the towel.

January 10, 2016

My legs and underarms are all itchy. It's most likely fungus. Death is creeping into me. It can't wait to feast on me.

January 12, 2016

Mercy showed me pictures of her sons and daughters. The sons are doing well faraway in the US. One of the daughters visits her once in a year. The other, what a beauty! Mercy doesn't know of her whereabouts, only that she married a drug addict and now has a daughter. She hasn't called in three years. I asked her how she felt looking at these pictures. She said she has almost forgotten what it means to be a mother.

January 15, 2016

There was shit in the washing machines in the laundry today. Some hooligans had messed it all up. The whole floor was filled with broken beer bottles and piss. I almost puked. It is humiliating, this poverty. Hunger I can take, but this, this makes me sick. Suicidal. Yes, I'd rather just end it all. What makes Mercy live?

❖

What seems deathly to you is life for me, Annie, this White Birch Street, with all its drunken louts, wasted single parents, and dying, diseased old people. It is all a reflection of my own state. You see, Annie, I am White Birch Street. That is why nothing here appals me. I can live here because I have the advantage of absolute acceptance. Do you know what that means, Annie? It means this is who I am and this is where I have landed. Do I deserve to be here? I could scream my head off crying No No No No and it wouldn't change a thing. Would it? You, Annie, my dear, on the other hand, have the disadvantage of hope. You come here, all loaded with paper and ink and stuffed with untold stories, you nurture your hungry stomach with charity, you think you can nourish your soul by giving away all your food, and then, as you sit to write, you think, Oh I don't deserve this, I can do better, I could have done better. Ha! I want to laugh at you in your face, Annie.

Beyond hope is acceptance and beyond acceptance is perhaps grace. You are far away from it because you are too busy hoping. Would it seem funny to you if I told you that I can bear my misery but I can't bear yours? I would have kicked you out but I know you have nowhere to go. Collect yourself, girl. Before one becomes present to others, one must be fully present to oneself. As for me, no, I don't wait for death. At my age, each day is time leased from death. I take what comes as it comes, without hopes, doubts, or regrets.

❖

Annie sits with Bill, Mercy, Rosa, and Bahareh, on an unbearably hot Sunday afternoon, helping them mend a small tub of socks, all the while moderating a discussion about a question Rosa has asked the group: What should work be? Rosa, being a fan of Socrates, is busy tearing apart statements from Mercy and Bill. Mercy has taken the stand that work should be whatever it needs to be; after all, not everyone has the privilege to choose one's work. Bill is busy arguing that humans have a duty to live an integral life, where hours are not wasted in meaningless work and producing goods that are by and large not needed by humanity. Bahareh, too upset with her own situation, sits shaking her head at every sentence spoken.

The mood is light, the arguments intense, the work at hand strenuous for stiff, old fingers. Annie is about to announce that she plans to leave White Birch Street in a few days. She doesn't know yet where she will head to but her face is radiant with the finality of this decision. Mercy knows about this too, having read about it in Annie's journal. She feels unburdened of a young woman's failed aspirations.

Bill has just finished telling them of his last day as a school teacher. The bell rings. Annie opens the door and sees a child of about four years of age. In her outstretched hands a large mustard envelope trembles with the breeze.

'This is for Mimma Mercy,' says the child.

Perplexed, Annie invites the child in. Mercy simply mumbles: 'Good Lord! Debbie! Where's your mum?'

'Uhmm, she told me to give you this and then she left.'

The group gets busy engaging with the child. Mercy opens the envelope, empties its contents on the couch and setting a large pack of neatly stapled papers aside, reads her daughter's handwriting scribbled on a lined piece of paper. In shocking pink ink, the thick capital letters announce:

MA TAKE CARE OF DEBBIE. THE PAPERWORK IS IN THERE. ALL MONEY IN MY ACCOUNT I HAVE TRANSFERRED TO YOU. THERE'S ENOUGH FOR A FEW YEARS. DON'T TRY TO FIND ME. HELP HER AS LONG AS YOU CAN. I KNOW SHE'LL FIND HER OWN WAY SOME DAY.

❖

The initial shock wears off in a day. There are papers to be signed, people to be met, opinions to be considered. Mercy prays, makes to-do lists, and tries to make sense of her children's long-distance sighs and grunts.

It takes a few days to sort out the accounts. Annie and Bahareh run around for Mercy's sake. At the end of a week, Mercy is ready to move to an affordable suburb where Bahareh has found a good school for Debbie. Rosa and Bill promise to visit once a month. Everything is arranged in a hurry because Bahareh has booked her tickets to go back home, not knowing yet if she will return. Annie has decided to move to Bahareh's room, agreeing to help Mercy with Debbie whenever needed.

On a cloudy Saturday morning, Mercy looks out of the small kitchen window and feels a pungent sense of loss and fear rising from her gut. Annie's bags are packed but she has enough time to take Debbie to the park for their usual evening playtime. Debbie sits on the couch sucking on a cookie and pulling it out often to probe it with her fingers.

'You are supposed to bite it and eat it, Deb,' says Annie, struggling to sound playful.

'If I make it wet, it tastes more tasty,' says Debbie, checking the wet part of the cookie again.

Annie smiles and, patting Debbie's hair, says: 'You are so cute, sometimes I just want to eat you.'

Debbie turns, the expression on her face horror-filled. 'If you eat me, Mimma Mercy will have no child.'

'Oh, Debbie, I was just kidding.'

Mercy listens to the conversation from the kitchen, continuing to cook. She can't wait to read Annie's last entry in the journal. As soon as Annie leaves for the park with Debbie, Mercy walks up to Annie's room and opens the last written page in the journal.

A single line sits in the middle of the page:

January 30, 2016

'Every child comes with the message that God is not yet discouraged of man.'

— Rabindranath Tagore

SUMEDHA IYER

Born in 1985 to parents of Bengali and South Indian backgrounds with ties to Bombay, but mostly raised in Australia, Sumedha Iyer recently completed a PhD at the University of New South Wales on white national sovereignty in selected works of Australian fiction. She has worked in the public sector for the last ten years, in policy and as a research assistant. Very occasionally, she writes poetry, this example appearing here for the first time.

Over the Rainbow

My father warned me before Mum and I left. At dusk,
we sat on the roof of our house, and he assumed an avatar
I had never seen before. 'They made me a murga instead of a Murugan.
Our gods are old and hard of hearing.' It made sense.
He had always been a compass, a confused rooster atop
a rusted weathervane, garlanded in bruised jacaranda.
'When I was young, the promise lay westward.
Even in a storm I pointed us there.' He gave a low guttural cluck.
'I had built that creaking idol
from scraps. Swept up by your mother's perfume,
we left our chappals at the temple door. But at customs,
they don't tell you that the cinemas don't smell
like pakoras and hair-oil, and that every time you go back to India
the amniotic sac of nostalgia cradling your heart bursts
as you step into the fetid heat outside the airport.'
We sat there all night.

With the red sky of the morning
My father crowed his warning.

West and East on tense terms meet
Especially when you roam

But Dorothy's red-slippered feet
Can never take you home

❖

You get off a plane and find yourself in a city that in every way resembles a fruit in an advanced state of decay. Everyone looks like you, but they at least speak ten million languages.

Children stare with saucer eyes.
You are scared too, and sweaty. Every face, every beeping Maruti
and gust of shitspice breeze is an affront.
Someone has blurred your edges with their thumb,
and your outline is indistinct. Without your edges,
you may disappear.
Your language, your precious English, when you hear it,
is syncopated and comical.

❖

Your Dida, she loves you. You can see it in her eyes, undulled by glaucoma.
Over tea and Parle-G
on well-worn imitation china,
your conversation moves like a long raincloud
over the mundane: do you watch TV, is your work interesting?
Mumbai been cold this year, beti. Did you bring sweaters?

Your soft toys from childhood visits are
meticulously assembled
around the telephone,
waiting.

The unsayable inhabits every movement,
the gurgle of brewing tea on a gas stove,
the (guilt laden) refusal of your toes
to make contact with the dusty floor,
the deferential nod when you ask for water.

You nap in the ripe mango afternoon,
You sleep, sweaty and dreamless, on the queen bed in your
    grandmother's flat. The ceiling fan clicks in its hinges.

❖

You wake at dusk in fullness of heat, heavy.
The marrow of your bones has melted, and your belly
is a growling tiger cub. Mum lies awake
next to you. Grinning,
she says you snored.
She drags Dida and you out of the flat
In search of plums. Children are playing.
Twice they let their ball roll towards Dida,
so she can throw it back.
The sun disappears into the evening.

❖

In the cab, your mother's eyes are disengaged,
wistful and wet. You cannot touch her.
Dida waves as you leave, her heart's busy thoroughfare
made suddenly still.

ABOUT THE EDITORS

Paul Sharrad

Paul first encountered Indian writing at Flinders University when Commonwealth Literature was a new study in the English curriculum and the Centre for Research in New Literatures in English organised visits by C. D. Narasimhaiah, R. K. Narayan, P. Lal, Kamala Das and many others. As a result, he wrote part of his doctorate on Raja Rao (that section was published in 1987 by Sterling Publishers as *Raja Rao and Cultural Tradition*) and has gone on to teach and write across most postcolonial literatures, including that of his own country, Australia. He edited *New Literatures Review* for ten years and most recently co-edited volume 12 of *The Oxford History of the Novel in English*. His work relating to Australian-Indian connections includes: 'Seen Through Other Eyes: Reconstructing Australian Literature in India', appearing in volume 10 of *Journal of the Association for the Study of Australian Literature* (*JASAL*) in 2010; 'Reconfiguring "Asian Australian" Writing: Australia, India and Inez Baranay', appearing in *Southerly* volume 70, issue 3, in 2010; and 'Les Murray in a Dhoti: Transnationalising Australian Literature', appearing in *Antipodes* volume 25, issue 1, in 2011.

Meeta Chatterjee Padmanabhan

Meeta is a lecturer in Learning Development at the University of Wollongong. Her work commitments include teaching research writing to doctoral students; academic skills and language across faculties and contributing to curriculum and subject design. She has degrees from India and Australia in English Literatures; Applied Linguistics and Teaching of English to Speakers of Other Languages. Humour in Indian women's writing in English was the topic of her

Masters Honours thesis. In her doctoral thesis, she explored identity projection in doctoral writing by multilingual writers. English language teaching in higher education, doctoral writing and Indian diasporic writing in Australia are some of her research interests. She is a published poet under her maiden name, Meeta Chatterjee (*Mascara Literary Review*, *Journal of Literature and Aesthetics*), and is working on a collection of poems. Her two homes—India and Australia—provide powerful inspiration for her poetry. She is an occasional blogger and a co-founding editor of *Southern Crossings*, a writers' collective based in Australia.